FORMATIVE MESOAMERICAN EXCHANGE NETWORKS
WITH SPECIAL REFERENCE TO
THE VALLEY OF OAXACA

Frontispiece. Jade figure from La Venta, Tabasco, shown wearing a small, flat iron ore mirror on his chest. (Museo Nacional de Antropología e Historia, Mexico City)

MEMOIRS OF THE MUSEUM OF ANTHROPOLOGY
UNIVERSITY OF MICHIGAN
NUMBER 7

PREHISTORY AND HUMAN ECOLOGY
OF THE VALLEY OF OAXACA

Kent V. Flannery, General Editor

Volume 3

FORMATIVE MESOAMERICAN EXCHANGE NETWORKS WITH SPECIAL REFERENCE TO THE VALLEY OF OAXACA

BY

JANE W. PIRES-FERREIRA

Appendix by B. J. Evans

ANN ARBOR
1975

© 1975 by the Regents of the University of Michigan
The Museum of Anthropology
All rights reserved

ISBN (print): 978-1-949098-44-0
ISBN (ebook): 978-1-949098-68-6

Browse all of our books at sites.lsa.umich.edu/archaeology-books.

Order our books from the University of Michigan Press at www.press.umich.edu.

For permissions, questions, or manuscript queries, contact Museum publications by email at umma-pubs@umich.edu or visit the Museum website at lsa.umich.edu/ummaa.

AN INTRODUCTION TO VOLUME 3

By Kent V. Flannery

This *Memoir* is the third in our series of final reports on the University of Michigan project, "Prehistoric Human Ecology of the Valley of Oaxaca," and it is the first of those reports to be based primarily on archeological data. Jane Wheeler Pires-Ferreira joined the project in 1967 and labored for more than half a decade in Oaxaca. Her contributions included archeological survey and excavation, analysis of animal bones, collection of zoological specimens, and studies of prehistoric trade. The fieldwork was made possible by National Science Foundation grants GS-1616 and GS-2121, and the publication of Volume 3 was supported by GN-35572.

Jane Wheeler came to Michigan with a background at Cambridge University, where Eric Higgs had stimulated an interest in faunal analysis, and fellow student Colin Renfrew had touched off an interest in tracing obsidian and other raw materials to their sources. She selected as a dissertation topic the exchange of obsidian, magnetite, and marine shell in Formative Mesoamerica. Work on this was alternated with archeological faunal analysis in the Near East, where she joined forces with a young Brazilian prehistorian, Edgardo Pires-Ferreira. (Applying for a teaching position under her married name, she was suddenly flooded with offers from universities which had been ordered to give more serious consideration to candidates with Spanish-American surnames.)

Studies of prehistoric trade have a long archeological history, and the tracing of obsidian to its source has been a major activity of the 1960s and 1970s. Techniques as different as optical spectroscopy, X-ray fluorescence, and neutron activation have been used, each with its vigorous supporters and each with its strengths and weaknesses. Mesoamerican obsidians have been analyzed at laboratories as far apart as Berkeley, Michigan, and Yale, and the exchange of information among labs has been of mutual benefit to all. For example, Pires-Ferreira at Michigan and Cobean at Yale agreed to analyze a series of identical samples by different techniques and compare the results. Only by such cooperative efforts can we expect to put archaeological trace element analysis on firm ground.

Because there are so many alternative ways to study prehistoric trade, I would like to set forth in this introduction what I see as the strengths of Dr. Pires-Ferreira's study. First, the ethnographic model she uses is one of the few that seem appropriate to the level of sociopolitical development of the Early and Middle Formative. In recent years we have seen Formative cultures explained in terms of models more appropriate for post-Renaissance Western states. Movements of products have been ascribed to Formative conquest empires, *pochteca* (professional traders of the Aztec period who were also political spies), and economic systems whose complexity would confound a Morganthau. Pires-Ferreira returns to a model based on the ethnography of cultures which may have some degree of hereditary ranking, but no true stratification and no state bureaucracy. For such cultures, exchange is still largely conceived as a series of gifts.

Second, Pires-Ferreira has devised an ellipse which establishes a 95 percent confidence level for scatter plots of obsidian trace elements. By removing confidence in points which fall outside the ellipse, this system introduces a level of rigor which was lacking in many previous studies. It immediately eliminates a whole series of anomalous results, which initially suggested that some Early Formative obsidian was coming from the distant "boondocks" of northern Mexico. The confidence ellipse narrows the range of sources used in the Early Formative to regions we can reasonably expect to have been occupied by village cultures at that time. Finally, it partially counters one of the legitimate criticisms leveled at this type of scatter plot, namely that it is based on only two trace elements. For example, use of the ellipse separates obsidian sources like Zinapécuaro, Guadalupe Victoria, and Cerro de las Navajas so widely that they could never be confused, even though only two elements are used.

Third, in the case of the Valley of Oaxaca, Pires-Ferreira has restricted her analysis to excavated obsidian whose provenience *and context* are known with absolute certainty. This may not seem like much of an innovation until one realizes that most obsidian analyzed so far from the Formative comes (a) from the surface of the site, or (b) from excavated proveniences which can only be designated in the grossest terms, for example, "deposits of the Tlaloc phase," or "Pit 3, Level 2." Many Mesoamerican archaeologists are satisfied with such proveniences, but designations like "Pit 3, Level 2" do not really tell us if the context is midden, structural fill, house floor, slope wash, or something else. In most cases we will never know whether the obsidian was *in situ,* redeposited during mound construction, or intrusive down a gopher hole.

There is a curious logical inconsistency here. Archeologists demand rigor from the chemists and physicists who analyze their material, and they will debate at length the merits of various physico-chemical techniques. Then they will hand those specialists a sample taken by arbitrary 20-centimeter levels from deposits whose nature is poorly understood. In other words, they expect from physicists and chemists a standard of rigor they themselves are not willing to provide. Yet no amount of physico-chemical "overkill" can correct for inadequacies in the way the sample was collected. If there is no science in our own archeology, our sister sciences cannot be expected to bail us out.

The samples chosen by Pires-Ferreira from Oaxaca were fragments of obsidian found resting on the floors of Formative houses or in isolated activity areas on courtyards immediately adjacent to houses. In all cases, the archeological context was known at the time the specimen was recovered, and its three-dimensional coordinates were established. No sample comes from construction fill, slope wash, or a deposit whose nature is unclear. This fact allowed Pires-Ferreira to do something totally new: compare one house with another. This in turn made it possible to focus down onto a previously uninvestigated activity, the distribution of obsidian among the households of a village.

Access to this level of analysis made it possible for Pires-Ferreira to make a fourth contribution: to show that not all products were exchanged by the same mechanisms. Obsidian exchange was universal, involving all households. Shell exchange involved primarily part-time craftsmen. Mirrors of iron ore moved between elites. In other words, prehistoric trade patterns tell us more than just which regions were in contact; when we focus on the household level, they open up a whole new world of intravillage social relations within a region.

Undoubtedly, many studies of Formative exchange will follow this one. New and more sophisticated techniques of trace element analysis will arise. Collaboration between institutions will make the whole pattern clearer and more reliable. Defects in this and in other studies will be uncovered and corrected. We can count on our colleagues in physics and chemistry to increase their contribution to archeology, and just as surely we can count on some archeologists to lean on such contributions like a crutch. I will always be grateful to Pires-Ferreira because she eschewed that crutch, and demanded the same level of rigor for the archeological data.

Ann Arbor, Michigan
April 1, 1975

CONTENTS

Figures ... ix
Tables ... x
Plates ... x
Agradecimientos ... xi

I. Formative Mesoamerican Archeology and Exchange Models

    Introduction ... 1
    Previous Models for Formative "Trade" ... 1
    The Varieties of Exchange in Formative Mesoamerica ... 3
    Exchange under Conditions of Reciprocity ... 5
    Exchange under Conditions of Redistribution ... 7
    Chronology of the Early and Middle Formative ... 8

II. Obsidian Exchange Networks in Formative Mesoamerica

    Obsidian: Methodology and Raw Data ... 11
    The Early Formative: Obsidian Exchange Networks Linking Villages ... 24
    The Middle Formative: Obsidian Exchange Networks Linking Villages ... 28
    The Distribution of Obsidian in Formative Oaxacan Households ... 31
    Summary ... 35

III. Iron Ore Mirror Exchange Networks in Formative Mesoamerica

    Iron Ore: Methodology and Raw Data ... 37
    The Early Formative: Magnetite Mirror Production and Exchange ... 57
    The Middle Formative: Localized Iron Ore Mirror Production ... 62
    Cañada Carreta Survey: Fluvial Dispersal of Iron Ore ... 63
    Summary ... 65

IV. Shell Exchange Networks

    Shells: Methodology and Raw Data ... 69
    The Early Formative: Shell Exchange Networks Linking Villages ... 73
    The Middle Formative: Shell Exchange Networks Linking Villages ... 75
    The Distribution of Shell among Formative Households: An Example from Oaxaca ... 77
    Summary ... 80

V. Additional Commodities Which Figured in Early and Middle Formative Exchange

    Ritual Paraphernalia ... 81
    "Specular Hematite" Pigment ... 81
    Ceramics ... 81

VI. Summary and Conclusions ... 83

Appendixes

    I. Other Reported Mesoamerican Obsidian Sources ... 85
    II. Mössbauer Spectroscopy, by *B. J. Evans* ... 87

Resumen en Español ... 103

References ... 107

FIGURES

1. Early and Middle Formative sites in Mesoamerica 8
2. Obsidian and iron ore sources 12
3. Obsidian sources 13
4. Confidence ellipse for Zinapécuaro 14
5. Confidence ellipse for Altotonga 15
6. Confidence ellipse for "Unknown Oaxacan" source 15
7. Confidence ellipse for Tulancingo 16
8. Confidence ellipse for El Chayal 16
9. Confidence ellipse for Cerro de las Navajas 17
10. Confidence ellipse for Barranca de los Estetes 17
11. Confidence ellipse for Guadalupe Victoria 18
12. Percentage of obsidian in the total chipped stone industry against distance from source for early Neolithic sites in the Near East, 6500 to 5000 B.C. 21
13. Q-type correlation matrix for Early Formative obsidian samples 23
14. Q-type correlation matrix for Middle Formative obsidian samples 24
15. Early Formative obsidian exchange networks as determined through correlation matrix analysis 25
16. Middle Formative obsidian exchange networks as determined through correlation matrix analysis 29
17. Geological sources of iron ore in the Valley of Oaxaca and Early Formative procurement routes 38
18. Mössbauer spectra of titaniferrous magnetite, magnetite, ilmenite and hematite 39
19. Mössbauer spectra, magnetite from Group I-A 49
20. Mössbauer spectra, magnetite from Loma de Cañada Totomosle-Loma de la Visnagra, Group I-A 53
21. Mössbauer spectra, magnetite from Group I-B 54
22. Mössbauer spectrum, magnetite mirror from La Venta, Group I-C 55
23. Mössbauer spectra, hematite mirrors from La Venta, Group II-A 56
24. Mössbauer spectra, ilmenite from Group III-A 57
25. Mössbauer spectra, mixed magnetite and ilmenite, from Group IV-A 58
26. Mössbauer spectra, mixed magnetite and ilmenite, from Group IV-B 59
27. Survey: Cañada Carreta fluvial dispersal of iron ore 64
28. Stages in the breakup of magnetite in the stream bed of the Cañada Carreta, Valley of Oaxaca 66
29. Stages in the breakup of magnetite in the stream bed of the Cañada Carreta, Valley of Oaxaca 67

Appendix II:

A1. Line profiles and relative energies of emitted and absorbed radiation for atomic resonance (visible and ultraviolet radiation) and nuclear resonance 88
A2. Nuclear level diagram for ^{57}Co 89
A3. Schematic of time-amplitude relationship between different components of a Mössbauer spectrometer 89
A4. A schematic diagram of a typical constant acceleration Mössbauer spectrometer 90
A5. Electric monopole interaction or isomer shift for ^{57}Fe 91
A6. Electric quadrapole interaction for ^{57}Fe 92
A7. Magnetic dipole interaction for ^{57}Fe 93
A8. Mixed magnetic dipole plus electric quadrapole interaction 94
A9. ^{57}Fe NGR spectrum of ilmenite ($FeTiO_3$) 95
A10. ^{57}Fe NGR spectrum of ulvöspinel (Fe_2TiO_4) 95
A11. ^{57}Fe NGR spectrum of titanohematites 96
A12. ^{57}Fe NGR spectrum of titanomagnetites 97
A13. Commercial backscatter detector showing relative positions of source, detector and absorber 99
A14. ^{57}Fe transmission and backscatter spectra of a polished iron ore mirror 100
A15. ^{57}Fe backscatter spectra obtained from two different orientations of a rectangular archeological artifact believed to be a compass needle 100

TABLES

1. Regional chronology: Formative Mesoamerica 9
2. Results of neutron activation analysis of Early and Middle Formative Mesoamerican obsidian sample: raw data 19
3. Results of neutron activation analysis of Early and Middle Formative obsidian sample; percentages by region 20
4. Obsidian as a function of distance: distance from primary obsidian source, compared with the percentage of obsidian used at various Formative villages 22
5. Comparative results of eight archeological samples from Tierras Largas, Oaxaca, analyzed by optical emission spectroscopy (Yale University) and neutron activation analysis (University of Michigan) 28
6. Results of neutron activation analysis of obsidian from Early and Middle Formative households at San José Mogote and Tierras Largas, Oaxaca 32
7. Results of neutron activation analysis of obsidian from Early Formative (San José Phase) households at San José Mogote 33
8. San José Mogote, Areas A and C: obsidian statistics 33
9. Valley of Oaxaca iron ore sources 40
10. Iron ore sources outside the Valley of Oaxaca sampled for Mössbauer spectral analysis 48
11. Group I-A: Loma de Cañada Totomosle-Loma de la Visnagra magnetite source, Tenango, Oaxaca 50
12. Group I-B: Loma los Sabinos magnetite source, Zimatlán, Valley of Oaxaca 50
13. Group I-C: unmatched magnetite source 50
14. Group II-A: Cerro Prieto hematite source, Niltepec, Isthmus of Tehuantepec 51
15. Group III-A: unmatched ilmenite source 51
16. Group IV-A: Loma del Arroyo Terrero mixed magnetite and ilmenite source, Arrazola, Valley of Oaxaca 52
17. Group IV-B: Loma Salinas mixed magnetite and ilmenite source, San Lorenzo Cacaotepec, Valley of Oaxaca 52
18. Provenience, date, context and probable source for 7 iron ore mirrors found by M. D. Coe at San Lorenzo, Veracruz 61
19. Mollusks found in Early Formative context: Valley of Oaxaca 70
20. Mollusks found in Early Formative context: other regions 72
21. Mollusks found in Middle Formative context: Valley of Oaxaca 76
22. Mollusks found in Middle Formative context: other regions 77
23. Numbers of identified shell taxa, by region of origin, for the Valley of Oaxaca and a small sample of other regions: Early and Middle Formative 78
24. Sources and utilization of shells: Early Formative House floors or Household Clusters at San José Mogote, Oaxaca 79
25. Sources of Early and Middle Formative shell found at Tierras Largas, Oaxaca 80
26. Utilization of shells: Early and Middle Formative Household Clusters at Tierras Largas, Oaxaca 80

A1. Atomic Resonance versus Nuclear Gamma-ray Resonance 87

PLATES

Frontispiece. Jade figure from La Venta, Tabasco, shown wearing a small, flat, iron ore mirror on his chest .. ii

1. Iron ore mirrors from Formative Mesoamerica 113
2. Figurines in the Museo Nacional de Antropología e Historia, Mexico City, wearing metal mirrors 114
3. Shells and shell ornaments from Formative sites in Oaxaca 115

AGRADECIMIENTOS

La realización de este trabajo hubiera sido imposible sin la ayuda y asistencia que recibí de los arqueologos, geologos y pobladores mexicanos, quienes siempre me recibieron con gran hospitalidad. En relación al estudio de los artefactos arqueologicos quiero expresar mis agradecimientos a los Arqueologos Roman Piña Chán, Arturo Romano y Roberto Garcia Moll del Museo Nacional de Antropologia, José Luis Lorenzo del Departamento de Prehistoria, I.N.A.H., y a Alfonso Medellin Zenil de la Universidad Veracruzana. Cuanto al estudio de la localización de los yacimientos de hierro agradezco en particular la ayuda del Ing. Ruben Pesquera Valezquez del Consejo de Recursos Naturales no Renovables y al Ing. Eliezer Ortiz Garcia del Plan Oaxaca. Sin la ayuda que recibí de los oficiales municipales del Valle de Oaxaca y del Istmo de Tehuantepec y en particular de los Señores Edmundo Matias Chavez y Eligio Martinez Sosa, poliglotas de Mitla en las lenguas zapoteco, español y inglés, el trabajo de campo hubiera sido arduo, si no imposible.

Varias personas contribuyeron con artefactos para analisis y como así tambien en la localización de yacimientos de obsidiana y hierro. Aprovecho el momento para expresar mi profunda gratitud a los doctores:

Jörg Aufdermauer, Proyecto Puebla-Tlaxcala, Fundación Alemana para la Investigación Científica,
Paul L. Cloke, Department of Geology and Mineralogy, The University of Michigan,
Charles DiPeso, Amerind Foundation,
Clifford Evans, Smithsonian Institution,
James Elwell, Plan Oaxaca,
Thomas Lee, New World Archaeological Foundation,
Gareth Lowe, New World Archaeological Foundation,
Richard S. MacNeish, R. S. Peabody Foundation for Archaeology,
Joseph Michels, Pennsylvania State University,
John Paddock, Centro de Estudios Oaxaqueños, Universidad de las Americas,
Jeffrey R. Parsons, The University of Michigan,
Michael Spence, University of Western Ontario, Canada,
Ronald Spores, Vanderbilt University,
Edward B. Sisson, R. S. Peabody Foundation for Archaeology,
Paul Tolstoy, Queens College,
Heinz Walter, Proyecto Puebla-Tlaxcala, Fundación Alemana para la Investigación Científica, y
Cecil Welte, Oficina de Estudios de Humanidad del Valle de Oaxaca.

También aprovecho la oportunidad para expresar mis agradecimientos a:

Profesor Pedro Armillas, University of Illinois at Chicago Circle,
Sr. Robert Cobean, Harvard University,
Dr. Michael D. Coe, Yale University,
Sr. Richard D. Drennan, The University of Michigan,
Dr. David C. Grove, University of Illinois at Urbana,
Dra. Anne V. T. Kirkby, Department of Geography, University of Bristol, England,

AGRADECIMENTOS

Dr. Michael J. Kirkby, Department of Geography, University of Bristol, England,
Sr. J. Thomas Meyers, The University of Michigan,
Dr. Joseph R. Morrison, Smithsonian Institution,
Sr. Chris Moser, The University of California at Los Angeles,
Dr. William O. Payne, Orange Coast College,
Dr. A. Colin Renfrew, Sheffield University, England,
Sr. Charles Sheffer, The University of Michigan
Dr. Marcus C. Winter, University of Arizona, y
Dr. Henry T. Wright, The University of Michigan.

A los doctores James B. Griffin, Billy J. Evans y Edwin N. Wilmsen, miembros de mi comité, mi reconocimiento profundo por la asistencia y ayuda que siempre recibí durante mis años en la Universidad de Michigan. Y finalmente mis agradecimientos especiales al Dr. Kent V. Flannery, director de mi tesis y del proyecto "La Ecología Humana Prehistórica del Valle de Oaxaca," quien en todos los momentos y circunstancias me ayudaron en la realización de este trabajo.

I
FORMATIVE MESOAMERICAN ARCHEOLOGY AND EXCHANGE MODELS

INTRODUCTION

The Early and Middle Formative periods in Mesoamerica (1500-500 B.C.) witnessed many significant changes from the Preceramic period in population growth, architecture, settlement patterns, and artifact categories. One of the most striking changes, however, was in the enormously expanded volume of material, both raw and finished, traveling between cultural regions and between environmental zones. Interregional movement of pottery, obsidian, jade, turquoise, iron pigments, iron ores, mica, mollusk shell, turtle shell, fish and stingray spines, shark teeth, and other commodities often reached impressive proportions. Many of these items were of ritual use, and, as pointed out by Drennan (n.d.), probably reflected an increasing role for rituals of sanctification on the part of Formative peoples. Others were "utilitarian" in nature, although the line between utilitarian and nonutilitarian is often hazy. Even ritual paraphernalia, insofar as it strengthened the integration of Formative communities and tightened the links between families who also exchanged foodstuffs and subsistence items, could be considered to have a utilitarian aspect.

In this paper, the term "exchange" has been used in preference to "trade," in much the same manner that Sahlins (1965) used it in his article, "On the Sociology of Primitive Exchange." The term "trade" has been used in so many different contexts—many of them associated with state societies, and the kinds of formal trade engaged in by Western states—that we prefer not to use it. The kind of "primitive exchange" described by Sahlins is more appropriate for the level of sociopolitical evolution we assume, on the basis of all available archeological evidence, to have characterized the Early and the Middle Formative periods. In such societies (corresponding roughly to the ideal types originally defined by Service [1962] as "tribes" and "chiefdoms" and by Fried [1967] as "egalitarian" and "rank" societies, respectively), exchange frequently takes the form of gift-giving, with the unstated assumption that the gift will be reciprocated at some time in the future, though not necessarily with the same commodity. Equivalences between commodities are generally not fixed, nor are the rates of exchange standard, although Sahlins (1972) has shown that participants do have ideas about the relative values of the goods exchanged. Much long-distance "primitive exchange" is facilitated by having the participants set up a fictive kin relationship or "trade partnership," and the usual means of escalating the volume of exchange is to produce an extraordinarily lavish gift requiring an extraordinary reciprocation. Apart from Sahlins' work, superb models for the operation of primitive exchange systems can be found in Rappaport's (1967) work on the Maring of New Guinea, Harding's (1967) work on the Siassi Islanders, and Leach's (1964) work on the Kachin of Burma.

PREVIOUS MODELS FOR FORMATIVE "TRADE"

With the exceptions of Sanders and Price (1968) and Flannery (1968), most writers on Formative Mesoamerica have not drawn their models from the ethnographic literature on egalitarian or "ranked" (but not stratified) societies. Rather, they have used models drawn from the Aztec state at the time of the Spanish Conquest, or the Classical archaic states of the Mediterranean region. Most of these models are unconvincing because they require institutions or mechanisms usually not found below the level of states, or truly stratified societies, a sociopolitical level for which there is no good evidence in Early and Middle Formative Mesoamerica. Expressions such as "merchant," "trade route," "trade center," "military outpost," or "(military) control of trade" abound in the literature, although such institutions have never been documented for the period 1500-500 B.C. in Mesoamerica. To a certain extent, such formularizations may result from the fact that the writers have underestimated the ability of ranked or even egalitarian societies to move large quantities of material over long distances.

Most models one finds in the Mesoamerican literature refer to the Formative peoples of southern Veracruz and western Tabasco as belonging to what has been defined (primarily on stylistic grounds) as the "Olmec" culture. The Olmec were first "discovered" at the lowland Gulf Coast sites of Tres Zapotes (Melgar y Serrano, 1869, 1871; Stirling, 1942a), La Venta (Blom and LaFarge, 1926; Stirling, 1942b, 1942c, 1947), and San Lorenzo (Stirling, 1955). At these sites, earth mound complexes oriented between 7 and 12 degrees west of true north—associated with sculptures, colossal basalt heads, buried caches containing sumptuary goods of serpentine and jade as well as concave mirrors and beads of polished iron ore—made up the corpus of what came to be called the Olmec culture or art style (Jones, 1963). From 1928 to 1933 (Vaillant, 1930a, 1930c, 1932a, 1935a, 1935b), excavations at Formative sites in the Valleys of Mexico and Morelos produced pottery and other artifacts which, though showing regional differences, were also in the Olmec style. Once the contemporaneousness and age of the Olmec stylistic horizon in both the Central Highlands and the Gulf Coast were realized, the error of attributing these artifacts to the later, historic "Olmec" of the Gulf Coast area became obvious (Sociedad Mexicana de Antropología, 1942). But despite such implicit error, the misnomer persists even to the present. Thus removed from history into prehistory, the origin of the artistically elaborate Olmec society and the explanation of its pervasive influence in Mesoamerica became one of the focal points for Formative research.

Because of the widespread distribution of stylistically Olmec objects, much theorizing has involved migration and trade route explanations. A West Mexican origin was proposed by Covarrubias (1950, 1957: 76, 110) based in part on the frequency distribution of Olmec jades. Others have seen the Gulf Coast area as the "homeland" or "metropolitan center" from which missionaries, commercial traders or armies (Coe, 1965a: 112-113, 1965b:764, 771; Grove, 1968a; Jiménez Moreno, 1966:14) spread out in search of certain luxury goods. But only through the recent excavations at San Lorenzo (Coe, 1968b and 1970) and La Venta (Drucker, Heizer and Squier, 1959; Heizer et al., 1968a, 1968b), in the Valley of Oaxaca (Flannery, 1968; Flannery et al., 1970) and in the Valley of Mexico (Tolstoy and Paradis, 1970), combined with the development of appropriate physical and chemical analytical techniques, has it become possible to evaluate the nature and extent of the exchange networks of this period, and their place in Mesoamerican prehistory. It is, in part, to this task that the present study is directed.

Among the many explanations for the "Olmec presence" in the Mexican Highlands which have been put forward, trade and trade-related hypotheses are currently the most popular. In 1965 M. D. Coe examined the activities of the Aztec *pochteca*, the merchant class, and their trade activities, as a possible model for explaining the "Olmec presence" in Central Mexico (1965b:122-123, 1965c:771). Jiménez Moreno, also utilizing historical evidence, has briefly discussed possible Early Formative access routes through Highland Mexico (1966:14). The essence of these hypotheses is briefly outlined below.

Sahagún deals at length with the pochteca, or merchant class, of Tenochtitlán-Tlateloco. The pochteca included a variety of merchant types, such as "vanguard merchants," "disguised merchants," "outpost merchants," and so forth, all of whom belonged to an almost separate hereditary social class, neither commoner nor noble

(Sahagún, 1959:3-8, 21-25; Chapman, 1957:120; Acosta Saignes, 1945:12-21). The pochteca generally went on long trading expeditions, often to areas where they were not always welcome. During these expeditions, goods were taken by the pochteca to trade, generally for luxury goods such as quetzal feathers, turquoise, "green stones," and cotton garments (Sahagún, 1959:1-2, 18-19); however, the pochteca often served as spies as well, bringing political information back with them (ibid.:22-23). The travels of the pochteca took them to regions throughout Mesoamerica, including the Gulf Coast (Anáhuac Xicalanco), the Pacific coast around Tehuantepec (Anáhuac Ayotlán), and, according to Acosta Saignes (1945:14), to the Chichimec country to the north of the Valley of Mexico, where certain towns were founded as trading bases. Some areas, such as Xicalanco on the Gulf Coast, were actually "ports of trade," Xicalanco serving as a trading center connecting the Maya region with the Central Highlands (Sahagún, 1959:17; Chapman, 1957:135-141). Sahagún notes that "jade" and "jadite" were brought from Xicalanco to the Valley of Mexico (1959:18-19) which suggests the source was located to the south. Other towns, such as Quauhtenanco and Ayotlán, because they resisted the Aztec pochteca, were conquered by the pochteca's private army, or by Aztec troops sent to the aid of the besieged merchants (Saghagún, 1959:3-4, 6, 18). In some cases, Aztec garrisons were probably established in these towns to protect trade or to establish tribute, and on occasion the Aztecs sent colonists into a subjected area. Therefore, it appears that there was a close relation between trade and militarism in the Late Postclassic, extending to the point of a "tribute empire" established by the Aztec Triple Alliance.

This apparent relation between trade and conquest in the Aztec pochteca model has led Coe (1965b:764) to see the expansion of Olmec influence in the Central Highlands as a direct result of military-trade expansion of an Olmec empire. A similar hypothesis of a militaristically-based Olmec empire was also proposed by Caso (1964). Coe (ibid.) relates the expansion to a theoretical demand for jade from Guerrero sources, while Bernal (1968) has distinguished between the Gulf Coast "metropolitan Olmec centers" and Highland "colonial" sites. In the latter category, sites such as Chalcatzingo are viewed as military settlements or trade centers related to the maintenance of control over indigenous populations.

Recently, however, workers in the Central Highlands have become dubious of this projection of the Aztec pattern backward in time. In 1968 Grove concluded that evidence for "...militarism during the Preclassic period is debatable, and... any militarism connected with Olmec trade must have been slight" (1968a:231). More recently he has stated that the concept of an "Olmec presence" in Morelos and the Central Highlands during the Early Formative is largely erroneous (1972b and in press:26). It now seems that the very concept of an "Olmec presence" in the Highlands must be revised.

Apart from their attribution of Aztec institutions to Formative societies, a major problem with the preceding theories is their emphasis on a one-way exploration and seeking of goods. "Olmec merchants" are seen as spreading through the Highlands in search of exotic materials, such as jade, to fulfill a demand for such goods at home. That this is probably not the situation was argued by Flannery in 1968, and will be supported by the data on Early and Middle Formative obsidian, iron ore mirror, and shell exchange presented in this paper. The networks of exchange we have defined do not show that the Gulf Coast held any position of primacy in Early and Middle Formative trade, and they suggest that models drawn from the ethnographic literature on egalitarian and rank societies are more appropriate for that period than models drawn from the Aztec state.

THE VARIETIES OF EXCHANGE IN FORMATIVE MESOAMERICA

Out of all the myriad types of exchange which exist in the ethnographic record, we feel that we can recognize four in the Formative Mesoamerican obsidian, iron ore, and marine shell data at our disposal. These four general types of exchange must be explained by different models.

1. *Reciprocal exchange of utilitarian commodities (excluding food-stuffs) to which every single villager had access.* An example of such exchange would be the movement of obsidian flakes and chunks during the Early Formative period. In spite of the abundance of native flints, cherts, or silicified tuffs in Highland Mesoamerica, hardly a household which has been carefully excavated is without obsidian, while some lowland villages, lacking local flint deposits, used obsidian exclusively.

Obsidian exchange probably was related to both (1) population density and distribution (Wright and Zeder, 1973), since the amount moving toward any area was partly a function of the number of villages in that area; and (2) distance, since the amount in any area was also partly a function of its distance from the nearest source. This exchange was probably analogous to the ethnographically-documented obsidian exchanges of the Siassi Islanders, in which the resource decreased in amount and increased in value as distance from the source increased (Harding, 1967:42).

In the Early Formative, obsidian trade was probably an egalitarian form of exchange in which all villagers participated. In the Valley of Oaxaca, where house-by-house data on obsidian are available, variation in the percentage of obsidian from different sources is usually so great as to suggest that each household obtained its obsidian on an individual basis. Unfortunately, comparable data cannot be provided for areas where only one source was used. Another important phenomenon is that the amount of obsidian found from village to village appears to decrease in rough proportion to distance from the source. Analogies with other regions of the world come to mind here. A linear regression analysis of the relationship between quantity of obsidian traded and distance from the source for Neolithic sites in the Near East, by Renfrew, Dixon, and Cann (1968), demonstrates a relatively log-constant reduction in the amount of obsidian found in sites as distance from the source area increases (Fig. 12). Beyond a "supply zone" (extending up to 300 kilometers from the primary source at Çiftlik, Turkey) the amount of obsidian decreases exponentially with distance, until at the site of Beidha, in Jordan, some 900 kilometers from the source, obsidian comprises only 0.1 percent of the lithic industry.

2. *Pooling of utilitarian commodities for later distribution to all members of the community.* An example of such exchange would be the movement of prismatic obsidian blades, beginning around 1000-900 B.C. in Mesoamerica. Although the quantity of prismatic blades exchanged was presumably related to the same population and distance factors affecting reciprocal exchange of utilitarian commodities, the type of exchange was different. In contrast to the variation in source utilization from household to household characteristic of reciprocal exchange, uniform distribution of obsidian from several sources among all households at large ceremonial-civic centers like San José Mogote, Oaxaca suggests pooling of obsidian by some central agency prior to distribution to members of the community.

Evidence of such pooling first appears around 1000 B.C., and is associated with the introduction of imported prismatic obsidian blades. Through time, as blades became more and more the object of exchange (and certain sources became more important as a result), such pooling became more the rule than the exception. By the Middle Formative, this pattern of obsidian distribution seems to be true even of small Oaxacan hamlets (Winter, 1972).

3. *Exchanges of unworked nonutilitarian commodities for conversion by part-time specialists, with most villagers having access to*

the finished product. Unmodified shell moved from the Pacific coast and tidewater estuaries to households at certain villages in Oaxaca (e.g., San José Mogote and Tierras Largas) where it was converted into ornaments. The range of artifacts on the house floors where the shell was found suggests that their occupants were farmers with a part-time speciality, not full-time shell workers. Finished ornaments, on the other hand, have been found at small neighboring sites where no evidence of shell working was found. Neither the mechanism by which the raw material reached the shell workers, nor the mechanism by which the finished products reached their users is fully understood. But the situation may be similar to that described for some Siassi Islanders who work raw material traded to them by another island, which they use themselves or pass on to still a third island (Harding, 1967).

4. *Conversion of exotic raw material into even more exotic commodities for exchange between chiefly elites.* The production of magnetite mirrors during the Early Formative period at one residential ward of one site in Oaxaca, evidently for exchange with sites in Morelos, Nochixtlán, and Veracruz, provides an example of this type. The distribution of these mirrors indicates an exchange which is not a function of distance from source. A very restricted number of sites (and of households within these sites) had access to mirrors, which, based on evidence from certain figurines, may have been worn on the chests of elite individuals. Analogous ethnographic situations might be the manufacture of tortoise-shell combs in Truk for wearing by members of highly-ranked lineages (David M. Schneider, verbal information) or the exchanges of jade in Burma between Kachin chiefs and Shan aristocrats (Leach, 1964). The mechanism for such exchanges may have been gifts between elites, perhaps sometimes set up by marriage alliances (Flannery, 1968).

These are the four modal types of commodity exchange we have outlined for Early and Middle Formative Mesoamerica. Although each of these types can be defined and examined as a distinct entity, eventual understanding of exchange processes must come from examination of the variation within, and interrelation between, the various types of commodity exchange. Utilitarian and nonutilitarian goods are assigned differential standing within the networks in which they move (Sahlins, 1972:277), so that a commodity moved by Type 2 exchange in one valley may, in fact, be handled by Type 3 exchange in the next. By examining the relative position of each commodity in relation to other commodities within the exchange sphere, it becomes possible to propose hypotheses about which products acted as "regulatory mechanisms," serving to maintain the system in spite of long-term fluctuations in population density or distribution.

EXCHANGE UNDER CONDITIONS OF RECIPROCITY

Rappaport's (1967) study of the egalitarian Maring tribesmen of New Guinea illustrates the mechanisms of exchange under conditions of reciprocity. Trade among the Maring is effected through direct exchanges between individuals on a reciprocal basis, and each trader or local group acts as one link in a "chain-like" structure (Rappaport, 1967:106-107). The producers and consumers of a particular commodity may be separated from each other by so many links that they are unknown to each other, just as the village of Beidha in Jordan probably had no knowledge of the Çiftlik obsidian source in Turkey and the village of Tierras Largas in Oaxaca no real knowledge of the Barranca de los Estetes obsidian source in the Valley of Mexico. In such a situation the material passes from kinsman to kinsman, or from valley to valley, through "trade partnerships" established by fictive kin ties. These ties are necessary because, as Sahlins (1972) points out, at a pre-state level, people generally do not like to trade with (and do not deal fairly with) non-relatives. As yet, however, we do not have a convincing methodology for demonstrating trade partnerships archeologically.

In the Maring system described by Rappaport, the two main locally-produced exchange items are salt (from saline springs in the Simbai Valley) and stone axes (from quarries in the Jimi Valley). Both are "utilitarian" items in the sense that they relate to eating on the one hand, and felling trees for agriculture on the other. They are, however, circulated in the same "sphere of conveyence" (Bohannan, quoted by Rappaport, 1967:106) with "nonutilitarian" goods such as ornamental feathers (from birds-of-paradise, parrots, and eagles), shells, and animal furs (used to decorate shields, headbands, and loincloths). (The ascription of "nonutilitarian" status here is perhaps arbitrary, because many of these latter items are used as bride wealth by the Maring, and hence are of great economic importance, but this fact need not concern us for the moment.)

Bird-of-paradise plumes and fur enter the Simbai Valley from the north. The local villagers keep some, and trade others south to the Jimi Valley, along with Simbai Valley salt. Shells of three types (gold-lip, sea-snail, and cowrie) enter the Jimi Valley from the south. The local villagers keep some, and trade the rest north to the Simbai Valley, along with Jimi Valley axes.

Such a chain-like reciprocal exchange structure, as Rappaport points out, has a number of weaknesses. First, the number of axes produced by the Jimi quarries is a function, not of the demand for axes, but of the Jimi Valley's need for salt. And if the Simbai Valley people have an adequate supply of axes, they may simply say, "we don't want any more," whereupon the Jimi Valley suffers a salt shortage. So many links separate the quarries from the salt springs that the Jimi axe-makers cannot shame, cajole, or wheedle the Simbai salt-makers into making more salt. Second, trade in "subsistence" items is related to population density; if population in the Jimi Valley drops, it will need less salt and the Simbai will probably be left with an axe shortage. Thus, "it may be questioned whether a direct exchange apparatus that moves only two or three items critical to subsistence would be viable" (Rappaport, 1967:106).

For these weaknesses, Rappaport (loc. cit.) offers a tentative solution: "It may be suggested that the inclusion of both the nonutilitarian valuables and utilitarian goods within a single 'sphere of conveyence' ... stimulated the production and facilitated the distribution of the utilitarian goods." Bird-of-paradise plumes fade, fur perishes, and the pressure for spectacular generosity in bride wealth is so great that demand for these items is constant, and they "could be freely exchanged for stone axes and native salt" (loc. cit.). Thus, so-called "nonutilitarian" or "exotic" exchange might act as a *systemic regulator*, which keeps trade in subsistence products going even when the balance of trade or demographic stability is in doubt. If this is the case, it is possible that, in the case of Formative Mesoamerica, such exotic items as Pacific Coast pearl oyster shells and lumps of magnetite ore moved north from Oaxaca through the Valleys of Nochixtlán and Morelos along the same chain-link route through which Barranca de los Estetes obsidian blades moved south to Oaxaca.

Recently, Henry T. Wright and Melinda Zeder (1973) have begun a computer simulation at the University of Michigan in which Rappaport's hypothesis will be tested. Hypothetical villages producing salt, axes, and other subsistence items are set in a demographically related exchange network into which exotic items are introduced. Thus far, the "nonutilitarian" goods seem to function best as regulators under conditions of expanding population—a model which is not without implications for Formative Mesoamerica. We await their future conclusions.

In a reciprocal economy, where individual households negotiated for their own obsidian, we would expect a great deal of variability between households, both in the sources used and the proportions of obsidian from various sources. The source of this variability would be differences between households or kin groups in their trade partnerships or contacts in areas nearer to the sources. This kind of variability is what most data for Early Formative obsidian flakes and chunks seem to show.

EXCHANGE UNDER CONDITIONS OF REDISTRIBUTION

As Rappaport points out, systemic regulators are needed because of the unsophisticated nature of reciprocal exchange and "chain-like" structures. In redistributive economies, where trade is coordinated by a chief or some managerial agency, "supralocal authorities may demand production and enforce deliveries" (Rappaport, 1967:108). In this case, exchange might continue in spite of demographic shifts in chain-like systems. "They might even work in 'reciprocal systems' in which the parties to the transactions are *groups* in which production might be commanded by a local authority who might, conceivably, take into consideration the requirements of other groups" (ibid.).

In redistributive economies, materials coming into a valley might be "pooled" by some administrative authority—either a paramount chief at the largest village, or a "head man" or high-status family at smaller villages. The pooler might then redistribute the material to his kinsmen or followers, according to their needs and the amount of pressure they are able to put on him. In the case of obsidian in Formative Oaxaca, the introduction of prismatic obsidian blades from the Barranca de los Estetes and Zinapécuaro source areas, beginning around 1000 B.C., is associated with a reduction of variation in source usage by households, suggesting that some form of pooling, probably associated with the rise of a managerial elite and reinforced by the increased value of prismatic blades over unstandardized flakes, was being practiced. For the Early Formative, evidence of such pooling comes only from the largest sites, but by the Middle Formative it had spread even to small hamlets (Winter, 1972).

Eventually, if the redistribution of utilitarian items came to be based on chiefly power, we would expect the authorities to "demand production and enforce deliveries" as Rappaport suggests. In this case, the exchange system would no longer need the "exotic" or "nonutilitarian" items as regulators. One might expect long-distance trade in exotic ores, shells, and plumes to diminish, except insofar as the elite needed these to enhance their status. The administration of a highly-developed chiefly authority should have been able to demand levels of production which would make it possible to derive most utilitarian items from within their own sphere of influence, or negotiate for them with the elites of other regions. One would therefore expect more regionalization and less long-distance trade in exotica on the level of the individual household. This does seem to be reflected in our Middle Formative data.

While some Mesoamerican Formative societies were egalitarian, others were complex chiefdoms or emergent chiefdoms, almost certainly with redistributive economies (Flannery, 1968). Whereas in egalitarian society most goods are equally available to all members of the community, in a chiefdom some goods are amassed by paramount chiefs for redistribution according to a hereditarily defined rank order (Service, 1962; Sahlins, 1972). The position of chief is an institutionalized office conferred by birth order within the ruling lineage, and often associated with the concept of divine descent from the gods. This exclusive chief-god relationship serves to legitimize the right of chiefly stewardship over the land, its people, and their produce. But concomitant with the chiefly right to demand community support and tribute is chiefly responsibility for accumulation, storage and redistribution of the produce. Negligence of these responsibilities may lead to the overthrow of a chief. Exclusive control over the exploitation and distribution of rare resources, insured by the power of chiefly *tabu,* further underwrites the position of the paramount chief in relation to his followers. Transformation of such rare resources into luxury goods is usually accomplished by craft specialists attached to the chiefly household; their products, together with the raw material itself, provide the chief with a basis for negotiating exchange with other chiefs. Such exchanges lead to the acquisition of both utilitarian and exotic sumptuary goods, which again are used to reinforce and legitimize chiefly status and power. Abstractly then, a chiefdom can be pictured as a sphere where lines of redistribution radiate out from the central paramount, according to social rank order, to integrate dependent villages. Two or more such spheres may be linked together in an exchange network as a result of exchange between their respective elites. In Formative Mesomaerica, magnetite mirrors may have been so exchanged.

Archeologically, it is a difficult matter to identify chiefdoms. The La Venta basalt column tomb containing the skeletons of two children accompanied by numerous sumptuary goods is often cited as evidence of ascribed status and, thus, of ranked society (Flannery, 1968). Better evidence has since come from bone strontium analysis of burials, which detects dietary differences (as early as the Middle Formative) which probably have a basis in hereditary rank (Brown, 1973). Such evidence of hereditary ranking is diagnostic of chiefdoms, but since most chiefdoms have a redistributive economy we can also look to artifact distributions for evidence of redistribution, and, thus, of a chiefly social system. The exchange of obsidian, shell and iron ore mirrors in Formative Mesoamerica has provided some evidence for the development and growth of redistributive systems.

CHRONOLOGY OF THE EARLY AND MIDDLE FORMATIVE

Mesoamerican archeologists are not in complete agreement on the chronology of the Formative period (ca. 1500 B.C.-100 A.D.). Disagreements stem from the history and development of archeological research at sites of this period in Mesoamerica. Recently, several books have presented reviews of this development (Ford, 1969; Bernal, 1968, 1969), and two doctoral dissertations have been devoted in great part to examina-

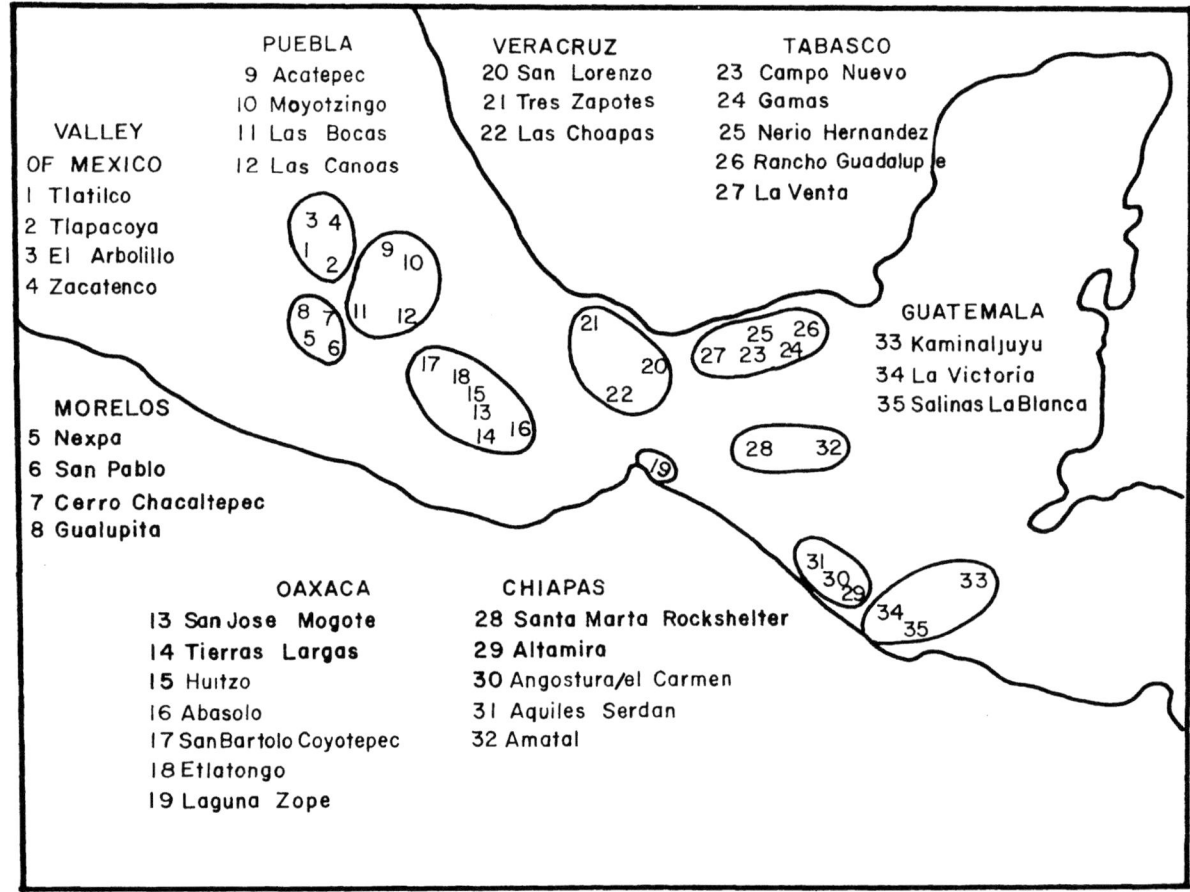

Fig. 1. Early and Middle Formative sites in Mesoamerica.

FORMATIVE MESOAMERICAN ARCHEOLOGY AND EXCHANGE MODELS

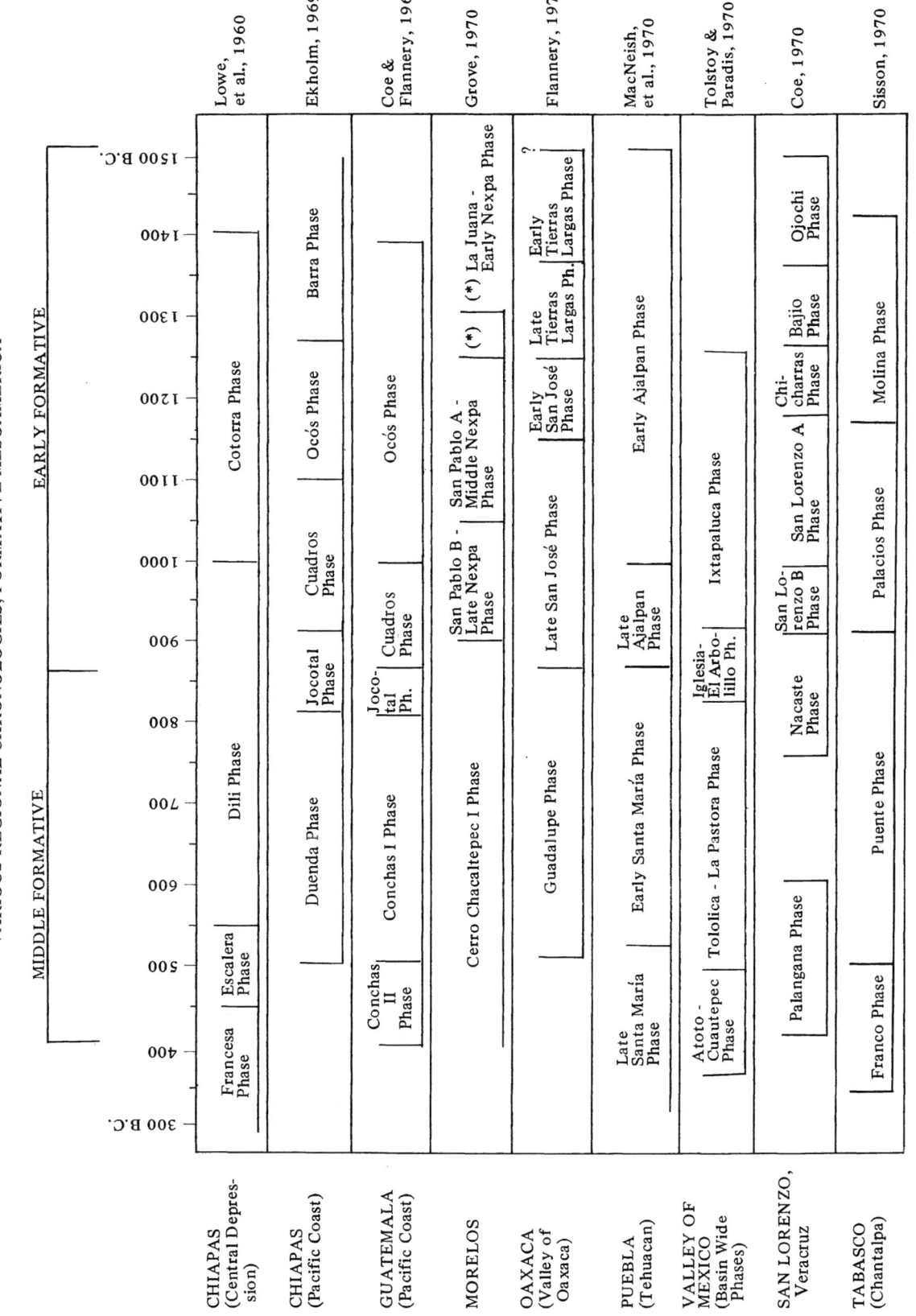

TABLE 1
VARIOUS REGIONAL CHRONOLOGIES, FORMATIVE MESOAMERICA

tion of this matter (Diehl, 1969; Grove, 1968a). Full consideration of this data is beyond the scope of the present paper, but a brief review of the most recent research and temporal phases currently proposed for the Formative period is necessary to provide a chronological framework for the exchange data presented here.

Table 1 presents the various regional chronologies published for the period 1500 to 400 B.C. Figure 1 shows the locations of important Formative sites mentioned in the text.

For the period from 1500 to 1250 B.C., much of our exchange data comes from sites located along the Pacific coast of Chiapas and western Guatemala. The Barra, Ocós and Cuadros phases at the sites of La Victoria (Coe, 1961), Salinas la Blanca (Coe and Flannery, 1967), Izapa (Ekholm, 1969), and Altamira (Green and Lowe, 1967) provide the bulk of our information on this early coastal farming region. The relationship between these Pacific coast phases and the contemporaneous Bajío and Ojochi phases at San Lorenzo on the Gulf Coast is not yet clearly understood, although Michael Coe (personal communication) considers the Ojochi ceramics of this period to be "country cousins" of the Ocós material. The Early Ajalpan and Tierras Largas phases of Puebla and Oaxaca are contemporaneous, and sherds from Ocós-like vessels appear in Tierras Largas deposits.

After 1250 B.C., the Gulf Coast area (and the ceremonial-civic center of San Lorenzo in particular) rose to prominence in Mesoamerica. Impressive earthen mound constructions and stone sculpture including colossal basalt heads date from 1200-900 B.C. at San Lorenzo. This was a period of extensive long-distance trade all over Mesoamerica. The question of the influence of San Lorenzo on other regions of Mesoamerica will be discussed elsewhere in this paper.

Near the end of the San Lorenzo B Phase (about 900 B.C.), defacement of monumental sculpture at San Lorenzo took place. This destruction preceded an eventual abandonment of the site, and was followed by a rise to prominence on the part of the ceremonial-civic center of La Venta between 900 and 500 B.C. This appears to be the first in a series of cyclical reorderings of sociopolitical structure which characterized the remaining Formative periods. Middle Formative development, from 850 to 400 B.C., was characterized by increasing regionalization and an actual decrease in the long-distance trade seen in previous periods.

II

OBSIDIAN EXCHANGE NETWORKS IN FORMATIVE MESOAMERICA

OBSIDIAN: METHODOLOGY AND RAW DATA

One of the most frequently studied prehistoric exchange items has been obsidian. Due to its widespread distribution in archeological sites and its finite number of geological sources, it can provide clear evidence for prehistoric exchange. Optical spectroscopy (Renfrew, Dixon and Cann, 1966; Cobean et al., 1971), x-ray fluorescence (Weaver and Stross, 1965; Jack and Heizer, 1968; Stross et al., 1968), and neutron activation analysis (Stross et al., 1968; Gordus et al., 1967; Gordus, Wright and Griffin, 1968; Wright, 1969) have been successfully utilized to characterize obsidian sources, and thus to determine the origin of obsidian artifacts found in archeological sites in the Near East, Europe, North America and Mesoamerica. The results of neutron activation analysis of some 600 samples from 20 geological sources in Mesoamerica and 422 archeological samples of Early and Middle Formative date in Mesoamerica are reported here.

Analytical Technique

The automated method of sodium (Na) and magnesium (Mn) neutron activation analysis has been described in detail previously (Gordus et al., 1967). Briefly, 25 samples of approximately 50 mgs. each are weighed, sealed in polyethylene tubing and irradiated together with Na and Mn standards for sixteen seconds. They are then placed in an automatic sample changer which is connected to a 2" by 2" well-type NaI(Tl) scintillation detector, as well as to a single channel analyzer. One-minute counts of the Na and Mn activity in each sample are taken every two hours and twenty-five minutes over a period of twenty-four hours, and the information is recorded on both teletype printout and punch paper tape. Actual Na and Mn percentages are calculated by comparison with the irradiated standards. Although certain refinements in technique have been made in order to obtain more accurate results (J. Thomas Meyers, personal communication), sampling and analysis procedures remain quite similar to those previously published.

Selection of Na and Mn as the elements for analysis was made by Gordus (Gordus et al., 1967) in accordance with the capabilities of his analytical equipment. Certain criticism has been leveled at the use of Na percentage to differentiate between geological sources. This element, one of the most common on earth, does exhibit considerable variability within any given geological source of obsidian, and serves to differentiate only four of the 20 Mesoamerican sources examined in this study. Clearly, Na has limited diagnostic utility.

Despite the suggestion from x-ray fluoresence that the percentage of Mn is widely variable within discrete obsidian sources (Stross et al., 1968), the results obtained through neutron activation analysis indicate the opposite to be the case. Utilizing improved technique (J. Thomas Meyers, personal communication) on samples from eleven geological sources, a maximum variation of 0.01 at a .95 confidence level was found to exist. The percentage of Mn in Mesoamerican obsidian is thus demonstrated to be a most useful element for distinguishing sources.

The Geological Sources

Obsidian is a volcanic glass created by rapid cooling of extrusive volcanic lava. Its distribution is generally restricted to areas of recent vulcan-

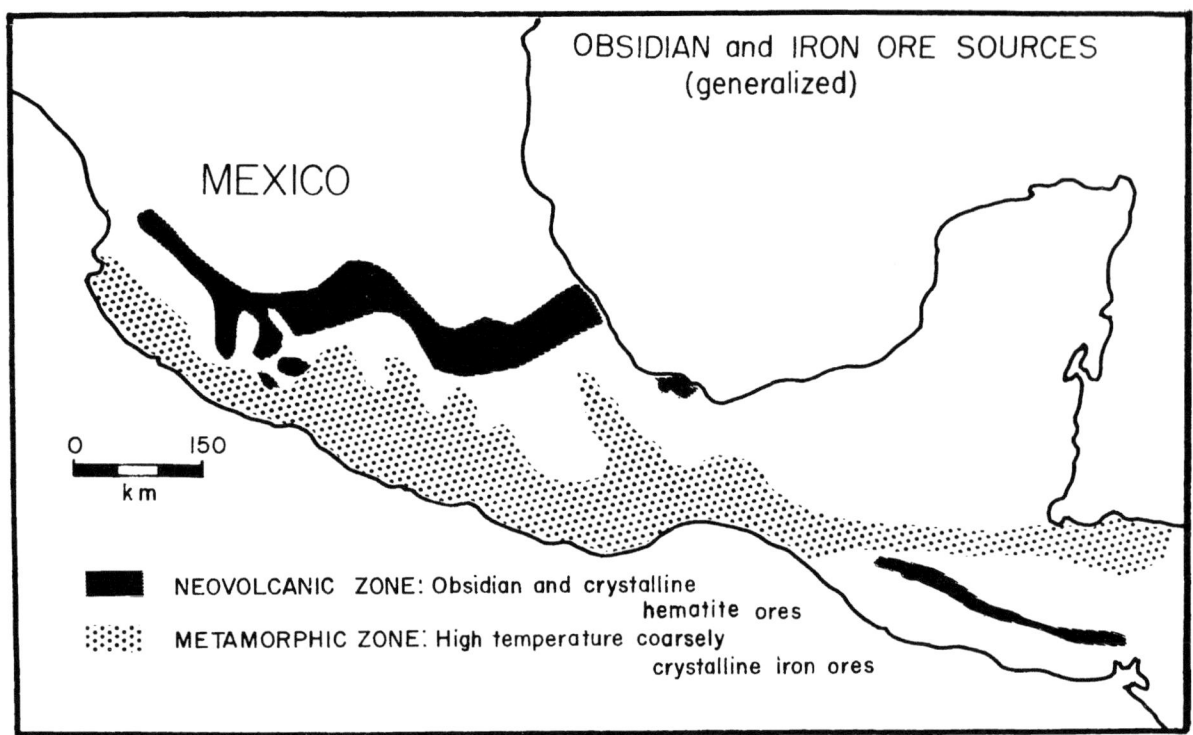

Fig. 2. Obsidian and iron ore sources.

ism. Mesoamerican obsidian occurs primarily in the east-west neovolcanic chain of Central Mexico and in the highlands of Guatemala (Fig. 2). Samples collected from twenty of these obsidian sources were examined in this study (Fig. 3).[1]

Geological source samples were obtained through field survey by the author and other members and associates of the University of Michgian Neutron Activation Analysis Laboratory, and through the assistance of several individuals and institutions. An attempt was made to obtain a representative series of samples for each source. However, lack of time and funds made this an impossibility, and extensive testing of five sources was substituted in order to examine the range of Na and Mn variability within sources. Each of the five sources—Barranca de los Estetes, Cerro de las Navajas, El Chayal, Guadalupe Victoria and Pénjamo—was extensively collected, with samples being taken at intervals across the surface exposure of the source. Thirty or more samples from each of these sources were analyzed.

Every geological source and archeological sample was irradiated and counted a minimum of five times, and the final Na and Mn percentage calculations represent an average of the five results. Multiple analyses insure an accuracy of better than $\pm 2.0\%$ at a .95 confidence level. The calculated percentages are plotted against each other with the percent Na scaled from 2.00 to 4.12 along the abcissa and the percent Mn $\times 10^2$ scaled from 0.00 to 14.40 along the ordinate. Percentage Mn $\times 10^2$ is utilized in plotting to facilitate visual differentiation between clusters, while reducing the plot size to conform with computer format specifications. The plotting parameters represent the observed range of variations in Na and Mn for Mesoamerican obsidian sources. All sources thus analyzed and plotted produced a roughly elliptical cluster of data points.

---

[1] Although these twenty sources do not include all of the known or reported sources in Mesoamerica, the major sources have been sampled in this study. Appendix I lists other sources reported for Mesoamerica which were not sampled in this study.

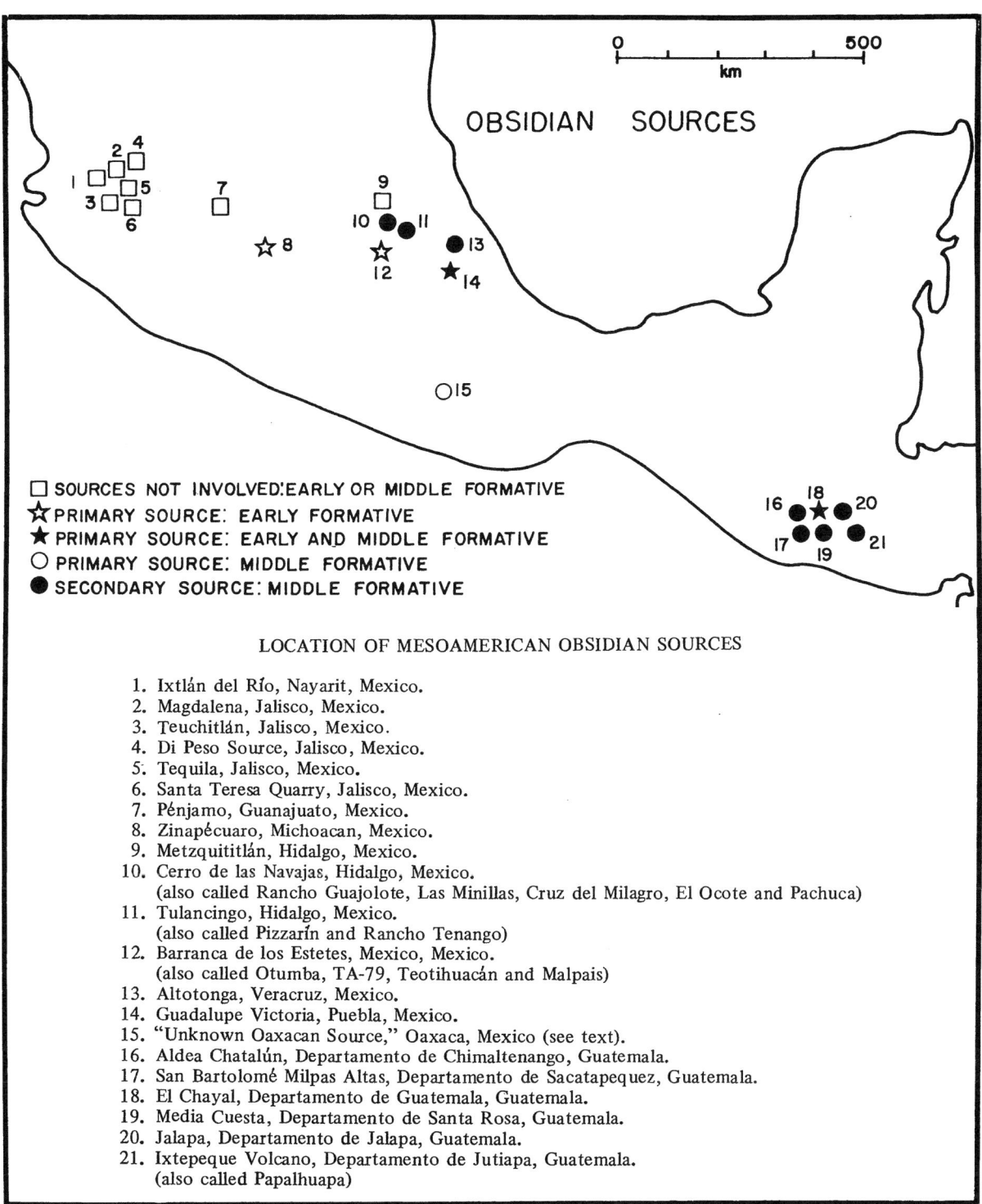

Fig. 3. Early and Middle Formative obsidian sources.

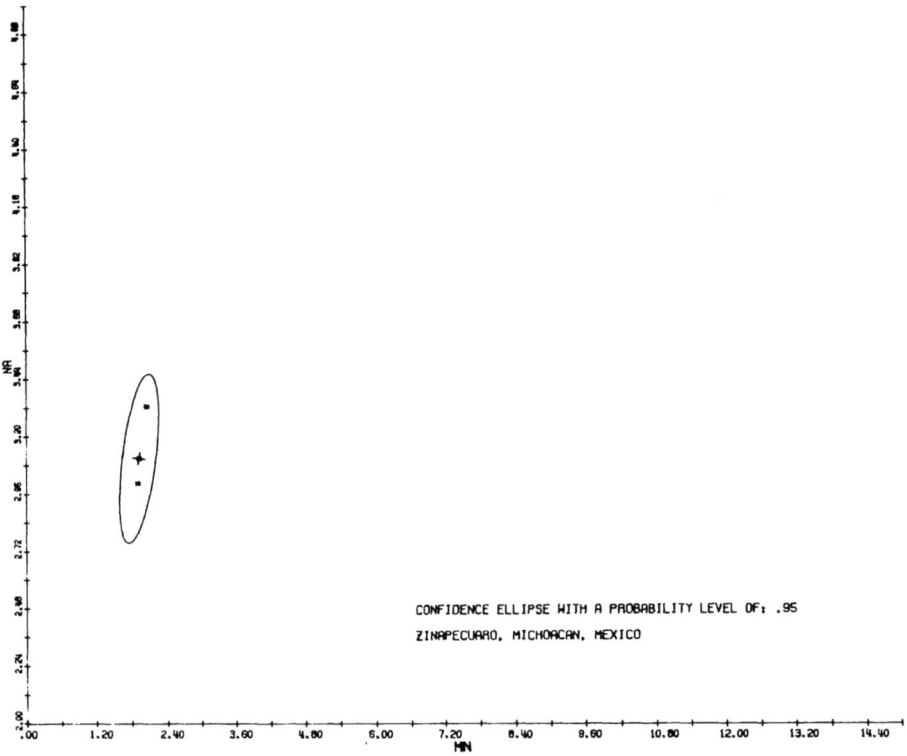

Fig. 4. Confidence ellipse for Zinapécuaro.

Definition of boundaries for each source cluster were calculated in a standard manner. Utilizing a computer-controlled digital plotter, a confidence ellipse with a probability level of .95 was drawn[2] based on the distribution of data points for each source with 20 or more samples (see Fig. 9, Cerro de las Navajas). When fewer than 20 samples were available for a source, the ellipse was determined from the degree of inclination and spread of the available points and the known maximum variations in the Na and Mn content for Mesoamerican obsidians (see Fig. 5, Altotonga). While the latter ellipses are not wholly satisfactory, because they tend to cover a larger range of variation than is characteristic of the source, they do provide a plausible basis for defining a source until such time as more samples can be analyzed. Adoption of the .95 probability level ellipse provides a standardized definition of source boundaries, elimination of erroneous data points, and an accurate tool for distinguishing between sources. Of the 20 geological sources analyzed, only nine were found to have been utilized during the Early and Middle Formative periods of Mesoamerican prehistory. Ellipses for eight of these nine sources are shown in Figures 4-11.

In one instance, we were able to document the existence of a geological source not actually sampled by our survey. When all the archeological samples which could not be assigned to a known source were plotted together, one distinctive elliptical cluster was noted. Samples from Early and Middle Formative period sites in the states of Oaxaca, Puebla, and the Valley of Mexico made up the cluster. The greatest number of samples in the cluster were from sites in the Valley of Oaxaca. In addition, twenty-one undated samples from a surface survey in the Valley of Nochixtlán, Oaxaca (these samples are

[2] The ellipse concept originated with the present author but was developed and programmed by Charles Sheffer, now at the Department of Anthropology, Temple University.

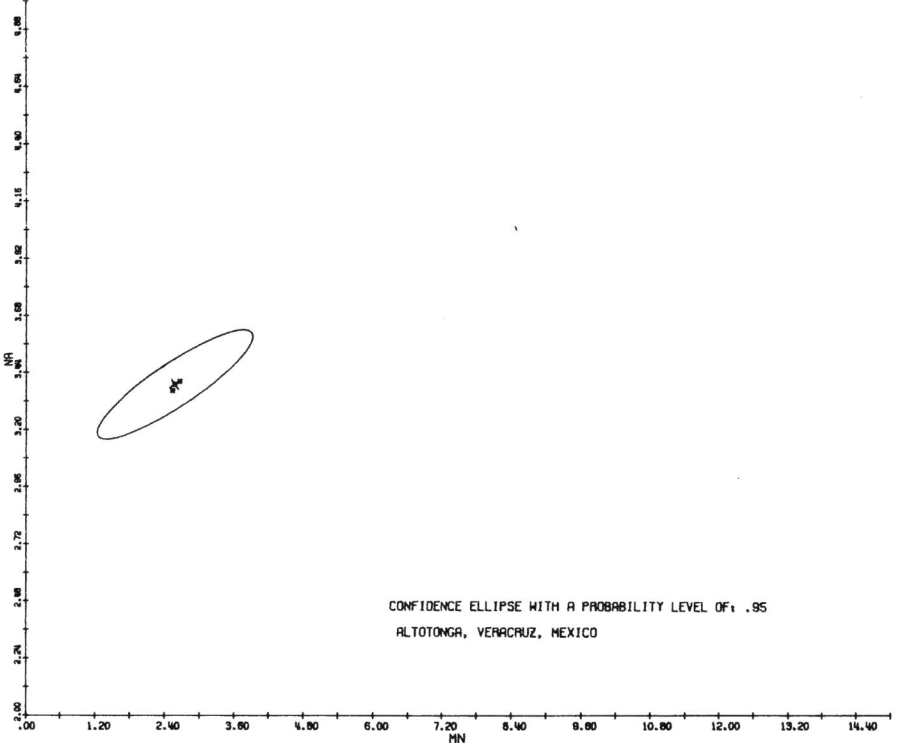

Fig. 5. Confidence ellipse for Altotonga.

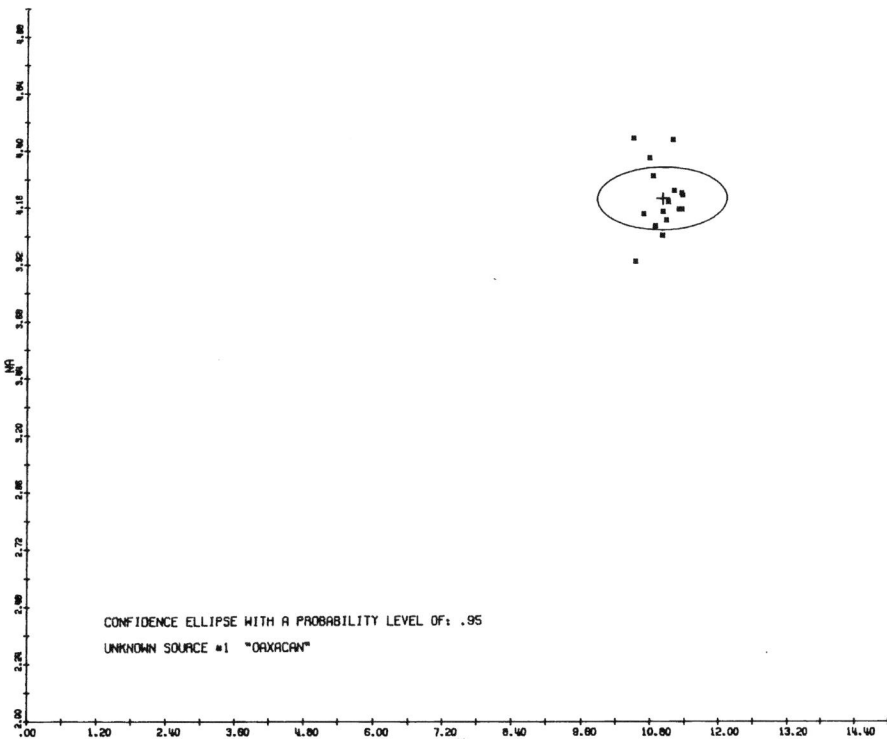

Fig. 6. Confidence ellipse for "Unknown Oaxacan" source.

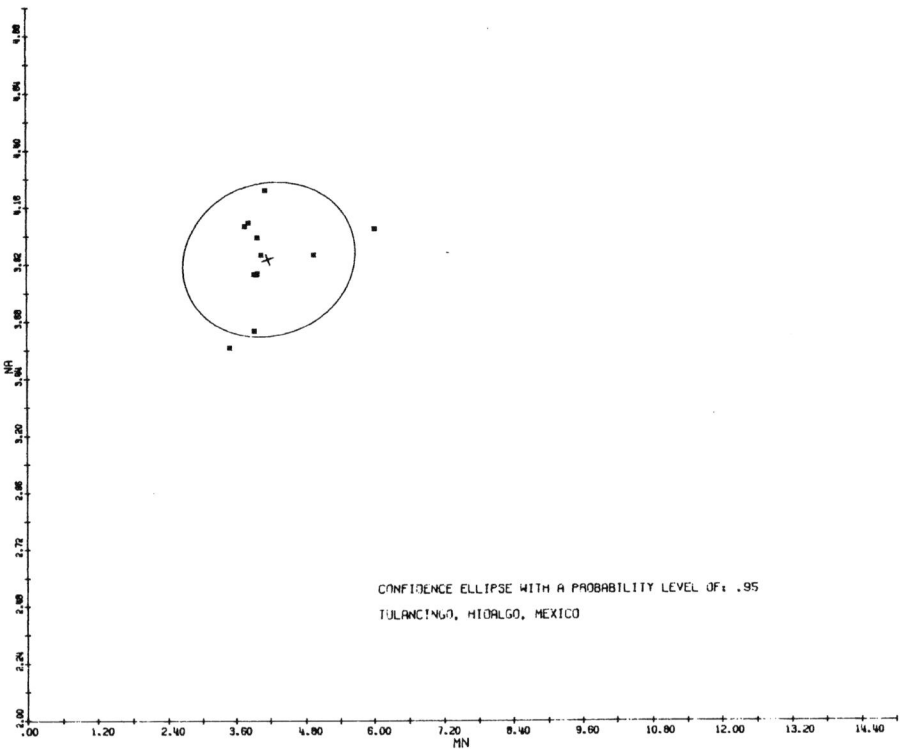

Fig. 7. Confidence ellipse for Tulancingo.

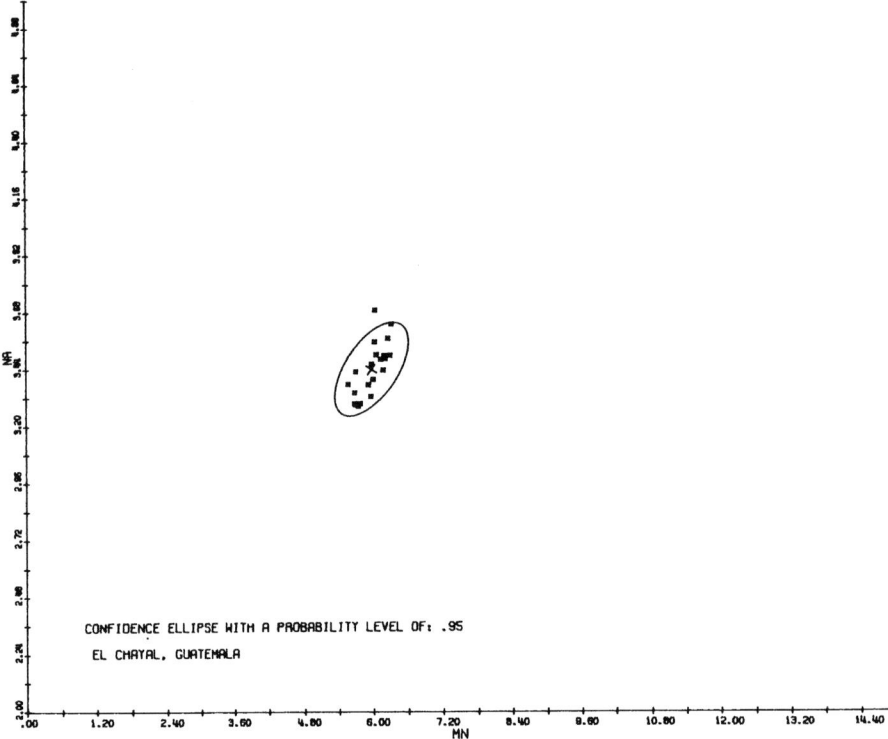

Fig. 8. Confidence ellipse for El Chayal.

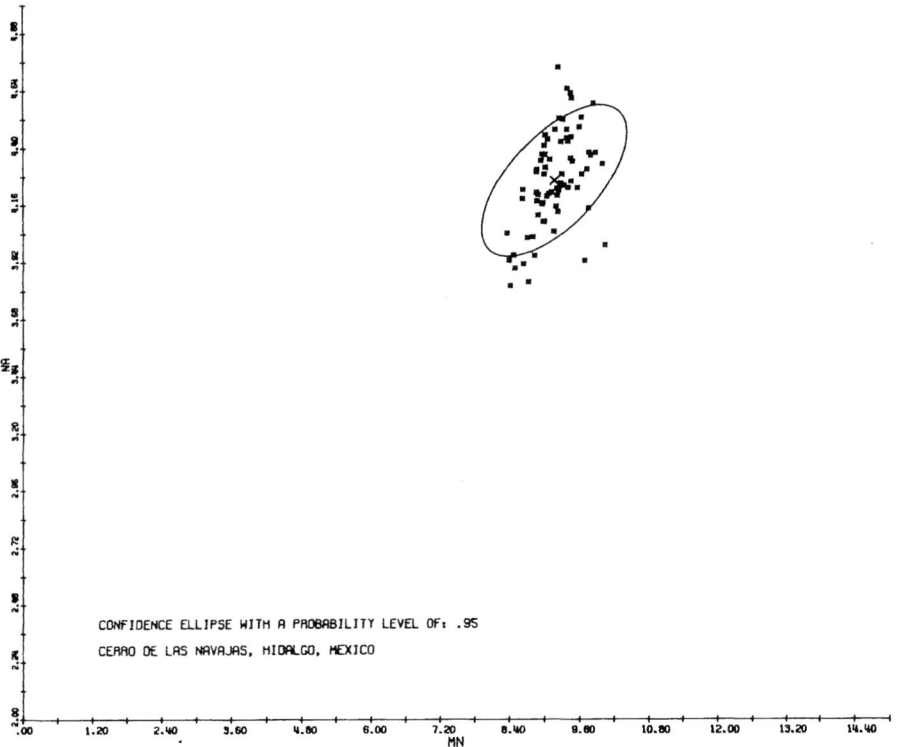

Fig. 9. Confidence ellipse for Cerro de las Navajas.

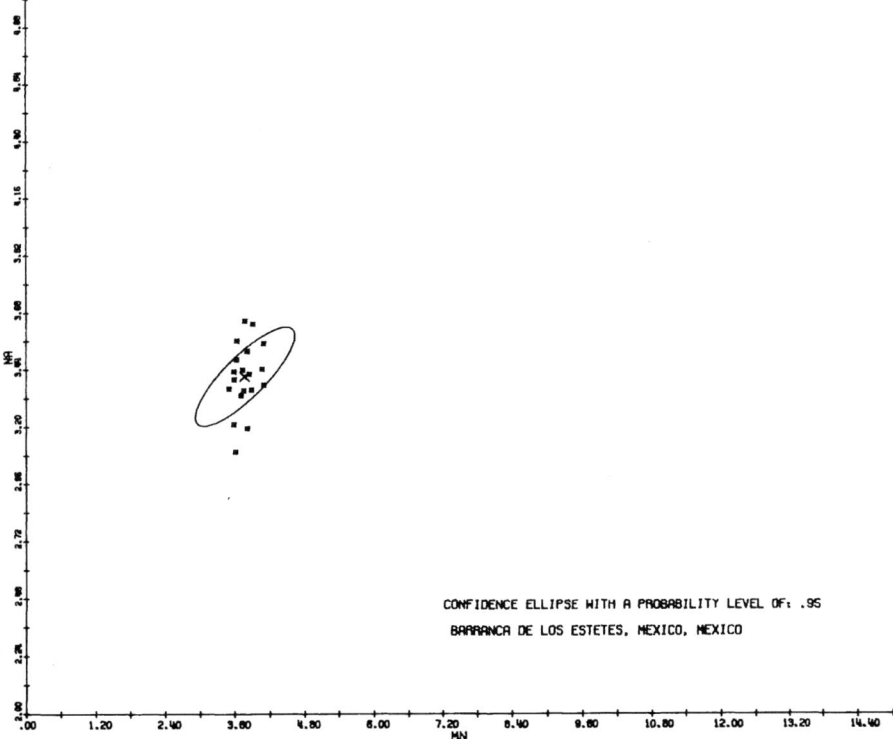

Fig. 10. Confidence ellipse for Barranca de los Estetes.

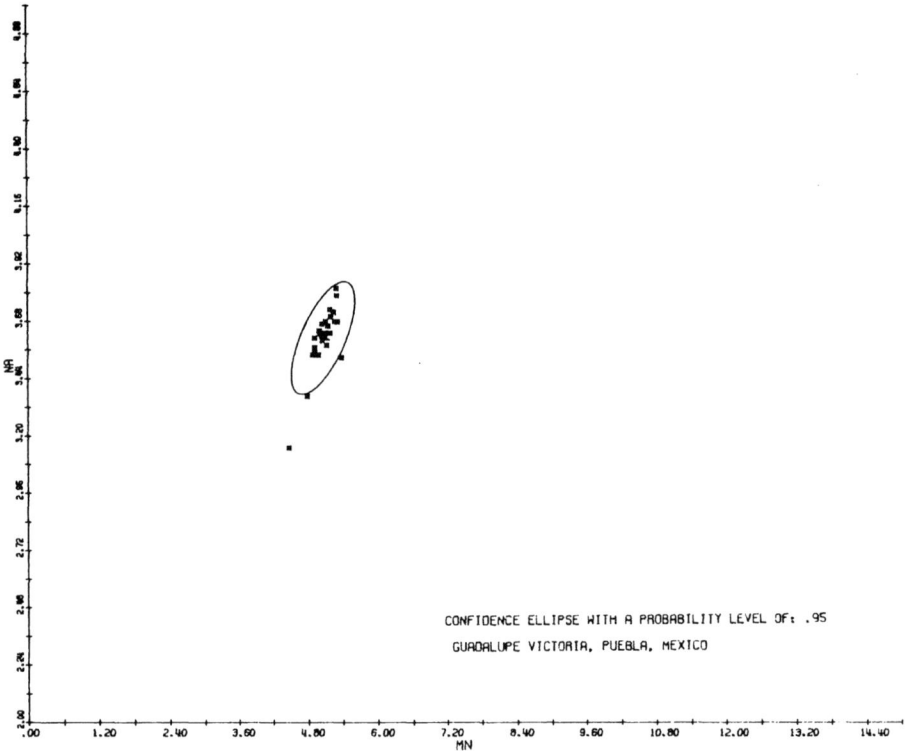

Fig. 11. Confidence ellipse for Guadalupe Victoria.

not included in the statistics given in this paper) also fall in this cluster. Given (1) the persistent verbal reports of an obsidian source in the Tlaxiaco-Yolomécatl area of the Mixteca Alta region, Oaxaca,[3] (2) the indication of a small zone of recent volcanic activity on geological maps of that area, and (3) the concentration of archeological artifacts from the above-mentioned unknown source in Oaxacan sites, it is tentatively suggested that these samples represent an "unknown Oaxacan source." The probable location of this source is recorded as number 15 on Figure 3, and the ellipse for the source is presented in Figure 6.

The Archeological Samples

Although more than 2000 obsidian artifacts have been analyzed by the University of Michigan Laboratory, only 988 of them could be assigned to a dated archeological context; the others are from surface collections. Among the 988 samples are 255 datable to the Early Formative, and 167 from the Middle Formative, which provide the data for this chapter. The remaining 566 samples dating to the Late and Terminal Formative, Classic and Postclassic periods, will be considered in a future paper. The ± 1150 undated samples will be disregarded, for the examination of artifacts of uncertain provenience is of interest only in testing the analytical technique.

Obsidian artifacts were obtained for analysis through the kindness of numerous individuals and institutions. When the total collection of obsidian from a site was available for analysis, a random selection of samples for each provenience unit was made by placing the obsidian in a bag and blindly selecting those pieces which would be sampled for analysis. No attempt was made to visually select samples according to color variations in the obsidian, as it was felt that this

---

[3]Information on this source has come from John Paddock, Centro de Estudios Oaxaqueños, Mitla, Oaxaca, and Ings. E. Ortiz García and J. Elwell of Plan Oaxaca de Juárez, Mexico. Two attempts by the author to reach the reported vicinity of the source were unsuccessful because of rain and mud.

might bias the statistics. Occasionally, however, selection of the artifacts to be analyzed was made by the excavator; this has perhaps introduced some bias into the results.

Archeological samples were analyzed and plotted as outlined above. Transparent overlays on which the .95 confidence ellipses for all sources had been drawn to the standard plot scale were used to determine the source origin of archeological samples. Those artifacts which did not fall within the area of any source ellipse were recorded as indeterminate, and set aside for reanalysis. Where two ellipses overlapped a cluster of archeological data points, as sometimes happened with the Barranca de los Estetes and Tulancingo ellipses, it was found that the samples would generally be distributed throughout the entire area of one or the other ellipse. For example, seventy-five samples from the site of Moyotzingo, Puebla, were densely packed within the Barranca de los Estetes ellipse, including an overlap zone with the Tulancingo elipse; but not one sample fell in any other part of the Tulancingo ellipse. Though obviously we cannot be 95% confident of the ascription, in such cases all samples were recorded as having come from the one ellipse which was completely filled. Where the sample size was too small, or the distribution

TABLE 2

RESULTS OF NEUTRON ACTIVATION ANALYSIS OF EARLY AND MIDDLE
FORMATIVE OBSIDIAN SAMPLES: RAW DATA

Period	Region	Site	Zinapécuaro, Michoacán	Barranca de los Estetes, Mexico	Cerro de las Navajas, Hidalgo	Tulancingo, Hidalgo	Guadalupe Victoria, Puebla	Altotonga, Veracruz	Unknown Oaxacan	El Chayal, Guatemala	Other Guatemalan	Indeterminate, to be Reanalyzed	Total Sample Size
Early Formative	Chiapas	Altamira								7			7
		Angostura-el Carmen								2			2
	Morelos	San Pablo		42				2	2			4	50
	Oaxaca	Huitzo						1					1
		San José Mogote	14	19			5	2	1	1	2		44
		Tierras Largas	8	20			26	6	1	1		4	66
	Puebla	Las Bocas		7									7
	Tabasco	Campo Nuevo					49			2	1		52
		Gamas					3						3
		Nerio Hernández					7						7
		Rancho Guadalupe					10			3	1		14
	Valley of Mexico	Tlapacoya		2									2
												Sub Total	255
Middle Formative	Morelos	Cerro Chacaltepec		3						2			5
	Oaxaca	Huitzo		1	1	3					2		5
		Tierras Largas	4	8		1	7	1	8				31
	Puebla	Acatepec		9	1				1			1	12
		Moyotzingo		75								17	92
	Valley of Mexico	El Arbolillo	1	7	2	1			1		1		13
		Zacatenco		3		1					2	3	9
												Sub Total	167
												Total	422

of points indicated that both sources were being utilized, samples falling in the overlap zone were simply recorded as being from "either source X or source Y." Table 2 lists by time period, region, site, and source, the results of the 422 analyses. In Table 3, the sites are grouped by geographic area, and the percentage of obsidian from each source is calculated.

Definition of Prehistoric Obsidian Exchange Networks

One of the most interesting uses of prehistoric obsidian exchange data is Renfrew, Dixon and Cann's (1968) linear regression analysis of the relationship between quantity of obsidian traded and distance from the source. Utilizing optical spectroscopic analysis, they identified 12 Neolithic villages in the Near East whose obsidian came from the Çiftlik flow in Central Turkey. The percentages of imported obsidian and locally available flint or chert in the lithic inventory was recorded, and the distance to Çiftlik from each site was calculated. This was then recorded on log-normal graph paper, with percent of obsidian on the logarithmic (Y) axis and distance from source on the arithmetic (X) axis. A linear regression line relating distance from the source to the percentage of the total chipped stone inventory which obsidian had contributed was then plotted.

The figures suggest that somewhat more obsidian was moving (and over greater distances) in the Neolithic Near East than in Formative Mesoamerica. Within 100 to 300 kilometers of Çiftlik, most chipped stone found at Neolithic sites is obsidian, at least 80 percent, with only 20 percent flint or chert. Outside this "supply zone," the proportion of obsidian falls off ex-

TABLE 3

RESULTS OF NEUTRON ACTIVATION ANALYSIS OF EARLY AND MIDDLE FORMATIVE OBSIDIAN SAMPLES: PERCENTAGES BY REGION

Archeological Period and Geographical Region	1. Zinapécuaro, Michoacán	2. Barranca de los Estetes, Mexico	3. Cerro de las Navajas, Hidalgo	4. Tulancingo, Hidalgo	5. Guadalupe Victoria, Puebla	6. Altotonga, Veracruz	7. Unknown Oaxacan	7. El Chayal, Guatemala	8. Other Guatemalan
EARLY FORMATIVE									
Chiapas								100.00	
Morelos		90.70				4.65	4.64		
Oaxaca	20.60	36.50			28.50	8.40	2.00	2.00	2.00
Puebla		100.00							
Tabasco					90.80			6.60	2.60
Valley of Mexico		100.00							
Veracruz[1]		4.82	4.82[2]		62.64			21.70	6.02
MIDDLE FORMATIVE									
Morelos	14.30	85.70							
Oaxaca	11.10	25.00	2.80	11.10	19.50	2.80	22.20		5.50
Puebla		79.60	1.20				1.20		
Valley of Mexico	4.50	45.40	9.10	9.10			13.70		18.20
Veracruz[1,3]		26.32	5.26		10.53	5.26		31.58	5.26

[1] Calculated from the analyses of Cobean et al. (personal communication) and eliminating all obsidians attributed to possible or probable source origins and to unknown obsidian source groups.
[2] The possibility that these samples are intrusive from more recent levels should be considered.
[3] Plus 15.79% from the Gueretaro obsidian source.

ponentially with distance. At Tabbat al-Hammam in Syria, 400 kilometers away, the percentage of obsidian is down to 5 percent; at Beidha, in southern Jordan, almost 900 kilometers away, the percentage is only 0.1 percent. In another paper, the authors suggest such a pattern would result if, for example, "villages were spaced at 90 kilometers apart, and... each village would pass to its neighbors down the line one half of the total it received" (Renfrew, Dixon, and Cann, 1968:329). Of course, there are many more villages than that, and a good deal of variation on either side of the regression line; but the model (percentage of obsidian is a function of distance to source) is useful (Fig. 12).

The model works in the Near East because there are sources only in the north, so that percentage of obsidian decreases as one moves south. In Mesoamerica, where obsidian sources form a mosaic pattern (in Central Mexico, Central Guatemala, the Gulf coast, etc.), the situation becomes more complicated. As one moves south, away from the Valley of Mexico sources, one comes gradually closer to the Guatemalan sources. Moreover, there are some coastal areas, such as the Ocós region of Guatemala (Coe and Flannery, 1967), where there is no available chert source, and thus 100 percent of the chipped stone is traded obsidian regardless of distance from source. In order to obtain figures

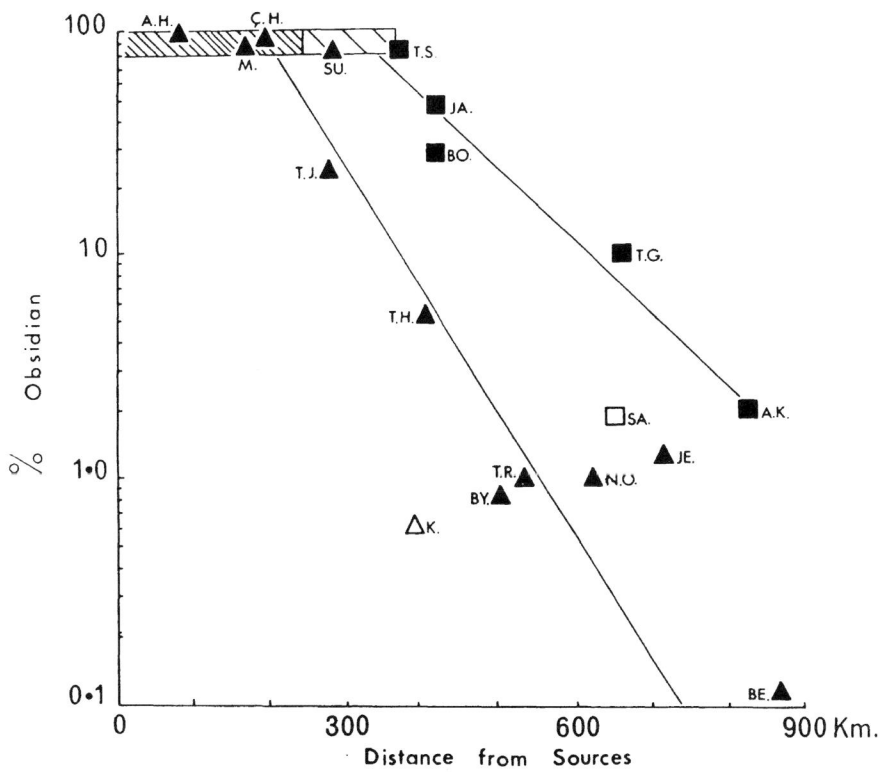

Fig. 12. Percentage of obsidian in the total chipped stone industry against distance from source for Early Neolithic sites in the Near East, 6500 to 5000 B.C. Triangles indicate sites in Central Anatolia and the Levant (supplied by the Cappodocian sources); squares those in the Zagros area (supplied by Armenian sources). Percentages are plotted on a logarithmic scale. Shaded areas indicate the supply zones, the straight lines show approximately exponential fall-off in the contact zones. Key to sites: Zagros: T.S.: Tell Shemsharah; JA: Jarmo; BO: Bouqras; T.G.: Tepe Guran; A.K.: Ali Kosh; SA: Sarab. Levant etc.: A.H.: Asilki Hüyük; C.H.: Çatal Hüyük; M: Mersin; SU: Suberde; T.J.: Tell al-Judaidah; T.H.: Tabbat al-Hammam; T.R.: Tell Ramad; BY: Byblos; N.O.: Nahal Oren; JE: Jericho; BE: Beidha; K: Khirokitia. Reproduced from Renfrew, Dixon and Cann, 1968:328, with permission of A. Colin Renfrew.

TABLE 4

OBSIDIAN AS A FUNCTION OF DISTANCE: DISTANCE FROM PRIMARY OBSIDIAN SOURCE, COMPARED WITH THE PERCENTAGE OBSIDIAN USED AT VARIOUS FORMATIVE VILLAGES

	Distance in Kilometers to Primary Source	Total Obsidian from all Sources Versus Flint	% Barranca de los Estetes Obsidian in Total Obsidian	% Barranca de los Estetes Obsidian in Total Lithic Assemblage	References
MIDDLE FORMATIVE SITES					
El Arbolillo I-II	30 (1)	80.20	53.84*	43.31	Vaillant, 1935
Zacatenco	30 (1)	86.60	30.00*	28.90	Vaillant, 1935
Las Canoas	100 (1?)	50.00	?	?	Flannery, 1964
Cerro Chacaltepec	135 (1)	?	60.00*	±56.00**	Grove, 1970
Huitzo	230 (3)	15.00	20.00*	3.00	Pires-Ferreira
Tierras Largas	400 (1)	16.00	25.80	4.10	Pires-Ferreira
EARLY FORMATIVE SITES					
Tlapacoya	40 (1)	?	100.00*	?	Tolstoy & Paradis, 1970
Gualupita	90 (1)	57.60	?	?	Vaillant, 1935
Las Bocas	120 (1)	?	100.00*	?	
San Pablo	130 (1)	?	90.70	±80.00**	Grove, 1970
Tierras Largas	245 (2)	15.00	30.30	5.00	Pires-Ferreira
San José Mogote	390 (1)	18.50	43.18	6.80	Pires-Ferreira

Primary Sources: 1. Barranca de los Estetes.
2. Guadalupe Victoria.
3. Tulancingo.

*This percentage is based on a small number of analyzed samples.
**Figures with ± are estimates made in lieu of actual percentages.

truly comparable to Renfrew's, we would have to calculate the percentage of obsidian from one specific source within the total chipped stone industry at many different sites in areas where flint is an available alternative, and this would require more neutron activation analyses than anyone has yet had the money or patience to perform. All these problems, coupled with the fact that most Mesoamerican excavators have not published the percentage of obsidian in their total chipped stone assemblage, make application of the Renfrew-Dixon-Cann model to Mesoamerica difficult, if not impossible, at present.

The few figures we have, however, suggest that it might be applicable if sufficient data were available. For example, in Table 4 we give the percentage of obsidian from all sources vs. flint, and the distance in kilometers to the nearest *primary* obsidian source known to have been used by each site. Data on the percentage of obsidian vs. flint is very scanty for the Early Formative. For the Middle Formative, the sites of El Arbolillo and Zacatenco in the Valley of Mexico, only 30 kilometers from the source, have obsidian percentages of 80 percent and 86 percent relative to "quartz."[4] Las Canoas in the Valley of Tehuacán, approximately 100 kilometers distant, has 50 percent obsidian; Barrio del Rosario Huitzo and Tierras Largas in the Valley of Oaxaca, at about 240 kilometers, have 15 percent and 16 percent respectively. These figures seem sufficient to suggest that Mesoamerica may also have had "supply areas," within which the obsidian percentage was close to 80 percent, and beyond which the proportion dropped exponentially with distance.

[4]This is the term Vaillant (1935a) used for flint or chert.

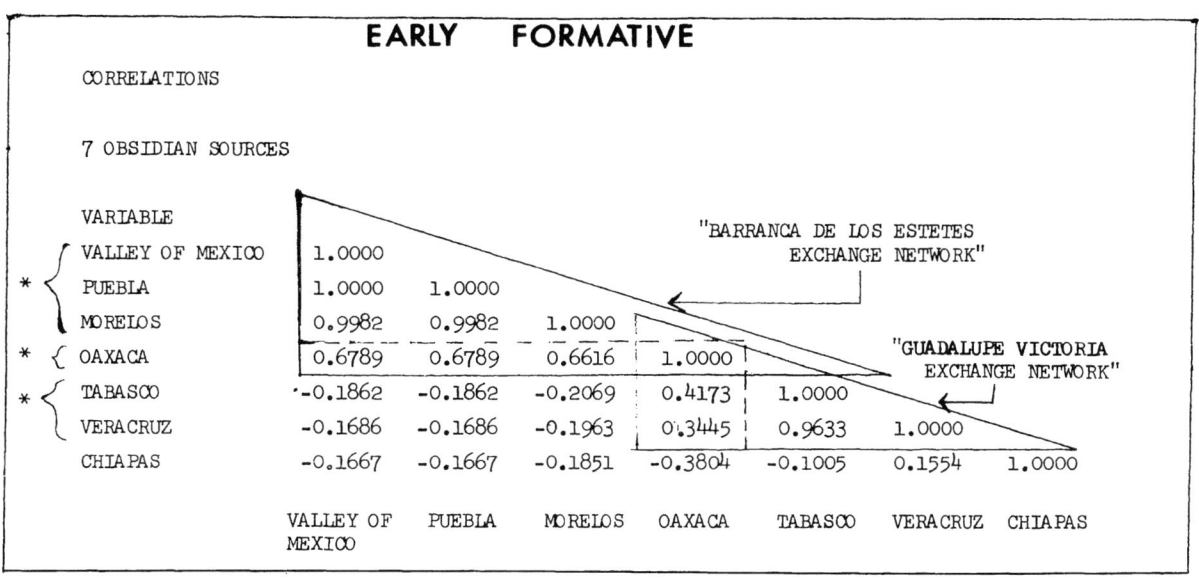

Fig. 13. Q-type correlation matrix for Early Formative Obsidian samples.

Missing data was the biggest problem encountered in constructing Table 4. In order to provide a point of reference, columns three and four provide data on the percentage of Barranca de los Estetes obsidian in relation to the total obsidian, as well as to the total lithic assemblage. At least limited neutron activation analyses are available for all but two other sites, Gualupita and Las Canoas. In both cases, the early appearance of obsidian prismatic blades—a phenomena directly associated with the utilization of Barranca de los Estetes obsidian—suggests that Barranca de los Estates was the primary source.

Because of the mosaic pattern of obsidian source location in Mesoamerica, a major concern in analysis of the Formative period exchange systems becomes what quantity of obsidian from each source, relative to all other sources, was moving in which direction, and at what time.

In order to determine the regions of Mesoamerica which utilized each obsidian source, and to suggest some of the sites within the network of exchange for each source, a series of Q-type sample-to-sample correlation matrices were calculated, utilizing the raw data counts presented in Table 2.[5] Each separate geological source observation was computed against the archeological data and cells of high correlation, suggesting participation in the "exchange sphere" for the source under consideration, were noted. Subsequently, the archeological site data was grouped according to geographic area (as in Table 3), and matrices including all the obsidian source observations were calculated. The composition of exchange networks determined by the grouped data matrix (Figs. 13 and 14) matches almost exactly the composition of exchange spheres previously determined by the individual source-archeological site matrices.

Definition of obsidian exchange networks through correlation matrix analysis is only as accurate as the data is complete. Where large samples from the major excavated sites for a given time period are available (as, for example, in the case of Early Formative Morelos, Oaxaca, Tabasco and Veracruz), we can be certain that the major exchange linkages within a network are

[5]The University of Michigan Statistical Research Laboratory "Midas Statistical Package" was used in calculation of the matrices.

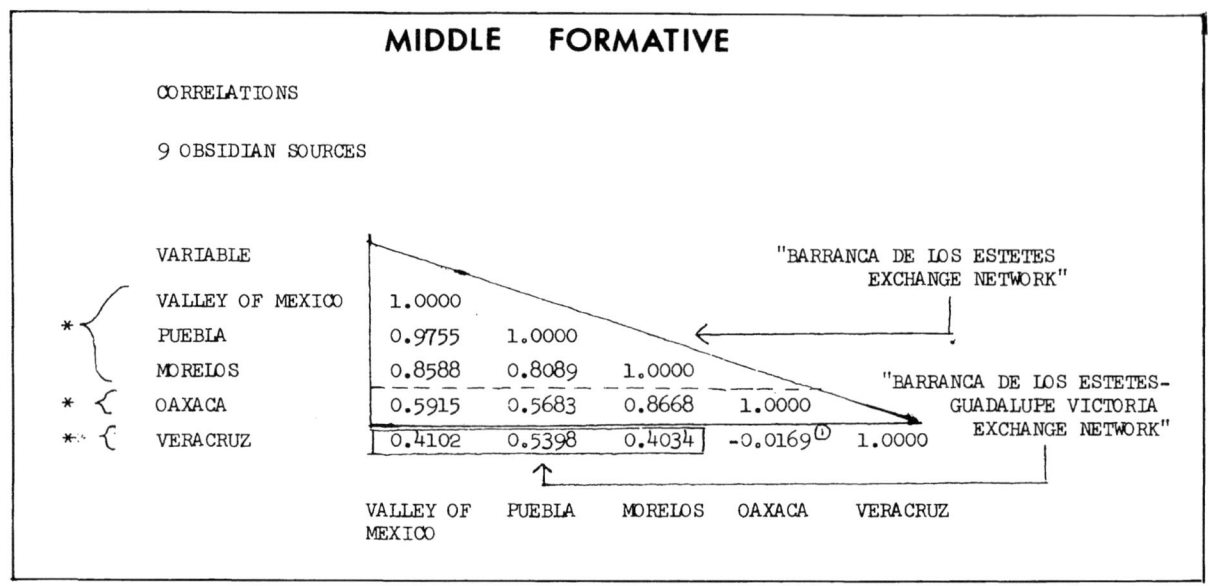

Fig. 14. Q-type correlation matrix for Middle Formative obsidian samples.

accurate in outline, although the exact boundaries of the network cannot be known. Where the data are incomplete because of insufficient sample size or the lack of archeological work in a given area, correlation matrix analysis will not produce good results. In three cases, Early and Middle Formative data show the utilization, within a given regional sphere, of significant quantities of obsidian from sources located in archeologically unknown or inadequately surveyed regions. In such cases, we do not know whether there were local sites controlling the source, or whether it was known and exploited by very distant villages. Although distance between the sites and sources in question must be known before we can resolve this question, provisional definition of an exchange network can be based on the relative importance of the source within the sphere where it is represented. Where obsidian from a given source amounts to more than 20 percent of the total obsidian supply for a given site, some degree of regularity in the supply, possibly involving an exchange network, is suggested. On a provisional basis, the 20 percent minimum is utilized in proposing hypothetical exchange network linkages between sites and archeologically unsurveyed source areas.

THE EARLY FORMATIVE: OBSIDIAN EXCHANGE NETWORKS LINKING VILLAGES

Four obsidian exchange networks have been identified for the Early Formative (see Fig. 15). San Lorenzo is involved in only two of these networks: the Guadalupe Victoria source network and the El Chayal source network. The two other networks, based on the Barranca de los Estetes and Zinapécuaro sources respectively, are virtually restricted to the Central Mexican Highlands and Oaxaca. In the following paragraphs, the archeological and geological evidence for each of the four networks, and the implications of this evidence for understanding the mechanics of prehistoric exchange systems, will be examined.

The Guadalupe Victoria Exchange Network

The Guadalupe Victoria obsidian source is located adjacent to the village of the same name in the eastern part of the state of Puebla. It is

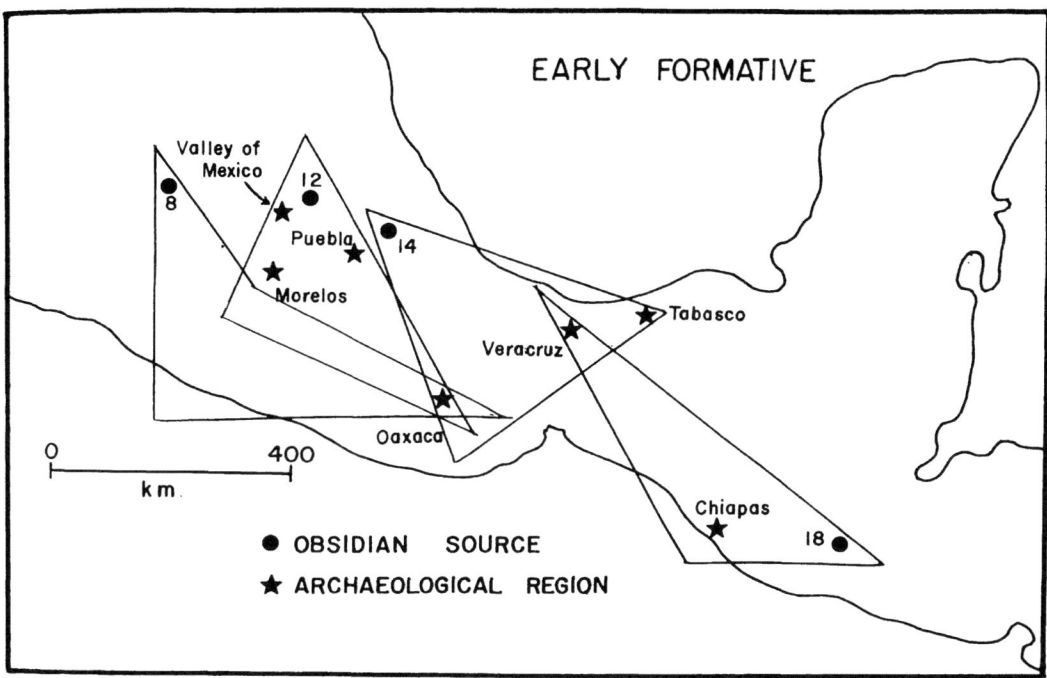

Fig. 15. Early Formative obsidian exchange networks as determined through correlation matrix analysis. The large triangles enclose the sites and sources linked in exchange networks and do not represent actual geographic boundaries. The sites which make up each archaeological region are listed in Table 2. The obsidian sources on which the exchange networks were based are 8: Zinapécuaro, 12: Barranca de los Estetes, 14: Guadalupe Victoria, and 18: El Chayal.

characterized by an extensive stream-laid deposit of weathered obsidian boulders, which may have eroded out of associated ash deposits. No obsidian flows were found by the author in a survey of the immediate region in 1970. Cobean et al. (1971) and J. L. Lorenzo (personal communication) have suggested that the Guadalupe Victoria obsidian boulders may be extrusive products of the Pico de Orizaba volcano, which is located immediately to the southeast. Whatever the origin of the obsidian, analysis of more than 100 samples from across the entire deposit characterize it as a single and unique source.

Guadalupe Victoria obsidian ranges from semi-transparent to banded and cloudy grey with abundant white inclusions. It is quite brittle, and experimental attempts to produce prismatic blades from the boulders were not successful. Core preparation was difficult, as the flakes consistently assumed anomalous and irregular forms due to the inclusions and the generally poor quality of this obsidian. The fact that this source was a poor one for prismatic blades is important in understanding the shifts in exchange networks subsequent to 1000 B.C. (see below).

No Early Formative sites have so far been discovered in the region of Guadalupe Victoria. Our sample from Las Bocas, approximately 100 kilometers to the west and one of the closest known early sites, contains no Guadalupe Victoria obsidian. Approximately 300 kilometers to the south, at the major Early Formative site of San Lorenzo, Guadalupe Victoria was found to be the source of 62.2 percent of the total obsidian (Table 3). At the four smaller sites of Campo Nuevo, Gamas, Nerio Hernández and Rancho Guadalupe, located in the Chontalapa region of Tabasco some 450 kilometers southeast of Guadalupe Victoria, 90.8 percent of the obsidians sampled came from that source. And, finally, 36.5 percent of the obsidians examined for the sites of Huitzo, San José Mogote, and

Tierras Largas in the Valley of Oaxaca, 200 kilometers away, were found to come from the Guadalupe Victoria source.

An interesting possibility is raised by the 62.2 percent Guadalupe Victoria obsidian at San Lorenzo and the 90.8 percent frequencies at the four small Chontalapa sites. If we assume that these small hamlets were dependencies of larger ceremonial and administrative centers, like San Lorenzo and La Venta, it may be that they obtained their obsidian from the larger centers. In this case, it would appear that the larger centers were holding on to larger amounts of the higher quality El Chayal obsidian (which is suitable for prismatic blade manufacture) and passing on more of the lower quality Guadalupe Victoria obsidian to dependent hamlets. This possibility could be checked by further analysis of the distribution of obsidian on a house-by-house basis (see below).

The El Chayal Exchange Network

Over 21 percent of the Early Formative San Lorenzo obsidian samples were found to have come from the El Chayal source in Guatemala, some 580 kilometers to the southwest (Table 3). This source, located in the central highlands near Guatemala City, is noted for its extensive deposits of high quality grey obsidian (Coe and Flannery, 1964). Early Formative sites are known to exist in nearby highland areas, and Shook and Proskouriakoff (1956:96) report Middle Formative (Las Charcas Phase) obsidian workshops in Kaminaljuyú, approximately 35 kilometers southwest of El Chayal. Unfortunately, however, no analyses of obsidian from Formative Guatemalan sites were available to me, and the networks of exchange through which San Lorenzo obtained El Chayal obsidian are not known.

Grove (in press) has suggested a Pacific coastal exchange route for the El Chayal obsidian. In fact, the exclusive presence of El Chayal obsidian at the Early Formative sites of Altamira and Angostura-el Carmen (Table 2) suggest that this source may have been the only one serving the abundant Early Formative sites of the Guatemalan and Chiapas coast. The chipped-stone assemblages of these sites are frequently 100 percent obsidian, a reflection of the total absence of flint sources in the Pacific Coastal Plain. It is possible that these coastal sites participated not only in the movement of El Chayal obsidian but also the shipment of local Pacific species of marine and estuary shells towards the Isthmus of Tehuantepec, and thence to the Gulf and the highlands of Oaxaca, but this remains to be demonstrated.

A second possibility is that the El Chayal exchange network may have involved the direct movement of obsidian northward from the source along the major rivers to the Gulf Coastal area. A high amount may have gone directly to San Lorenzo for later distribution. Although the recent work of Hammond (1972) suggests this route may have been in use as early as the Middle Formative period, no Early Formative sites have ever been reported for the area. Evaluation of this hypothesis must therefore await further field work and analysis.

Secondary distribution of El Chayal obsidian after it reached San Lorenzo is also of interest because it evidently followed the linkages of the Guadalupe Victoria exchange network. El Chayal obsidian represents 5.6 percent of the total at the small Tabasco sites, and 2.0 percent of the total in Oaxaca. No El Chayal obsidian has yet been identified from any site located outside the linkages of the Guadalupe Victoria and El Chayal exchange networks.

The Barranca de los Estetes
Exchange Network

The Barrance de los Estetes obsidian flows are located in the Teotihuacán Valley, near the village of Otumba in the State of Mexico. These deposits, in an area locally referred to as Malpais, are extensive and contain a highly silicified grey obsidian of uniform quality. Experimental knapping with Barranca de los Estetes obsidian shows that its flaking properties are ideally suited for controlled pressure flaking and blade production. The distribution of Barranca de los Estetes obsidian during the Early Formative is densest in the Central Highlands region of Mexico. Although no Early Formative period sites have been reported from the Teotihuacán Valley proper, they are numerous elsewhere in the Valley of Mexico, and David Grove (1972a) has recently suggested that further analysis of the ceramics from W. T. Sanders' survey of the Teotihuacán Valley may yet reveal the presence of Early Formative pottery.

When the percentage of Barranca de los Estetes obsidian in the total obsidian sample is calculated (setting aside for the moment the percentage of flint), it suggests a "supply zone" extending up to 130 kilometers from the source, and including the sites of Tlapacoya, Valley of Mexico (with 100 percent Barranca de los Estetes obsidian), Las Bocas, Puebla (with 100 percent Barranca de los Estetes obsidian), and San Pablo, Morelos (with 90.7 percent Barranca de los Estetes obsidian). Beyond the "supply zone," Early Formative sites in the Valley of Oaxaca, approximately 375 kilometers to the south, contain 36.5 percent Barranca de los Estetes obsidian. Similar proportions of Barranca de los Estetes obsidian in the Central Highlands continue during the Middle Formative, and indeed are characteristic of all periods except, perhaps, the Aztec era (unpublished data). The reasons for this almost unique homogeneity in obsidian exploitation patterns during Central Highlands prehistory probably lie in the richness of the source and its suitability for blade-making.

Considerable exchange between the Central Highlands and Oaxaca is indicated by the presence of 36.5 percent Barranca de los Estetes obsidian (with a +.67 average matrix correlation) found in the Early Formative Oaxacan samples. Barranca de los Estetes obsidian was also found at San Lorenzo, but composed only 4.8 percent of the total obsidian industry. The −0.17 average matrix correlation for San Lorenzo suggests that San Lorenzo may have received Barranca de los Estetes obsidian only indirectly, as a byproduct of its established Guadalupe Victoria exchange linkages with Oaxaca. The possible position of Oaxaca as a point of overlap between the Central Highland-Barranca de los Estetes network and the Gulf Coast-Guadalupe Victoria network suggests that Oaxaca may have played a kind of "middle man" role in the transmission of some Gulf Coast materials to the Central Highlands and vice versa.

Increasing movement of Barranca de los Estetes obsidian to distant regions in subsequent periods reflects the increasing demand for prismatic blades. The earliest evidence of manufacture of prismatic obsidian blades comes from the Valley of Mexico, where they were found in association with the Iztapan mammoth (Aveleyra, 1952). In Morelos, in Oaxaca, and along the Gulf Coast, the earliest known prismatic blades date to about 1000-900 B.C. and are made of Barranca de los Estetes obsidian. The rare blade cores found at these sites are insufficient in size and number to have produced the quantities of blades which were recovered. This suggests that much of the Barranca de los Estetes obsidian was exported from the Central Highlands in the form of finished blades. Certainly this was the case in later periods; MacNeish (personal communication) reports finding obsidian blades wrapped in bark cloth, presumably to prevent breakage during transportation, in one Tehuacán cave.

The Zinapécuaro Exchange Network

The Zinapécuaro obsidian flows, located in the state of Michoacán, produce a cloudy grey obsidian of high quality. The area surrounding the source is archeologically unknown, so that the network of sites through which Oaxaca obtained the 20.2 percent of its total obsidian supply from this source (located at a distance of approximately 530 kilometers) cannot be determined. The only other piece of Zinapécuaro obsidian identified from the sites considered in this paper is one artifact from mixed levels at the site of San Pablo, Morelos; it has not been included in the statistics.

Considering Grove's suggestion (in press) that the Central Highland "Tlatilco culture" contains "West Mexican influences," it is surprising that more Zinapécuaro obsidian was not found there, but the explanation may lie in the more readily-available Barranca de los Estetes source. It is suggested by this author that the apparent absence of Zinapécuaro obsidian at San Lorenzo

TABLE 5
COMPARATIVE RESULTS OF EIGHT ARCHEOLOGICAL SAMPLES FROM TIERRAS LARGAS, OAXACA, ANALYZED BY OPTICAL EMISSION SPECTROSCOPY (YALE UNIVERSITY) AND NEUTRON ACTIVATION ANALYSIS (UNIVERSITY OF MICHIGAN)

Sample	Sample Number	Analysis of Yale University (Cobean et al.)	Analysis of the University of Michigan Laboratory
1. Tierras Largas B74C/feature 151/depth 75-95/N small unused flake	OB-3861	Guadalupe Victoria, Puebla	Guadalupe Victoria, Puebla
2. Tierras Largas B74B/feature 152/depth 90-120 small unused flake	OB-3862	Guadalupe Victoria, Puebla	Guadalupe Victoria, Puebla
3. Tierras Largas B74B/feature 116/depth 100 small unused flake	OB-3863	Guadalupe Victoria, Puebla	Guadalupe Victoria, Puebla
4. Tierras Largas B74B/feature 130/depth 70-90/W blade fragment	OB-3864	Possibly El Paraíso, Queréraro	Zinapécuaro, Michoacán
5. Tierras Largas B74/square 3796/feature 112/depth 50-90	OB-3865	Possibly El Paraíso, Queréraro	Barranca de los Estetes, Mexico
6. Tierras Largas B74A/house 1/square C13 small unused flake	OB-3866	Probably Barranca de los Estetes, Mexico	Zinapécuaro, Michoacán
7. Tierras Largas B74A/house 1/square E15 small unused flake	OB-3867	Unknown source	Barranca de los Estetes, Mexico
8. Tierras Largas B74A/house 1/square D14 blade fragment	OB-3868	Possibly El Paraíso, Queréraro	Zinapécuaro, Michoacán

may be an analytical anomaly.[6] A suggestion of the possible importance of the Zinapécuaro source area as a second center of prismatic blade manufacture and export is seen in the nearly equal proportions of Barranca de los Estetes and Zinapécuaro prismatic blades in San José Mogote (Table 7).

THE MIDDLE FORMATIVE: OBSIDIAN EXCHANGE NETWORKS LINKING VILLAGES

The defacement of basalt monuments at San Lorenzo around 900 B.C. (Coe, 1968b) falls near

[6]See Table 5 for a comparison of the results of duplicate samples analyzed by Cobean at Yale and the University of Michigan Neutron Activation Analysis Laboratory. Our results, based on the .95 confidence ellipse, would suggest that the Yale samples listed as "possibly El Paraíso" are from Zinapécuaro.

the beginning of the Middle Formative period. This partial destruction, followed by the rise of La Venta, is probably the first of a cycle of such political readjustments which characterizes the Formative periods. The effects of political realignment after this event were felt throughout Mesoamerica. Some of the existing obsidian exchange networks broke down, others were modified, and new ones were established as new villages rose to prominence. The "pan-Mesoamerican" aspect of the Early Formative long-distance exchange patterns disappeared, the frequency and intensity of long-distance exchange was reduced, and a period of increasing insularity and regionalization followed. Perhaps paradoxically, this regionalization took place during a period of great political evolution in the highland regions of Mexico.

For example, despite the position of La Venta

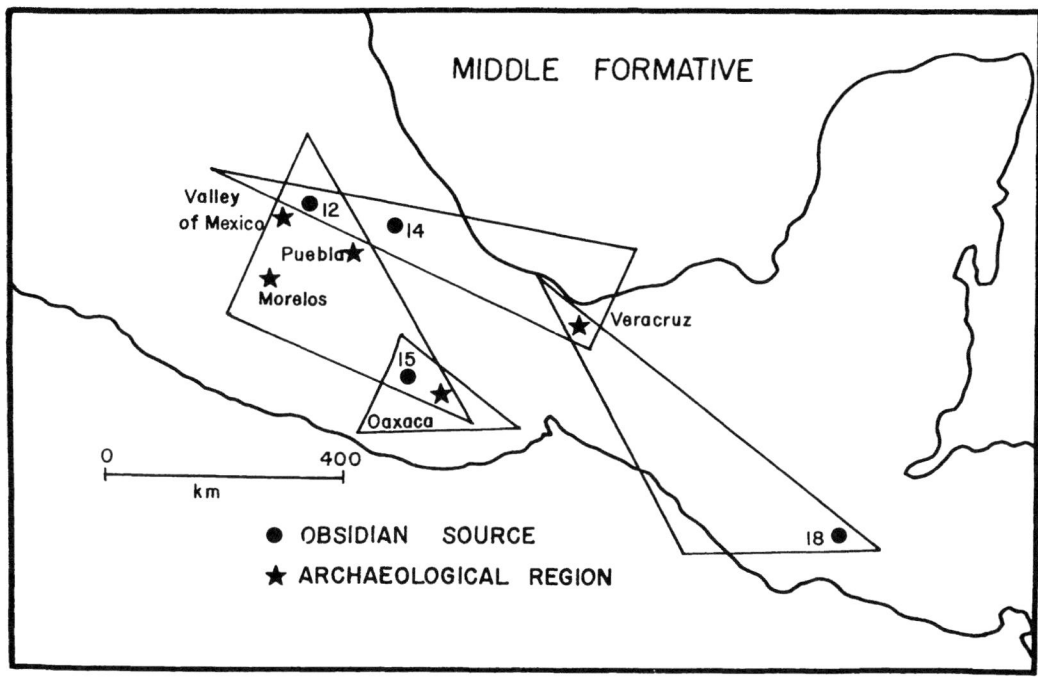

Fig. 16. Middle Formative obsidian exchange networks as determined through correlation matrix analysis. The large triangles enclose the sites and sources linked in exchange networks and do not represent actual geographic boundaries. The sites which make up each archaeological region are listed in Table 2. The obsidian sources on which the exchange networks were based are 12: Barranca de los Estetes, 14: Guadalupe Victoria, 15: Unknown Oaxacan, and 18: El Chayal.

as the dominant center succeeding San Lorenzo (a position reflected in amassed luxury items), La Venta remained a regional site. The excavators have suggested that the bulk of the raw material found at La Venta was probably obtained within 100 miles of the site (Heizer, 1961). A similar trend toward regionalization is noted for Middle Formative sites in the Valley of Mexico (Tolstoy and Paradis, 1971), Morelos (Grove, 1970a) and the Valley of Oaxaca (Winter, 1972). Four obsidian exchange spheres have been identified for this period (Fig. 16).

The Guadalupe Victoria-Barranca de los Estetes Exchange Network

The most significant modification of exchange network patterns from the Early Formative to the Middle Formative period centers on the breakdown and realignment of the Early Formative Guadalupe Victoria exchange system. A dissolution of traditional exchange ties between the Gulf Coast and the Valley of Oaxaca followed the destruction of monuments at San Lorenzo and the rise of La Venta to political dominance. The San Lorenzo-Oaxaca Q-type matrix correlation drops from an Early Formative +0.38 average to a −0.01 average during the Middle Formative, clearly reflecting the weakening of ties between these spheres. Unfortunately, obsidian percentage data for La Venta are not available,[7] and we can only guess what its role in the Middle Formative obsidian exchange networks might have been.

The second important change in obsidian exchange during the Middle Formative involves an increase in obsidian moving between the Valley of Mexico and the Gulf Coast. Barranca de los

[7] Only twelve excavated obsidian samples from La Venta have been analyzed (Jack and Heizer, 1968). Three of the samples were identified as Cerro de las Navajas obsidian, two as unknown source B, six as unknown source C, and one as possibly coming from El Chayal. Unknown sources B and C are grey obsidians, and may possibly represent the same Barranca de los Estetes and Guadalupe Victoria sources found in the Middle Formative samples from San Lorenzo (Table 3).

Estetes obsidian jumps from 4.8 percent to 26.3 percent of the total at San Lorenzo, and the average correlation coefficient between the two areas changes from −0.17 to +0.47. The increase of direct contact between these two areas may in part reflect the weakening of Oaxaca-San Lorenzo exchange relations; but a more compelling factor is that by the Middle Formative well-made prismatic blades were in great demand throughout Mesoamerica, thus increasing the importance of the Barranca de los Estetes source. Our first Middle Formative obsidian exchange network thus links the Gulf Coast (San Lorenzo and probably La Venta) with the Guadalupe Victoria and Barranca de los Estetes sources. The Guadalupe Victoria-Barranca de los Estetes exchange network included a one-way movement of obsidian from Barranca de los Estetes to the Gulf Coast which, while it represented a change in patterns of obsidian utilization for the coast, does not seem to have involved a comparable change in the patterns of distribution within the Central Highlands.

The El Chayal Exchange Network

The percentage of El Chayal obsidian at San Lorenzo increased from 21.7 percent to 31.6 percent during the Middle Formative. At La Venta, one of the twelve excavated obsidians analyzed by Jack and Heizer (1968) was identified as coming from this source (see footnote 7, above). Although a series of Chiapas Pacific Coastal sites near Aquiles Serdán, Izapa, and Pijijiapan flourished during this period, this region is of minor importance here because no obsidians from Middle Formative sites in the Guatemalan Highlands or the Pacific coast are included in our sample.

The Barranca de los Estetes Exchange Network

The original network of Central Highland sites associated with the Barranca de los Estetes source during the Early Formative remain essentially intact during the Middle Formative period. The predominant importance of Barranca de los Estetes obsidian in the Central Highlands continues; 85.7 percent of the obsidian at Cerro Chacaltepec, Morelos, and 97.6 percent of the obsidian at Acatepec and Moyotzingo, Puebla come from this source. In the Valley of Mexico, however, an interesting diversity of sources is seen at El Arbolillo and Zacatenco. Although these sites are the closest to the Barranca de los Estetes source of all the sites analyzed, they contain only 45.5 percent Barranca de los Estetes obsidian. Small amounts of obsidian from other sources compose the balance: Zinepécuaro 4.5 percent, Cerro de las Navajas 9.1 percent, Tulancingo 9.1 percent, "Unknown Oaxacan" 13.7 percent, and Guatemalan (other than El Chayal) 18.2 percent. This apparent diversity could be a function of small sample size, or might be the result of pooling (see below). Since we do not have house-by-house data for Valley of Mexico sites, this cannot be confirmed.

Twenty-five percent of the obsidian samples from Middle Formative levels in Oaxaca were of Barranca de los Estetes obsidian, indicating a continuity of exchange ties with the Central Highlands from the Early to the Middle Formative periods. The average correlation coefficient between the two areas changes only slightly, from +0.58 to +0.50. A diversification of source utilization, similar to that in the Valley of Mexico, is also seen in Oaxaca at this time. Obsidian from six different sources is represented in Middle Formative deposits in both Oaxaca and the Valley of Mexico. It is in this period that pooling of obsidian by some central agency, seen only at major villages during the Early Formative period, spreads to include even the small hamlets (see below).

The "Unknown Oaxacan" Exchange Network

Although obsidian from eight geological sources is found in Middle Formative Oaxaca, five of the sources could have been obtained through contact with the already-established Barranca de los Estetes exchange system; two suggest some continued contact with the Gulf Coast, and one source is a local one. Definition of the "Unknown Oaxacan" source has already been discussed. The obsidian is consistently green in color, and the irregular shape of the artifacts suggests it may not be of very high quality. It represents 22.2 percent of the total Oaxacan obsidian, 13.7 percent of the Valley of Mexico obsidian, and 1.2 percent of the Puebla Middle Formative obsidian. The source was already known during the Early Formative (1.1 percent in Oaxaca and 4.6 percent in Morelos), but was not extensively exploited at that time. The reasons for this may lie partly in the apparent poor quality of the source, and partly in Oaxaca's position as "middleman" in the exchange of obsidian from higher quality sources. Increased use of this Oaxacan source is further evidence for the Middle Formative regionalization already mentioned.

Indeed, during the Middle Formative, for the first time, each of the major settlement areas we have mentioned—the Central Mexican Highlands, the Gulf Coast, Highland Guatemala, and Oaxaca—apparently concentrated most heavily on its own local obsidian source. Individually-negotiated long-distance trade, a form of "foreign relations" characteristic of simpler societies like the previously-described Maring and Siassi, was gradually replaced by more intensive regional exploitation, and by regional specialization in blade-making. In the case of the latter, Barranca de los Estetes and El Chayal rose to prominence because of the suitability of their raw material. In later times, Teotihuacán and Kaminaljuyú were to monopolize blade making in those areas.

THE DISTRIBUTION OF OBSIDIAN IN FORMATIVE OAXACAN HOUSEHOLDS

Analysis of the distribution of obsidian in Formative Oaxacan households comes from excavations at San José Mogote (Flannery et al., 1970) and Tierras Largas (Winter, 1972) in the Valley of Oaxaca. Determination of the sources of obsidian samples from eighteen house floors at these two sites provides information on the changing patterns of source utilization from 1300 to 500 B.C.

Excavations at the small site of Tierras Largas (Winter, 1972) produced three "household clusters" (units composed of a house plus its associated features and burials) for the periods dating from 1300 to 1150 B.C. (Late Tierras Largas Phase) and 1150 to 850 B.C. (San José Phase). Thirty-three obsidian samples from these household clusters were analyzed, and considerable variation from house to house in the percentage of various sources used was observed, implying that all households probably did not draw on a common pool of obsidian. Based on the data presented in Table 6 (and see also Winter, 1972:177), Winter suggested that during the Early Formative each household may have directly and independently obtained the obsidian which it used. The mechanism for such exchange may have been "trade partnerships" based on fictive kinship relations of the type previously discussed. This form of obsidian distribution contrasts with that shown at San José Mogote for the period from 1200 to 850 B.C.

San José Mogote, located approximately ten kilometers northwest of Tierras Largas, is the largest Early Formative period site discovered so far in the Valley of Oaxaca. Some of the thirteen household clusters excavated at San José Mogote as of 1970 provide a possible contrast to those from Tierras Largas, although the samples are small and our conclusions should be taken as tentative. Forty-four obsidian artifacts from eleven house floors at San José Mogote were analyzed. The results, presented in Tables 6 and 7 indicate that the percentages of obsidian from various sources are unexpectedly uniform from house to house in at least one residential ward, Area A. This suggests that some form of centralized pooling, which resulted in a mixture of the incoming obsidian prior to its distribution, may have been taking place.

The four household clusters in Area A show a number of stratigraphic continuities in shell-working, mica-working, and other craft activities over four "generations" of house construction in one residential ward (Flannery et al., 1970). They contain a wide variety of exotic items, as well as evidence of manufacture of small flat magnetite mirrors which were exchanged with communities as far away as Morelos, Nochixtlán, and the Gulf Coast (see Chapter III). The evidence for pooling suggests that the part-time

TABLE 6

RESULTS OF NEUTRON ACTIVATION ANALYSIS OF OBSIDIAN FROM EARLY AND MIDDLE FORMATIVE HOUSEHOLDS AT SAN JOSÉ MOGOTE AND TIERRAS LARGAS, OAXACA

Time Period	Provenience	Zinapécuaro (Michoacán)	Barranca de los Estetes (Mexico)	Guadalupe Victoria (Puebla)	Altotonga (Veracruz)	Unknown Oaxacan	El Chayal (Guatemala)	Other Guatemalan	Total
Rosario Phase	Tierras Largas								
	Cluster R-1	3	7	9		7			26
Guadalupe Phase	Cluster G-3	2	2			2			6
	Total	5	9	9		9			32
San José Phase	Tierras Largas								
	Cluster LSJ-1	12	4	2	1				19
	Cluster LSJ-2	2	5	4					11
	Cluster ESJ-1	1	3	3	1	1			9
	Total	15	12	9	2	1			39
San José Phase	San José Mogote								
	Area A								
	Cluster C1	2	2	2			1		7
	Cluster C2	3	3						6
	Cluster C3	3	3	1	1				8
	Cluster C4	2	2						4
	Area C								
	House 1		1					1	2
	House 2		1						1
	House 5	1	1						2
	House 6		1						1
	House 8	1	3					1	5
	House 9	2		2	1				5
	House 10		2			1			3
	Total	14	19	5	2	1	1	2	44
Tierras Largas Phase	Tierras Largas								
	Cluster LTL-1		3	21	1				25
	Cluster LTL-2			1					1
	Cluster LTL-3		7	2			1		10
	Total		10	24	1		1		36

craft-specialists whose handiwork is seen in Area A may have been affiliated with an important individual or family from whom they received their obsidian. We are struck by the fact that this early evidence of obsidian pooling is also contemporaneous with the earliest importation of prismatic blades from the Barranca de los Estetes and Zinapécuaro sources, beginning about 1000 B.C. A causal relationship between the two events could be suggested, although the evidence from San José Mogote suggests that flakes and chunks were being pooled as well (Table 7). The obsidian sample from a contemporary residential ward, Area C, is too small to indicate whether

TABLE 7
RESULTS OF NEUTRON ACTIVATION ANALYSIS OF OBSIDIAN FROM EARLY FORMATIVE (SAN JOSÉ PHASE) HOUSEHOLDS AT SAN JOSÉ MOGOTE

	Zinapécuaro (Michoacán)	Barranca de los Estetes (Mexico)	Guadalupe Victoria (Puebla)	Altotonga (Veracruz)	Unknown Oaxacan	El Chayal (Guatemala)	Other Guatemalan	Total
Area A								
Cluster C1	BB	BB	CD			D		7
Cluster C2	BDD	BDD						6
Cluster C3	BBB	FDD	F	F				8
Cluster C4	DD	DD						4
Area C								
House 1		B					F	2
House 2		F						1
House 5	B	C						2
House 6		F						1
House 8	B	BFF					F	5
House 9	FK		FF	F				5
House 10		BB			F			3
Total	14	19	5	2	1	1	2	44

Note: B=Blade, C=Flake Core, D=Debitage, F=Flake, K=Chunk.

TABLE 8
SAN JOSÉ MOGOTE, AREAS A AND C: OBSIDIAN STATISTICS

AREA A

Household Cluster C1:
- obsidian = 15 of 40 artifacts or 37.50%
- Used: 12 blade fragments; 1 core, bullet or blade with cortex, fragment
- Not Used: 2 blade fragments

Household Cluster C2:
- obsidian = 9 of 65 artifacts or 13.85%
- Used: 8 blade fragments; 1 rectangular flake with cortex

Household Cluster C3:
- obsidian = 11 of 83 artifacts or 13.25%
- Used: 5 blade fragments; 2 flake fragments, indeterminate form; 1 oval flake fragment; 1 core preparation piece, face with cortex
- Not Used: 1 blade fragment; 1 core preparation piece, face with cortex

Household Cluster C4:
- obsidian = 6 of 57 artifacts or 10.53%

TABLE 8 (Continued)

Household Cluster C4 (Continued)
- Used: 5 blade fragments; 1 core on a flake or flake fragment

AREA C

House 1:
- obsidian = 12 of 91 artifacts or 13.19%
- Used: 1 contracting flake; 3 flake fragments, indeterminate form
- Not Used: 1 chunk; 1 blade fragment; 5 flake fragments, indeterminate form; 1 expanding flake

House 2:
- obsidian = 40 of 318 artifacts or 12.57%
- Used: 3 flakes, indeterminate form; 1 expanding flake; 1 rectangular flake; 10 flake fragments, indeterminate form; 9 blade fragments; 1 chunk; 1 core preparation piece, edge of platform
- Not Used: 9 flake fragments, indeterminate form; 1 blade fragment; 3 chunks; 1 chunk with cortex

TABLE 8 (Continued)

House 4:	obsidian =	120 of 532 artifacts or 22.56%
	Used:	3 expanding flakes 1 rectangular flake 1 oval flake 1 oval flake with cortex 17 flake fragments, indeterminate form 3 flake fragments, indeterminate form with cortex 30 blade fragments 1 blade fragment with cortex 6 rectangular flake fragments 2 chunks 2 nodule fragment cores 2 split nodule cores 1 core preparation piece, chunk
	Not Used:	1 expanding flake 2 rectangular flakes 2 oval flakes 25 flake fragments, indeterminate form 1 flake fragment, indeterminate form with cortex 1 expanding flake fragment 5 blade fragments 1 rectangular flake fragment 6 chunks 2 split nodule cores 2 core preparation pieces, faces 1 core preparation piece, face with cortex 1 core preparation piece, chunk
House 5:	obsidian =	5 of 21 artifacts or 23.80%
	Used:	1 blade fragment
	Not Used:	2 flake fragments, indeterminate form 1 blade fragment 1 chunk with cortex
House 6:	obsidian =	4 of 17 artifacts or 25.53%
	Used:	3 blade fragments
	Not Used:	1 chunk
House 7:	obsidian =	1 of 14 artifacts or 7.14%
	Used:	1 blade fragment
House 8:	obsidian =	46 of 207 artifacts or 22.06%
	Used:	1 flake, indeterminate form 2 expanding flakes 1 expanding flake with cortex 2 contracting flakes 1 contracting flake with cortex 1 rectangular flake 1 rectangular flake with cortex 4 flake fragments, indeterminate form 1 contracting flake fragment with cortex 9 blade fragments 1 blade fragment with cortex 2 rectangular flake fragments

TABLE 8 (Continued)

House 8: (Continued)		
	Used:	1 chunk 1 core preparation piece, face
	Not Used:	6 flake fragments, indeterminate form 1 expanding flake fragment 1 rectangular flake fragment 5 chunks 2 chunks with cortex 1 nodule fragment core 2 core preparation pieces, faces
House 9:	obsidian =	52 of 306 artifacts or 16.99%
	Used:	1 flake, indeterminate form 1 expanding flake 2 rectangular flakes 2 oval flakes 12 flake fragments, indeterminate form 1 expanding flake fragment 3 rectangular flake fragments
	Not Used:	1 expanding flake 1 contracting flake 2 rectangular flakes 1 rectangular flake with cortex 2 oval flakes 12 flake fragments, indeterminate form 1 expanding flake fragment 3 contracting flake fragments 1 rectangular flake fragment 3 chunks 2 core on flake or flake fragments 1 core preparation piece, face
House 10:	obsidian =	7 of 28 artifacts or 25.00%
	Used:	4 flakes, indeterminate form with cortex 1 blade 1 contracting flake with cortex
	Not Used:	1 expanding flake with cortex 1 contracting flake with cortex

SUMMARY: Area A and Area C Obsidian Statistics.

Of the 1779 artifacts analyzed, 328 are obsidian; that is, a total of 18.47%.

The 328 obsidian artifacts are subdivided as follows:

182 or	55.49%	flakes and flake fragments (excluding blades)
95 or	28.96%	blades and blade fragments
28 or	8.53%	chunks
22 or	6.72%	flake cores and core preparation pieces
1 or	.30%	blade cores

Of the 328 obsidian artifacts, 27 or 8.23% had cortex; these are subdivided as follows:

17 or	9.34%	of all 182 flakes and flake fragments (excluding blades) have cortex
2 or	2.10%	of all 95 blades and blade fragments have cortex
4 or	14.20%	of all 28 chunks have cortex
3 or	18.18%	of all 22 flake cores and core preparation pieces have cortex
1 or	100%	of the one blade core has cortex

pooling went on there or not. The absence of evidence of pooling at Tierras Largas (and its very different source percentages) suggests that it probably did not obtain its obsidian from San José Mogote at this period. Perhaps pooling at the latter site was restricted to a few important individuals or families, who brought in obsidian for distribution to their affines.

By the Middle Formative period (850 to 500 B.C.), some evidence of pooling of obsidian is found even in small hamlets. At Tierras Largas, the few available analyses suggest that pooling may have been practiced in the Guadalupe and Rosario-Monte Albán I Phases (Table 6). This phenomena is associated with the probable establishment of a resident elite household at the site (Winter, 1972:121) and an increasing demand for high-quality prismatic blades. Thus, the pooling of imported obsidian should probably be seen as a gradual process, beginning in the Early Formative among important families at the largest sites and spreading as the demand for high quality obsidian and prismatic blades grew. By Middle Formative times, elite families probably controlled, pooled, and "redistributed" obsidian to their affines even at small hamlets. This suggestion needs to be checked, and, needless to say, this will require house-by-house data on obsidian source variation.

SUMMARY

The Early Formative period in Mesoamerica was characterized by four major obsidian exchange networks. The first, referred to as the Barranca de los Estetes network, linked the Central Highlands of Mexico with the Oaxacan Highlands. This network brought to Oaxaca prismatic blades of Barranca de los Estetes obsidian, some of which were probably passed on to Veracruz via the second major network. The latter, referred to as the Guadalupe Victoria network, linked the Oaxacan Highlands to the Gulf Coast. This network circulated a poor quality obsidian from the Guadalupe Victoria, Puebla source, little or none of which was passed on by Oaxaca to the obsidian-rich Central Mexican Highlands. A third network, based on the El Chayal source, linked the Gulf Coast with the Guatemalan Highlands, most probably by a Chiapas-Guatemalan Pacific Coast route. The fourth, or Zinapécuaro network, involved the movement of prismatic blades from Michoacán to the Oaxacan Highlands.

The defacement of monuments at San Lorenzo about 900 B.C., combined with political evolution in Oaxaca and the Central Highlands, was accompanied by a breakdown and realignment of the Early Formative exchange networks. A growing demand for well-made prismatic obsidian blades increased the importance of the Barranca de los Estetes and El Chayal sources, while the Guadalupe Victoria source faded into the background. The demand for blades also led increasingly to the pooling of imported obsidian for redistribution by local elites, a phenomenon accompanied by regionalism and considerable construction of public buildings in the respective regions.

III

IRON ORE MIRROR EXCHANGE NETWORKS IN FORMATIVE MESOAMERICA

IRON ORE: METHODOLOGY AND RAW DATA

The discovery of an iron ore mirror-producing residential ward at the site of San José Mogote in the Valley of Oaxaca during 1966 (Flannery, 1968), coupled with Michael Coe's discovery of nearly identical mirrors of the same age at San Lorenzo, Veracruz (Coe, 1968b) has led to the suggestion of an exchange relationship between the two sites based in part on San Lorenzo's importation of Oaxacan mirrors (Flannery, 1968:106). The mirrors at both sites date to roughly 1000-800 B.C. (San José phase in Oaxaca; San Lorenzo and Nacaste phases in Veracruz), thus predating the well-known concave iron mirrors from La Venta, which come from Middle Formative Construction Phases II-IV (Drucker, Heizer and Squier, 1959:177-186). In order to examine both the origin and distribution of the mirrors, samples were obtained from geological sources in the Valley of Oaxaca and the Sierra Madre del Sur, as well as from the archeological sites.

Previous physico-chemical measurements made on the La Venta mirrors (Curtis *in* Drucker, Heizer and Squier, 1959:284-288) had determined only their gross petrologic characteristics. No quantitative measurements of the relative amounts of hematite, ilmenite and magnetite, or of the composition of individual mineral phases in the different specimens were made. Such data is necessary in order to determine the geologic origin of ores used in mirror production, and to distinguish between mirrors derived from different ores. Attempts at obtaining this information through neutron activation analysis and x-ray fluoresence produced generally intractable results, and nondestructive sample preparation for the electron microprobe proved an insurmountable problem.[8] Wet chemical analysis was impossible because the mirrors could not be destroyed or marred by sampling.

Recent developments in the instrumentation for Mössbauer spectroscopy, and the large number of carefully-executed fundamental studies of magnetites (Evans, 1968), ilmenites (Greenwood and Gibb, 1971; Shirane et al., 1962), and hematites (Artman et al., 1968) using this technique made conditions propitious for the application of Mössbauer spectroscopy to a study of the iron ore sources and mirrors from archeological sites in Mesoamerica. It was crucial to the undertaking of the present investigation that correlations between various probable source materials and the mirrors be possible by a visual inspection of the primary data, thus eliminating the complex data-reduction programs necessary to other techniques, which often bar the non-technical archeologist from participation in reading and interpreting the results of his analyses.

Analytical Technique

Mössbauer spectral analysis of twenty-five geological sources and thirty-eight archeological iron ore samples was completed in collaboration with Dr. B. J. Evans of the Department of Geology and Mineralogy, University of Michigan. A report by Dr. Evans on the techniques and procedures

---

[8]The neutron activation analysis studies were carried out in conjunction with J. Thomas Meyers at the University of Michigan Neutron Activation Analysis Laboratory. The x-ray fluorescence studies were carried out in conjunction with Dr. Paul Cloke at the Department of Geology and Mineralogy, University of Michigan. The electron microprobe studies were completed by Dr. Cloke at the University of Michigan.

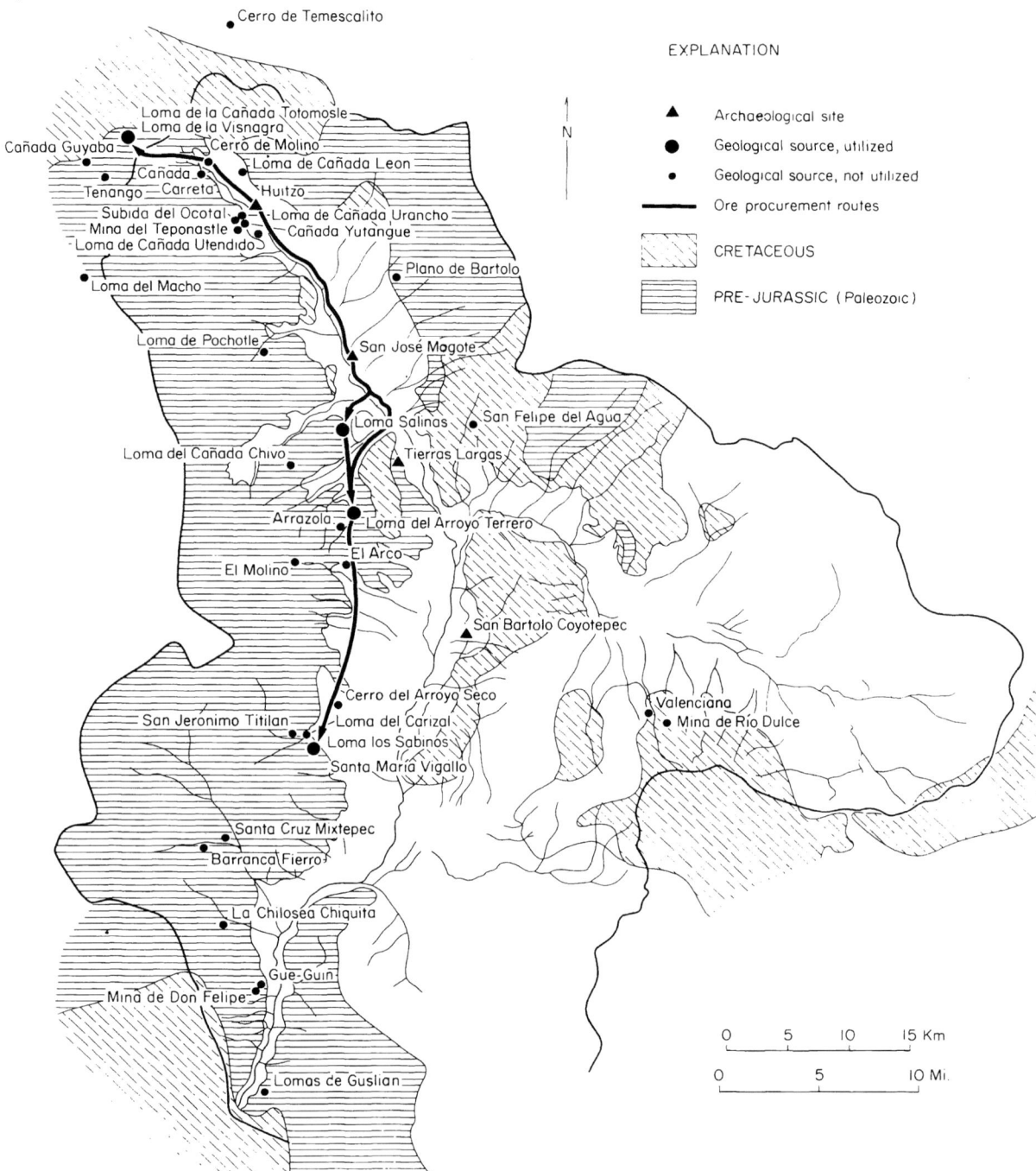

Fig. 17. Geological sources of iron ore in the Valley of Oaxaca and Early Formative procurement routes. Map prepared by Derwin Bell.

used in analysis of these samples is included in Appendix II.

The Geological Sources

A systematic survey of all potential iron-bearing geologic zones in the Valley of Oaxaca was completed during a five month period in 1967. Surveys in the Isthmus of Tehuantepec, the Central Depression of Chiapas, and the Valley of Morelos were completed in 1968 and 1970. A sampling procedure designed to test physical variation within the iron ore at each source was used for all fifty-four sources examined. This involved definition of the surface exposure at the source and collection of samples from across the entire exposure. The Mössbauer analytical technique used in testing variation is also described in Appendix II.

Thirty-six major surface exposures of iron ore were discovered in the Valley of Oaxaca, and are shown in Figure 17. Table 9 provides a detailed description of the location and characteristics of the sources, and Table 10 lists geological sources outside the Valley of Oaxaca which were also sampled for analysis.

On comparison of the Mössbauer spectra of the archeological samples with those of pure magnitite, hematite and ilmenite (Fig. 18), it is readily observed that these are the predominant mineral phases in the samples, as they were in the geological samples (see Pires-Ferreira, 1973: Figs. 28-56). Further, it is clear that in most cases one

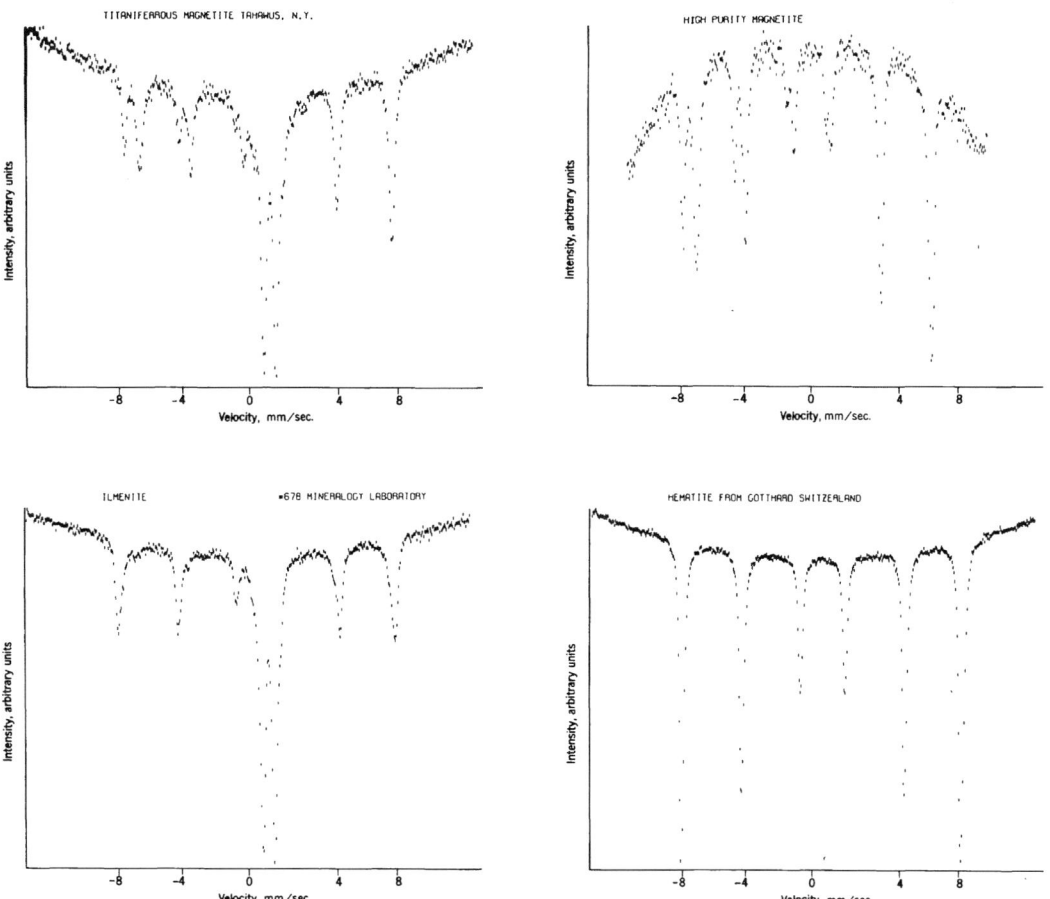

Fig. 18. Mössbauer spectra, showing differences between various types of iron ores. Upper left, titaniferrous magnetite from New York State. Upper right, high purity magnetite. Lower left, ilmenite. Lower right, hematite from Switzerland.

TABLE 9

VALLEY OF OAXACA IRON ORE SOURCES

1. ARRAZOLA Sample #59

Arrazola (Etla). A small surface scatter of iron ore is found on the lower slopes of the southwest side of Monte Albán. The source is located on the north side of the road, halfway between Arrazola and Hacienda San Francisco Javier.

Hardness: 6.5
Specific Gravity: 4.0
Streak: black
Luster: metallic
Fracture: irregular
Magnetism: strong

2. BARRANCA FIERRO

Barranca Fierro, ranchería of San Miguel Mixtepec, approximately one and one half kilometers west of Santa Cruz Mixtepec. Surface scatter of ore sparse but extensive. Ploughed up in fields and in arroyos. In an area of typical weakly metamorphosed quartz-granite.

Hardness: 5.5
Specific Gravity: 5.0
Streak: black
Luster: metallic
Fracture: irregular
Magnetism: strong

3. CAÑADA CARRETA Sample #18, 163

San Francisco Telixtlahuaca. Referred to as Cañada Peras in old publications. 2300 meters at 20° northwest of the Telixtlahuaca church. Surface exposure 20 meters by 15 on a spur above the Cañada Carreta stream, a tributary of the Río Atoyac. See below for description of the survey of fluvial dispersal of ore from this source. Fairly pure ore in rotting gneiss matrix.

Hardness: 5.5
Specific Gravity: 3.9-6.0
Streak: black
Luster: metallic
Fracture: irregular along crystal faces
Magnetism: strong

4. CAÑADA GUYABA

Santiago Tenango. 75° northwest, one kilometer distant from the Municipio of Santiago Tenango on the hillside of Cañada Guyaba. Fairly pure pieces of ore coming out of rotting gneiss and quartz bed rock.

Hardness: 5.5
Specific Gravity: 4.9
Streak: cherry red
Luster: earthy
Fracture: crumbles
Magnetism: absent

5. CAÑADA YUTANGUE

Santa María Tenexpan. 20° southwest of the church of Tenexpan and due south approximately one and one half kilometers from the archeological site of Barrio del Rosario Huitzo (OS64). Small crystals of ore found in pockets in a pegmatite formation. Plan Oaxaca assay: TiO_2 29.90%; Fe 26.90%; CaO 13.05%; SiO_2 8.32%; and P 3.40%.

Hardness: 5.5
Specific Gravity: indeterminate
Streak: brown-red
Luster: earthy
Fracture: irregular along crystal faces
Magnetism: absent

Table 9 (Continued)

---

6. CERRO DEL ARROYO SECO — Sample #62

La Ciénaga. 40° northeast of the Zimatlán church at eight kilometers distance. Located at the end of the road to Santa Inez del Monte on a southerly hill demarcated by two branches of the Arroyo Seco, one and one half kilometers at 60° northwest from the end of the road. Small crystals of ore embedded in a quartz feldspar gneiss, compact and fairly pure ore.

Hardness: 5.5
Specific Gravity: 5.0
Streak: black
Luster: metallic
Fracture: irregular
Magnetism: strong

---

7. CERRO DE MOLINO — Sample #44

San Francisco Telixtlahuaca. 30° north of the Telixtlahuaca church at approximately two kilometers distance. Leaving Telixtlahuaca on the road to the Cañada Tomellín (north), just beyond the second bridge the red talus from the mines can be seen on the hillside to the left of the road. Surface scatter samples eroding from gneiss bedrock.

Sample 1.
Hardness: 5.5
Specific Gravity: 4.8
Streak: black
Luster: metallic
Fracture: irregular along crystal faces
Magnetism: strong

Sample 2.
Hardness: 5.5
Specific Gravity: 5.1
Streak: black
Luster: sub-metallic
Fracture: irregular
Magnetism: strong

Sample 3.
Hardness: 5.5
Specific Gravity: 4.4
Streak: red
Luster: metallic
Fracture: irregular
Magnetism: absent

---

8. CERRO DE TEMESCALITO — Sample #45

San Francisco Telixtlahuaca. 12.3 miles from the Panamerican Highway on the road to Telixtlahuaca and San Sebastian Sedas (2.3 miles beyond the Monumento la Carbonera crossroads). The deposit covers three large hills just to the right of the road when facing north. Rotting gneiss bedrock, pure ore.

Hardness: 5.5
Specific Gravity: 5.0
Streak: black
Luster: metallic
Fracture: irregular
Magnetism: strong

---

9. EL ARCO — Sample #60

Cuilapan. Located on the road from Zimatlán to Zaachila, at the junction of the Arroyo El Arco. Small pieces of ore are found eroding out of gneiss bedrock on the Cerro El Arco on the north side of the Arroyo El Arco, and approximately two kilometers west of the road.

Hardness: 5.0
Specific Gravity: indeterminate
Streak: black

TABLE 9 (Continued)

---

9. EL ARCO (Continued)

Luster: metallic
Fracture: irregular
Magnetism: weak

---

10. EL MOLINO   Sample #65

Cuilapan. Located approximately twelve kilometers due west of the convent at Cuilapan, adjacent to the remains of a colonial hacienda. Surface scatters of small iron crystals are found on the southern bank of the Arroyo Cuilipan in gneiss bedrock.

Hardness: 5.5
Specific Gravity: indeterminate
Streak: reddish brown
Luster: metallic
Fracture: irregular
Magnetism: weak

---

11. GUE-GUIN

Santa María Ayoquezco. On the south slope of Loma Ayoquezco, 30° southeast of the Loma Ayoquezco archeological site and 40° southwest at two kilometers distance from the church of Ayoquezco. Bedrock is weakly metamorphosed quartz-granite, surface scatter small.

Hardness: 5.5
Specific Gravity: 3.4
Streak: red
Luster: metallic
Fracture: irregular
Magnetism: absent

---

12. LA CHILOSEA CHIQUITA   Sample #26

Guegovela de Tlapacoyan. Three kilometers west of Agua Blanca, between the Arroyos Aguacate and Chilosea Chiquita. A vein deposit of more or less pure ore sticking up from poorly metamorphosed quartz-granite bedrock. Surface exposure of five by five meters.

Hardness: 5.5
Specific Gravity: 5.0
Streak: black
Luster: metallic
Fracture: irregular
Magnetism: strong

---

13. LOMA DEL ARROYO TERRERO   Sample #67

Arrazola (Etla). On the road from Tiracoz to Arrazola, approximately 700 meters before entering Arrazola, a small surface scatter of ore is found to the north of the road. This is due south of the main pyramid on Cerro de Azompa. Rotten gneiss bedrock and pure ore.

Hardness: 5.5
Specific Gravity: 5.1
Streak: black
Luster: metallic
Fracture: irregular
Magnetism: strong

---

14. LOMA DEL CAÑADA CHIVO

San Felipe Tejalapam (Etla). 37° west-northwest of Jalapa at approximately four kilometers distance, and 55° southwest of Tejalapam at approximately 5 kilometers distance. A sparse scatter of ore is found on the lower slopes of the Loma del Cañada Chivo, below the mica mine. Rotten gneiss bedrock.

Hardness: 5.5
Specific Gravity: 4.5

TABLE 9 (Continued)

14. LOMA DEL CAÑADA CHIVO (Continued)

Streak: black
Luster: metallic
Fracture: irregular
Magnetism: weak

15. LOMA DE CAÑADA LEON

San Francisco Telixtlahuaca. At the junction of the Ríos Verde and Rosa, above the Telixtlahuaca dam. The source is exactly due north of Telixtlahuaca, and approximately 1 kilometer north-northeast of the dam. An abundant surface scatter of very large pieces of ore.

Hardness: 5.5
Specific Gravity: 3.2
Streak: brown
Luster: earthy
Fracture: irregular
Magnetism: absent

16. LOMA DE CAÑADA TOTOMOSLE

Santiago Tenango. Two and one half kilometers from Tenango to the northeast, above the Río Grande. The Mogote del Sol is 10° east of magnetic north from the source. A surface scatter of 350 by 200 meters, containing very high quality ore eroding out of rotting gneiss.

Hardness: 5.5
Specific Gravity: 5.0
Streak: black
Luster: metallic
Fracture: irregular
Magnetism: strong

17. LOMA DE CAÑADA URANCHO

Santa María Tenexpan. One half kilometer at 65° southwest of the church of Tenexpan, on the west side of the Cañada Urancho and approximately 150 meters above the river bed. A small scatter of iron crystals on the surface associated with a pegmatite formation. Plan Oaxaca assay: TiO_2 29.90%; Fe 26.90%; CaO 13.05%; SiO_2 8.32%; P 3.40%.

Hardness: 5.5
Specific Gravity: 4.0
Streak: black
Luster: non-metallic to sub-metallic
Fracture: irregular
Magnetism: weak

18. LOMA DE CAÑADA UTENDIDO

Santiago Suchilquitongo. Following the road to Tenexpan west from Suchilquitongo, turn south up the Cañada Utendido river bed for approximately one kilometer to the first hill due south of the end of the road. The source is located on the second flank up the hill. This is approximately two kilometers due west of the Suchilquitongo church. The small iron crystals are found in a pegmatite feldspar, quartz, mica and ilmenite deposit.

Hardness: 5.5
Specific Gravity: indeterminate
Streak: grey
Luster: submetallic
Fracture: irregular
Magnetism: absent

TABLE 9 (Continued)

19. LOMA DEL CARRIZAL   Sample #68

San Jerónimo Titilán. Located on the road from Zimatlán to San Jerónimo, 10° northwest and seven kilometers distance from the Santa María Vigallo church. A small surface exposure of heavy high quality ore associated with gneiss bedrock.

Hardness: 5.5
Specific Gravity: 4.8
Streak: black
Luster: metallic
Fracture: irregular along crystal faces
Magnetism: absent

20. LOMA DEL MACHO

Tejocotes, Santiago Tenango. 30° northwest of El Poleo at kilometer 489.5 of the Panamerican highway. Approximately one-half kilometer from the house of Ruben Vivas at El Poleo, along the trail adjacent to the house to the north. A surface scatter of high quality iron ore associated with rotting gneiss bedrock. *In situ* veins of ore can be seen.

Hardness: 5.5
Specific Gravity: 5.5
Streak: black
Luster: metallic
Fracture: irregular along crystal faces
Magnetism: strong

21. LOMA DE POCHOTLE

Santo Tomás Mazaltepec. Two kilometers at 80° southwest of the Mazaltepec church, and 47° southwest of Zautla. A very small scatter of ore in association with gneiss and quartz bedrock.

Hardness: 5.5
Specific Gravity: 5.1
Streak: grey
Luster: sub-metallic
Fracture: irregular
Magnetism: weak

22. LOMA DE LA VISNAGRA   Sample #54

Santiago Tenango. 55° southwest at three kilometers distance from the Municipio of Santiago Tenango on the Loma de la Visnagra, facing the Mogote del Sol and above a tributary of the Río Grande. Pure heavy ore weathering out of rotting gneiss on surface. The ore is dense with no inclusions or interior weathering along crystal faces.

Hardness: 5.8
Specific Gravity: 5.0
Streak: black
Luster: metallic
Fracture: irregular
Magnetism: strong

23. LOMA LOS SABINOS   Sample #70, 71

Zimatlán. Located adjacent to the road from Zimatlán to San Jerónimo Titilán, approximately four kilometers at 60° northwest of the Zimatlán church. This extensive source consists of a surface ore exposure covering approximately one square kilometer. The ore is eroding out of a quartz-gneiss formation which is deeply cut by three arroyos. The size of the ore lumps ranges from boulders (the largest approximately 30 by 20 centimeters) to small fragments. The ore is dense, compact and of high quality, with very little evidence of surface or interior oxidation.

TABLE 9 (Continued)

23. LOMA LOS SABINOS (Continued)

Hardness: 5.5
Specific Gravity: 5.4
Streak: black
Luster: metallic
Fracture: irregular
Magnetism: strong

24. LOMA SALINAS   Sample #14, 164

San Lorenzo Cacaotepec. One-and-one-half kilometers southwest of the Cacaotepec church at 35°. Small pieces of ore are scattered across the surface of the hill and pockets of ore are exposed in gneiss bedrock where arroyo cutting has occurred. A Monte Albán IA site covers part of the source area. The arroyo bed below the source provides part of the clay utilized in the ceramic industry at Santa María Atzompa (W. O. Payne, personal communication).

Hardness: 5.5
Specific Gravity: 5.2
Streak: black
Luster: metallic
Fracture: irregular
Magnetism: strong

25. LOMAS DE GUSLIAN   Sample #69

Ranchería Rio "Y." On the east bank of the Río Atoyac at the Ranchería. A vein of ore can be seen running from the river to the top of the hill and an abandoned mine is located on the lower slope of the hill. Large lumps of ore mixed with quartz and feldspar are eroding from the exposed vein. The ore is impure.

Hardness: 5.5
Specific Gravity: 5.2
Streak: black
Luster: metallic
Fracture: crumbles irregularly
Magnetism: strong

26. MINA DE DON FELIPE   Sample #74

Loma de Ayoquezco, Santa María Ayoquezco. Above the Arroyo de la Cucharita on the south flank of the Loma Ayoquezco, 20° and approximately twelve kilometers northeast of San Andrés Zabache. In typical poorly metamorphosed quartz-granite deposit, the deposit of ore has largely been removed by mining. A few fragments of ore found in the mine and on the surface of fields immediately below the entrance. Impure ore.

Hardness: 3.0
Specific Gravity: indeterminate
Streak: red
Luster: earthy
Fracture: crumbles
Magnetism: absent

27. MINA DE RIO DULCE

Magdalena Teitipac. One-and-one-half kilometers at 30° east of Magdalena Teitipac in the Cañada de Río Dulce. Following the road through Teitipac to Río Palasalina, turn on the road to the left immediately after crossing the river. Follow the road for one half kilometer along the Río Dulce, cross the river again, and proceed 500 meters up the hill to the mine. The mine was operated in the 1930s by an American company and is very large. Deposits of ochre occur on the surface adjacent to the mine, but it is impossible to determine if the ore found in and around the mine occurred on the surface.

Sample 1.
Hardness: 3.5
Specific Gravity: 3.3
Streak: cherry red
Luster: earthy
Fracture: crumbles, uneven
Magnetism: absent

TABLE 9 (Continued)

27. MINA DE RIO DULCE (Continued)

Sample 2.
Hardness: 5.0
Specific Gravity: 4.0
Streak: red
Luster: earthy
Fracture: uneven
Magnetism: absent

28. MINA DEL TEPONASTLE

Santiago Suchilquitongo. Approximately two-and-one-half kilometers due west of the church of Suchilquitongo. Magdalena Apasco is due east of the source, and Tenexpan is due north. Small crystals of ore found in a pegmatite deposit with feldspar, quartz and mica. Plan Oaxaca assay: TiO_2 29.90%; Fe 26.90%; CaO 13.05%; SiO_2 8.32%; P 3.40%.

Hardness: 5.5
Specific Gravity: 3.0
Streak: red-brown
Luster: earthy
Fracture: irregular
Magnetism: absent

29. PLANO DE BARTOLO

San Juan Bautista Guelache. A one-hour walk north from the village of Guelache up the Cañada Plano de Bartolo. The mines of La Hundida and Mina del Agua, reported by González Reyna (1962) as iron ore mines, are located here, but survey of the mines recovered no ore. The Plano de Bartolo is a third mine located one half kilometer north of the others along the course of the river bed. Lumps of poor quality ore were found here adjacent to the mine entrance. The bedrock is a rotting gneiss with quartz.

Hardness: 5.5
Specific Gravity: 4.5
Streak: cherry red
Luster: earthy, sub-metallic
Fracture: irregular
Magnetism: absent

30. SAN FELIPE DEL AGUA   Sample #57

San Felipe del Agua. In the grounds of the State of Oaxaca plant nursery, located on the northern edge of the village of San Felipe del Agua. Lumps of dense ore are found in association with iron oxide stained earth adjacent to the stream bed. The surface scatter is small and widely scattered.

Hardness: 5.6
Specific Gravity: 4.2
Streak: red
Luster: earthy
Fracture: irregular
Magnetism: absent

31. SAN JERONIMO TITILAN   Sample #75

San Jerómino Titilán. Lumps of ore were found eroding from gneiss deposits exposed in the main street of this village. Follow the road from Zimatlán to the northwest, past the Loma los Sabinos source to the village. The surface scatter is small and the ore pieces are also small.

Hardness: 5.5
Specific Gravity: 4.5
Streak: black
Luster: metallic
Fracture: irregular
Magnetism: strong

TABLE 9 (Continued)

32. SANTA CRUZ MIXTEPEC

Santa Cruz Mixtepec. A mine is located one-half kilometer due west of the Santa Cruz church. A few ore lumps were found inside the mine, but no surface scatter of ore was found outside the mine. The bedrock is typical poorly metamorphosed granite.

Hardness: 5.5
Specific Gravity: 5.2
Streak: red
Luster: metallic
Fracture: irregular
Magnetism: absent

33. SANTA MARIA VIGALLO   Sample #77

Santa María Vigallo. A sparse surface scatter of ore covers the hills between one and two kilometers northwest of the municipio of Santa María. The ore is mixed with the gneiss bedrock.

Hardness: 5.5
Specific Gravity: indeterminate
Streak: red
Luster: sub-metallic
Fracture: irregular
Magnetism: absent

34. SUBIDA DEL OCOTAL   Sample #58

Santa María Tenexpan. 60° southwest of the Tenexpan church at one half kilometer distance on the east side of the Cañada Urancho. Small crystals of ore are exposed in the gneiss bedrock. Plan Oaxaca assay: TiO_2 29.90%; Fe 26.90%; CaO 13.05%; SiO_2 8.32%; P 3.40%.

Hardness: 5.5
Specific Gravity: indeterminate
Streak: black
Luster: sub-metallic
Fracture: irregular
Magnetism: weak

35. TENANGO   Sample #24

Santiago Tenango. Outcrop on the road from Santiago Tenango to La Carbonera (on the Panamerican highway), three-fourths of a mile after leaving the municipio of Tenango. A very low grade ore is found in rotting gneiss.

Hardness: 5.0
Specific Gravity: indeterminate
Streak: red
Luster: earthy
Fracture: uneven, crumbly
Magnetism: absent

36. VALENCIANA

Magdalena Teitipac. Located in the barrio of Valenciana of the village of Teitipac; ore deposits are exposed in the roads of the barrio. Ore lumps are found in the gneiss bedrock and are mixed with the gneiss.

Hardness: 6.5
Specific Gravity: 3.5
Streak: red
Luster: sub-metallic
Fracture: irregular
Magnetism: absent

TABLE 10

IRON ORE SOURCES OUTSIDE THE VALLEY OF OAXACA SAMPLED FOR MÖSSBAUER SPECTRAL ANALYSIS

1. CERRO DEL MERCADO
   Durango

2. CERRO ESTAQUIO
   La Ventosa, Isthmus of Tehuantepec, Oaxaca

3. CERRO GRACIAS A DIOS   Sample #81
   Hacienda La Razón, Chiapas

4. CERRO PEÑELA
   San Juan Guichicovi, Isthmus of Tehuantepec, Oaxaca

5. CERRO PRIETO   Sample #82
   Niltepec, Isthmus of Tehuantepec, Oaxaca

6. EL ENCINO
   Pihuamo, Jalisco

7. EL NORILLO
   Tamaulipas

8. EL TAMARINDO   Sample #25
   Jalapa del Marquez, Isthmus of Tehuantepec, Oaxaca

9. LA HUERTA
   Jalisco

10. LA MINA   Sample #84
    Colonia Lópes, Chiapas

11. LA NEGRA
    Chihuahua

12. LA PERLA
    Chihuahua

13. LA VENTOSA
    Isthmus of Tehuantepec, Oaxaca

14. LAS CUEVAS   Sample #83
    Jalapa del Marquez, Isthmus of Tehuantepec, Oaxaca

15. LAS TRUCHES
    Michoacán

16. NIZADUGA
    Salinas, Isthmus of Tehuantepec, Oaxaca

17. PEÑA COLORADA
    Colima

18. RINCON MORENO
    Isthmus of Tehuantepec, Oaxaca

of these mineral phases predominates, thereby facilitating the division of samples into generalized groups according to iron oxide types. In order to simplify the referencing of spectra, the results were divided into the following five general iron oxide groups: I, samples composed mainly of magnetite; II, samples of relatively pure hematite; III, samples of ilmenite; IV, samples containing a mixture of magnetite and ilmenite; and V, samples composed of a mixture of magnetite and hematite. In the case of the archeological samples, shown below, these groups were later subdivided according to the most probable geologic source.

One question of particular interest in the study of the geological sources was just how widely the Mössbauer spectra of samples collected from different parts of a source would vary. Two series of five samples each from the Loma los Sabinos and Cerro de Temescalito sources were analyzed. The results in both cases showed that there was virtually no variation in the major phase composition of ore throughout the source. Once this was established, the probability of accurately identifying the geologic origin of mirror ores was greatly increased.

The Archeological Samples

Archeological samples from the Early Formative sites of San José Mogote, San Bartolo Coyotepec, and Tierras Largas in the Valley of Oaxaca; Etlatongo in the Valley of Nochixtlán; San Pablo, Morelos; and San Lorenzo, Veracruz were analyzed. Middle Formative samples come only from La Venta, Tabasco; Las Choapas, Veracruz; and Amatal, Chiapas.

Several spectral details were used in matching the archeological and geological source samples. For the magnetite samples, the relative intensity and separation of the doublet structure of the peaks in the extreme negative velocity region were used to distinguish between the various sources which make up this group. For mirrors containing hematite and ilmenite, the spectra are so distinctive that the choices were obvious. For the mixed magnetite and ilmenite group, the presence of magnetite is evidenced by the doublet structure in the region of the high channel numbers (see Appendix II). In some cases (as in IV-B below), a significant amount of titanium has dissolved in the magnetite, and the doublet structure has been reduced to a strong outer peak and a weak inner peak. The relative intensity of these two peaks, however, serves to distinguish sources.

The largest number of archeological samples are of magnetite (Group I). Utilizing the spectral

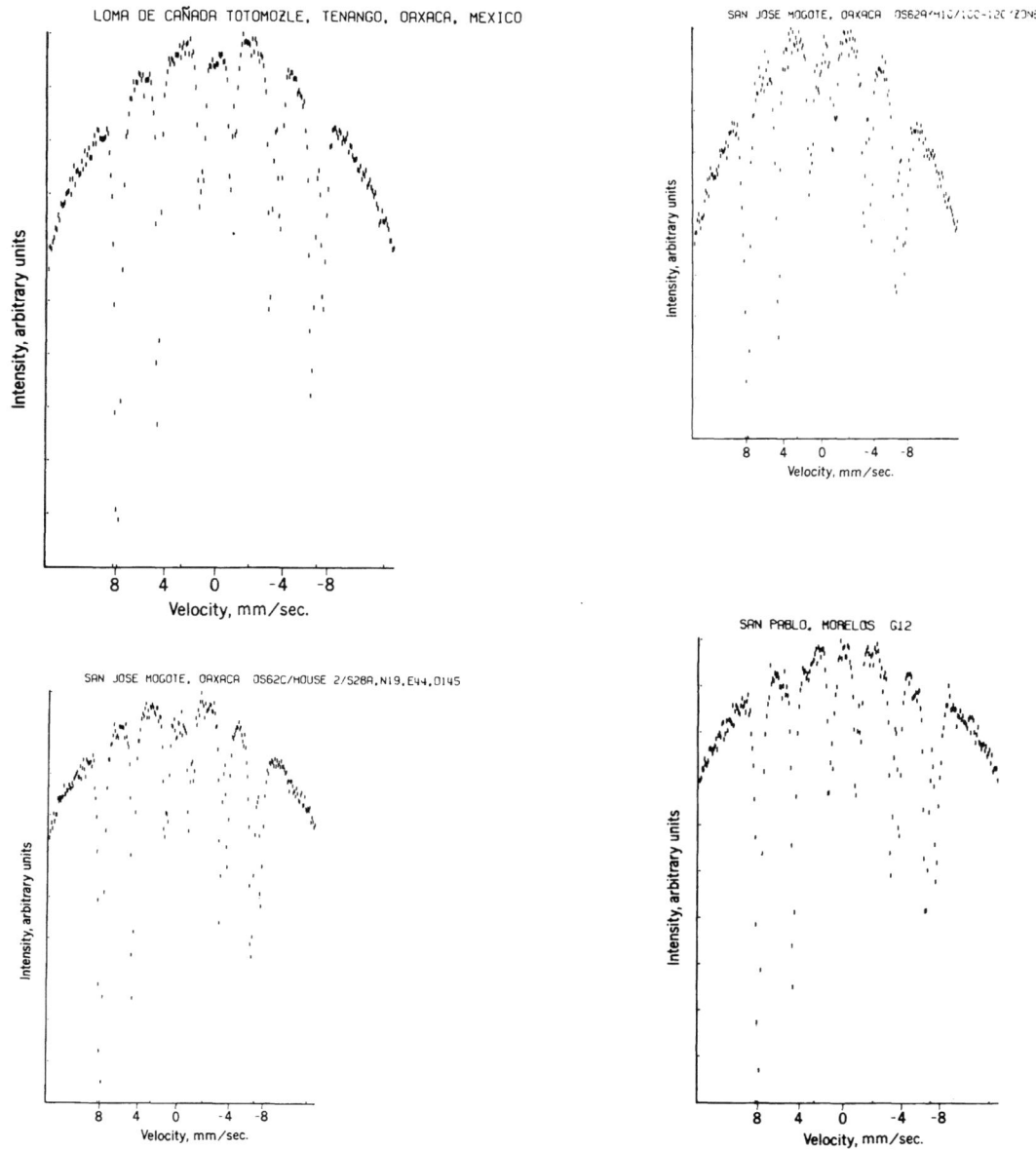

Fig. 19. Mössbauer spectra for four magnetite specimens from Group I-A. Upper left, ore from the Loma de Cañada Totomosle source, Tenango, Oaxaca. Upper right, ore lump from Household Cluster C1, Area A, San José Mogote. Lower left, ore lump from House 2, Area C, San José Mogote. Lower right, ore lump from San Pablo, Morelos.

details outlined above, we defined three probable geologic sources, designated I-A, I-B, and I-C in order to distinguish them from other geological sources in group I. A listing of the archeological samples, divided into the probable source groups, is presented in Tables 11-17, and the sample spectra are given in Figures 19-26.

Six Early Formative (San José phase) samples from San José Mogote in the Valley of Oaxaca and one Early Formative (San Pablo phase) sample from the site of San Pablo, Morelos, make up magnetite group I-A.[9] These nearly identical

[9] Only a portion of the archaeological samples are illustrated here. Mössbauer spectra and descriptions of all archaeological samples are given in Pires-Ferreira, 1973:238-247, Figs. 57-94.

50 FORMATIVE MESOAMERICAN EXCHANGE NETWORKS

TABLE 11

GROUP I-A: LOMA DE CAÑADA TOTOMOSLE-LOMA DE LA VISNAGRA MAGNETITE SOURCE, TENANGO, OAXACA

Site	Provenience	Period	Sample Number	Description	Reference
San José Mogote, Valley of Oaxaca	Area A, Platform 1 & 2, surface debris	San José Phase	8	Unfinished mirror	cf. Flannery, 1968
San José Mogote	Area A, Platform 2, East, redeposited debris	San José Phase	133	Ore lump	cf. Flannery, 1968
San José Mogote	Area A, Zone B1 alluvium	San José Phase	103	Ore lump	cf. Flannery, 1968
San José Mogote	Area A, Household Cluster C1	San José Phase	7	Ore lump	cf. Flannery, 1968
San José Mogote	Area A, Household Cluster C2	San José Phase	105	Unfinished mirror	cf. Flannery, 1968
San José Mogote	Area A, Household Cluster C3	San José Phase	2	Ore lump	cf. Flannery, 1968
San José Mogote	Area A, Household Cluster C3	San José Phase	4	Ore lump	cf. Flannery, 1968
San José Mogote	Area A, Zone D1 midden	San José Phase	108	Ore lump	cf. Flannery, 1968
San José Mogote	Area A, Zone D3 midden	San José Phase	12	Ore lump	cf. Flannery, 1968
San José Mogote	Area C, House 2 floor	San José Phase	5	Ore lump	cf. Flannery, 1968
San Pablo, Morelos	G 12	San Pablo Phase	93	Ore lump	Grove (unpub.)

TABLE 12

GROUP I-B: LOMA LOS SABINOS MAGNETITE SOURCE, ZIMATLÁN, VALLEY OF OAXACA

Site	Provenience	Period	Sample Number	Description	Reference
San José Mogote, Valley of Oaxaca	Area A, Zone A1 debris	San José Phase ?	6	Ore lump	cf. Flannery, 1968
San José Mogote	Area A, Zone A2 debris	San José Phase ?	11	Ore lump	cf. Flannery, 1968
San José Mogote	Area A, Household Cluster C4	San José Phase	1	Ore lump	cf. Flannery, 1968
San José Mogote	Area A, Zone D1 midden	San José Phase	10	Ore lump	cf. Flannery, 1968
San José Mogote	Area A, Zone D2 midden	San José Phase	13	Ore lump	cf. Flannery, 1968
San Bartolo Coyotepec, Valley of Oaxaca	Surface of site	Found with Early Formative sherds	96	Ore lump	cf. Flannery, 1968
Etlatongo, Valley of Nochixtlán, Oaxaca	Platform fill	Cruz Phase	97	Mirror	Spores (unpub.)

TABLE 13

GROUP I-C: UNMATCHED MAGNETITE SOURCE

Site	Provenience	Period	Sample Number	Description	Reference
La Venta, Tabasco	Mound A2 fill, 1942 (Museo Nacional de Antropología e Historia, #13-207 7451)	Construction Phase I-IV, Middle Formative	147	Reworked concave mirror fragment with scalloped edge	Drucker, Heizer & Squier, 1959: 182, Fig. 50

TABLE 14

GROUP II-A: CERRO PRIETO HEMATITE SOURCE, NILTEPEC, ISTHMUS OF TEHUANTEPEC

Site	Provenience	Period	Sample Number	Description	Reference
La Venta, Tabasco	Drucker, 1955 (Museo Nacional de Antropología e Historia, #13-375 8100)	Middle Formative	144	Concave mirror fragment, illustrated	Drucker, Heizer & Squier, 1959
La Venta, Tabasco	Offering #9. 1955 (Museo Nacional de Antropología e Historia, #13-374 8099)	Construction Phase IV, Late Middle Formative	143	Complete concave mirror perforated for suspension	Drucker, Heizer & Squier, 1959: 180, Fig. 49
San Lorenzo, Veracruz	SL-PNW-I-1a	Nacaste Phase (850 B.C.)	—	Thick flat mirror	Coe, pers. comm.
San Lorenzo, Veracruz	LS-PNW-I-1b	Nacaste Phase (850 B.C.)	—	Thick flat mirror	Coe, pers. comm.

TABLE 15

GROUP III-A: UNMATCHED ILMENITE SOURCE

Site	Provenience	Period	Sample Number	Description	Reference
La Venta, Tabasco	Drucker, 1955 (Museo Nacional de Antropología e Historia, #13-355 8080)	Middle Formative	146	Fragment of flat, poorly polished mirror—not illustrated	Drucker, Heizer & Squier, 1959
La Venta, Tabasco	Offering 1943-F (Museo Nacional de Antropología e Historia, #13-328 7552)	Middle Formative	148	Fragment of concave mirror perforated for suspension	Drucker, Heizer & Squier, 1959: 182, Fig. 50
Las Choapas, Veracruz	Arroyo Pesquero	Middle Formative	92	2 fragments of concave mirror	Collections of Museo de Xalapa, Veracruz
San Lorenzo, Veracruz	Cache associated with colossal head, Monument 17	Early Formative	141	Multi-drilled bead	Coe, pers. comm.
San Lorenzo, Veracruz	SL-PNW-I-3e	Nacaste Phase (850 B.C.)	—	Small flat mirror	Coe, pers. comm.
San Lorenzo, Veracruz	SL-PNW-ST-IIc ⓑ	Nacaste Phase (850 B.C.)	—	Small flat mirror	Coe, pers. comm.
San Lorenzo, Veracruz	SL-NW-MI-2zc	San Lorenzo Phase	—	Small concave mirror	Coe, pers. comm.
Amatal (near Chiapa de Corzo), Chiapas	Isolated cache	?	94	Multi-drilled bead	T. Lee, pers. comm.

TABLE 16

GROUP IV-A: LOMA DEL ARROYO TERRERO MIXED MAGNETITE AND ILMENITE SOURCE, ARRAZOLA, VALLEY OF OAXACA

Site	Provenience	Period	Sample Number	Description	Reference
San José Mogote, Valley of Oaxaca	Area A, Household Cluster C1	San José Phase	3	Ore lump	cf. Flannery, 1968
San José Mogote	Area A, Household Cluster C2	San José Phase	9	Ore lump	cf. Flannery, 1968
San José Mogote	Area A, Feature 2, Household Cluster C2	San José Phase	109	Ore lump	cf. Flannery, 1968
Tierras Largas, Valley of Oaxaca	Main site area, surface collection	Early Formative (?)	114	Ore lump with quartz inclusions	Winter (unpub.)

TABLE 17

GROUP IV-B: LOMA SALINAS MIXED MAGNETITE AND ILMENITE SOURCE, SAN LORENZO CACAOTEPEC, VALLEY OF OAXACA

Site	Provenience	Period	Sample Number	Description	Reference
San José Mogote, Valley of Oaxaca	Area A, Household Cluster C4	San José Phase	107	Ore lump, worked	cf. Flannery, 1968
San Lorenzo, Veracruz	SL-CC-13B	Redeposited, probably Nacaste Phase	—	Small flat mirror	Coe, pers. comm.
San Lorenzo, Veracruz	SL-PNW-ST-IA	Nacaste Phase	—	Small flat mirror	Coe, pers. comm.

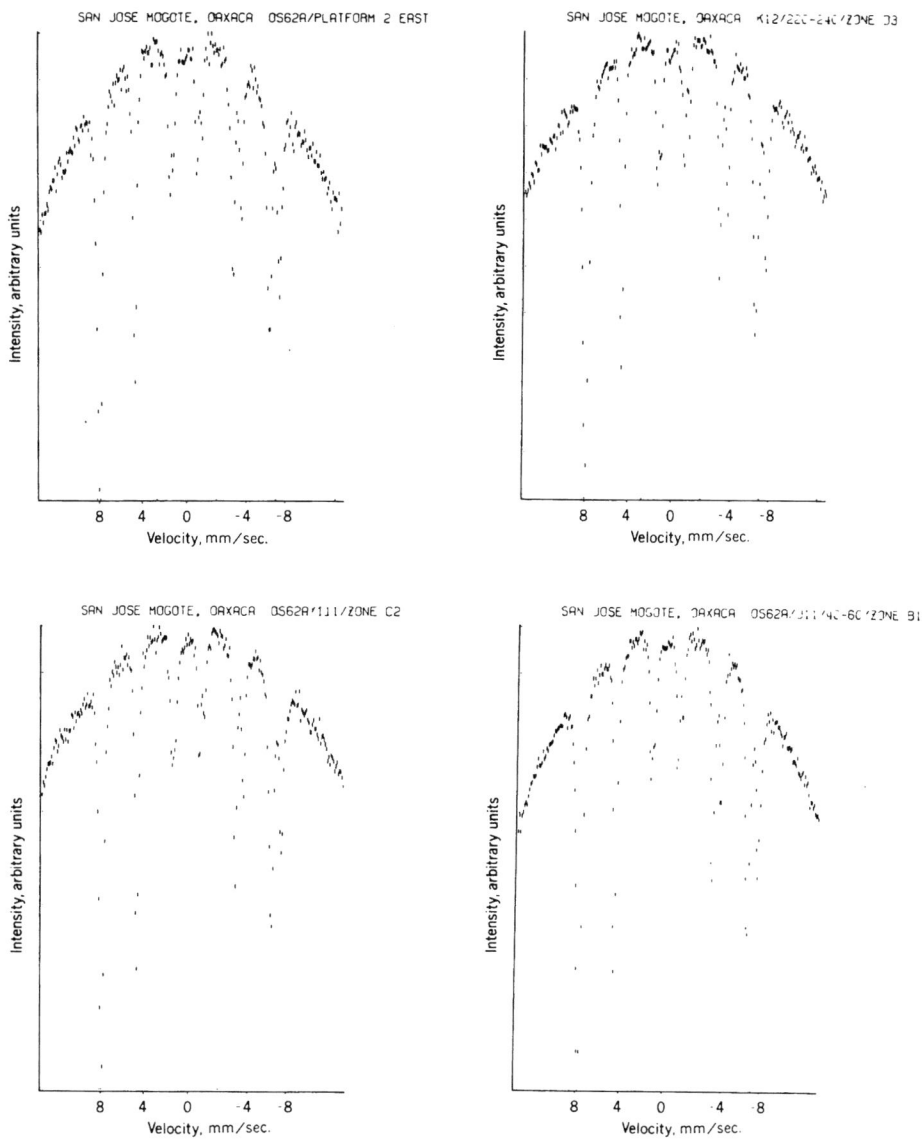

Fig. 20. Mössbauer spectra for four specimens of magnetite from the Loma de Cañada Totomosle—Loma de la Visnagra source (Group I-A), San José Mogote. Upper left, ore lump, Platform 2 East, Area A. Upper right, ore lump, Zone D3 midden, Area A. Lower left, unfinished mirror, Household Cluster C2, Area A. Lower right, ore lump, Zone B1 (stream alluvium which eventually covered Platform 2).

spectra of a quite pure magnetite, free from any ilmenite contamination, appear to match the spectrum obtained for the source of Loma de Cañada Totomosle (Fig. 19, upper left) in the municipio of Santiago Tenango, located two kilometers to the northwest of the headwaters of the Río Atoyac and just outside the Valley of Oaxaca. This source is located on the side of a mountain which has been cut through by a stream. A similar ore deposit, called Loma de la Visnagra, was encountered on the mountainside directly opposite the first source, and yielded a very similar (though not quite so ilmenite-free) spectrum. The geographical proximity and spectral similarity point towards a probable common origin of the two ore deposits, and so they will be referred to as

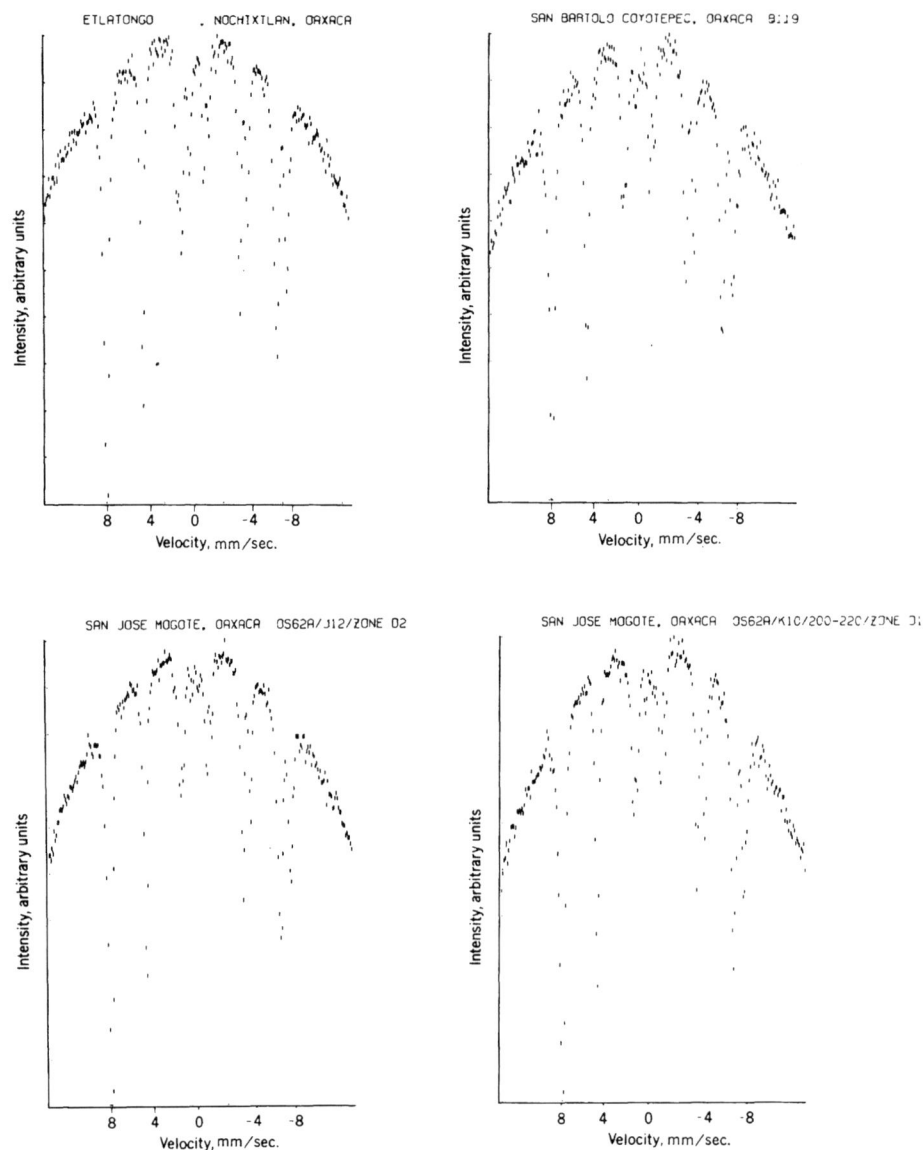

Fig. 21. Mössbauer spectra, magnetite samples of Group I-B. Upper left, mirror from Etlatongo, Nochixtlán, Oaxaca. Upper right, ore lump from San Bartolo Coyotepec, Valley of Oaxaca. Lower left and right, ore lumps from Zone D2 and D1 midden, respectively, Area A, San José Mogote.

the Loma de Cañada Totomosle-Loma de la Visnagra source. The ore found here is compact and non-friable. In section, it presents inclusion-free faces ideally suited for mirror making.

The second magnetite group, I-B (Fig. 21), includes two Early Formative (San José phase) samples from San José Mogote; one probable San José phase sample from San Bartolo Coyotepec; and one sample from early Cruz phase fill at the site of Etlatongo in the neighboring Valley of Nochixtlán. The spectra are similar to those of group I-A, but a significant amount of ilmenite contamination serves to distinguish between the two groups. The spectra match those from both Loma los Sabinos and Cerro de Temescalito sources in the Valley of Oaxaca on all points. Although it is impossible to distinguish visually between these two sources without resorting to spectrum-stripping procedures, we feel that the following arguments are sufficient to disqualify Cerro de Temescalito as a likely source, leaving Loma los Sabinos as the point of origin for Group I-B.

The Loma los Sabinos (Zimatlán) source is located in the Valley of Oaxaca in an area where archeological evidence of Early Formative occupation is abundant (Flannery et al., 1970). The ore—which occurs on the surface in large lumps—is very compact, showing few large fissures and fractures, and little or no weathering. In section, it presents essentially inclusion-free regions which would be ideal for mirror making. The Cerro de Temescalito source, on the other hand, is located outside the Valley of Oaxaca in a mountainous area where no permanent occupation has been found until the Classic period (R. D. Drennan, personal communication). In addition, the ore at this latter source, whether from the surface or sub-surface, contains severely weathered zones along both internal and external fractures and fissures, which would cause the ore to be too friable for mirror making.

The third magnetite group, I-C, is made up of the Middle Formative scalloped-edge concave mirror from La Venta, mentioned above (Fig. 22). The spectrum of this mirror does not match any of the sources we have examined. It is possible that this ore comes from one of several sources in the Isthmus of Tehuantepec which were not reached in our survey (see Ojeda Rivera et al., 1965 for location of sources).

Only two of our archeological samples proved to be of hematite—two concave mirrors from Middle Formative context at La Venta (Fig. 23). These, along with two thick, flat mirrors from Nacaste phase San Lorenzo, will be referred to as group II-A. They present nearly identical spectra, and

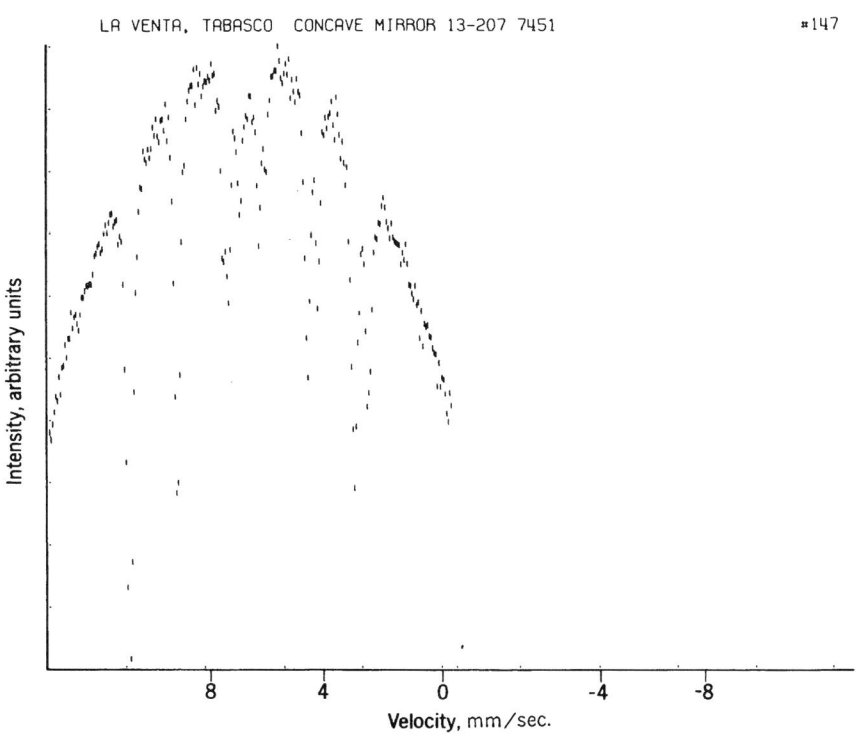

Fig. 22. Mössbauer spectrum, concave magnetite mirror from La Venta, Group I-C.

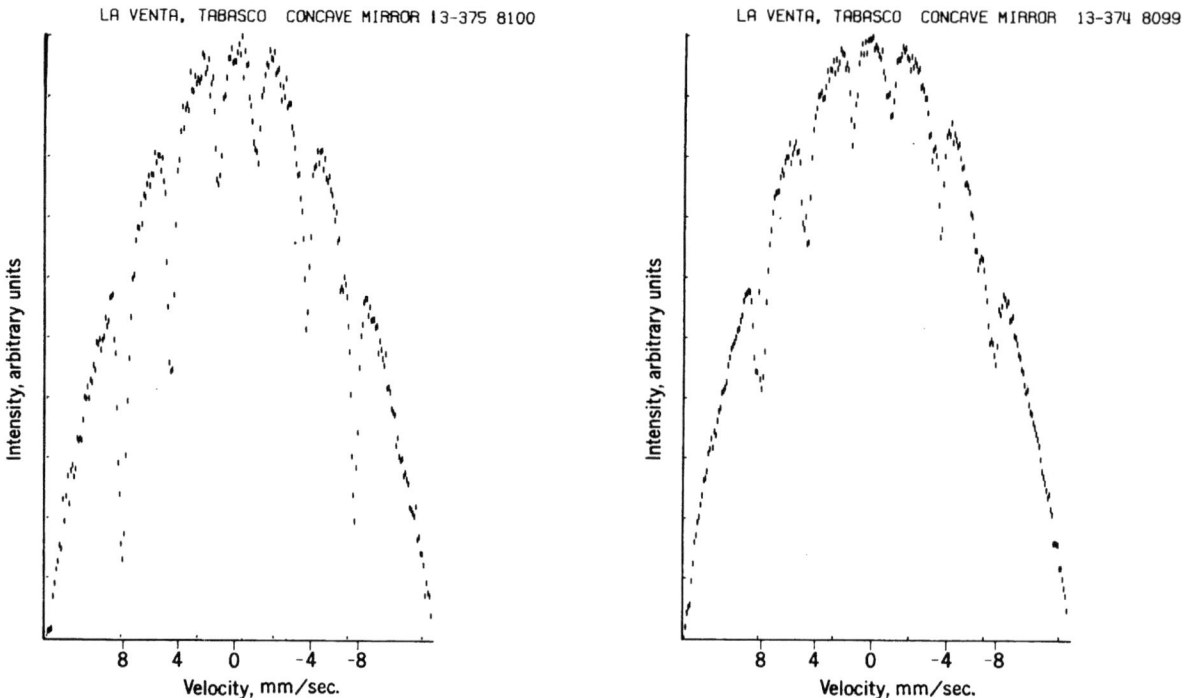

Fig. 23. Mössbauer spectra of two large concave hematite mirrors from La Venta. The ore is of Group II-A, probably from Cerro Prieto in the Isthmus of Tehuantepec.

are tentatively identified as being made of ore from the source of Cerro Prieto, located at Niltepec in the Isthmus of Tehuantepec. Although this is the source suggested by Heizer and Williams (1965:12) as the probable origin of La Venta mirror ore, other iron ore sources are known to exist in the region, not sampled in this survey (Ojeda Rivera et al., 1965); for this reason, the identification must be considered tentative. However, the Cerro Prieto ore is dense and compact, showing little weathering and containing few fissures or fractures, and would have served well for mirror making.

Eight of the archeological samples examined produced such nearly-identical ilmenite spectra that they are almost certainly made of ore from a single geologic source. The spectra, which do not match any of the sources we examined, will be referred to as group III-A. Four are shown in Fig. 24. One is a flat, poorly-polished (unfinished?) mirror from La Venta and two are concave mirrors: one from Middle Formative La Venta, and one from an undated deposit at Arroyo Pesquero near Las Choapas, Veracruz. Among the remaining samples are two unique multi-drilled beads. One of the beads comes from an Early Formative cache associated with the Monument 17 colossal head at San Lorenzo and the other from an undated cache at Amatal near Chiapa de Corzo in Chiapas.

The mixed magnetite and ilmenite samples are subdivided into two different source groups. Group IV-A (Fig. 25) consists of three Early Formative (San José phase) pieces from San José Mogote, and one probable San José phase piece from the nearby site of Tierras Largas. The spectra correspond with that obtained for the Loma del Arroyo Terrero source which is located on lands of the municipio of Arrazola, just off the western slope of Monte Albán in the Valley of Oaxaca. The surface exposure of the ore is not extensive, and the small

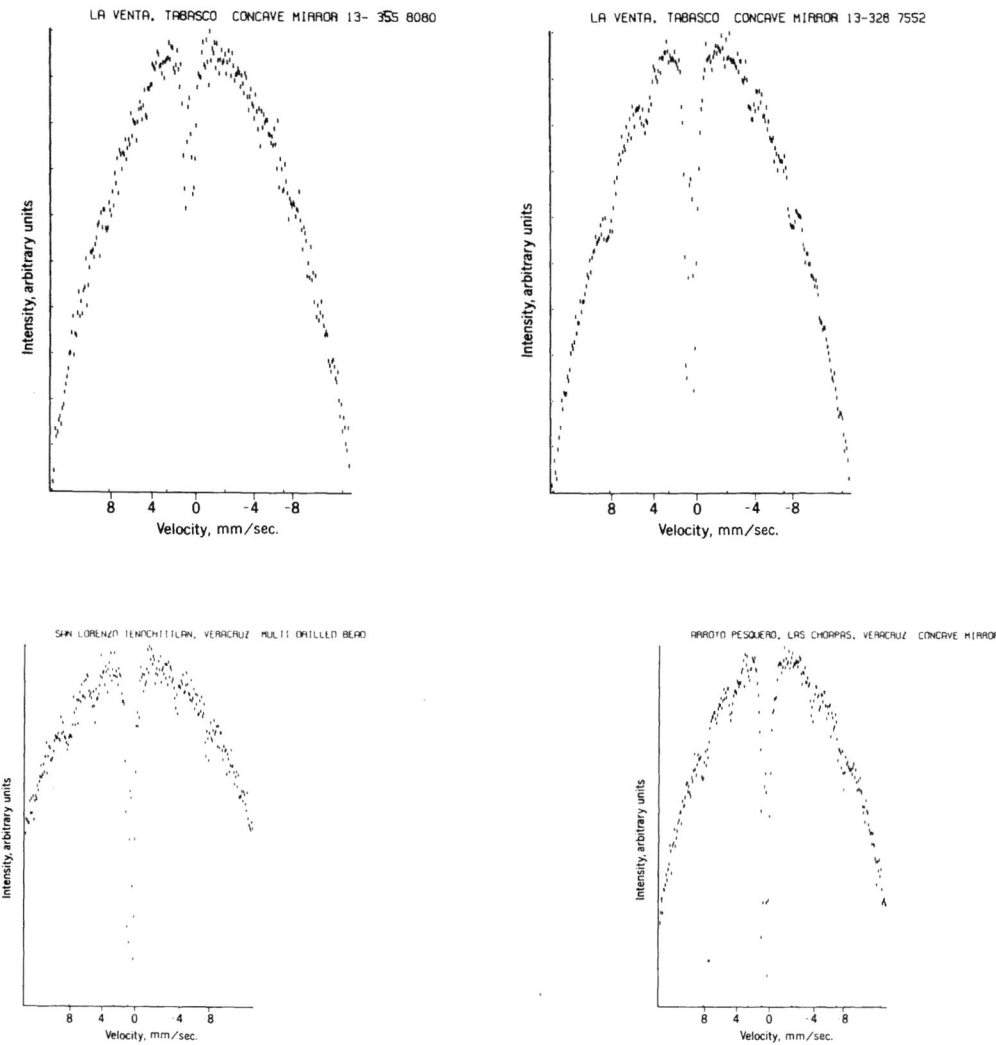

Fig. 24. Mössbauer spectra, ilmenite samples from Group III-A. Upper left and right, concave mirrors from La Venta. Lower left, multi-drilled bead from cache, Monument 17, San Lorenzo. Lower right, concave mirror from Las Choapas, Veracruz.

lumps found are probably not of sufficient quality for mirror making.

Group IV-B contains three samples of Early Formative date—two small, flat mirrors from Nacaste phase San Lorenzo, and a partly-worked ore lump from San José Mogote. The spectra match one obtained for the Loma Salinas source (Fig. 26) at San Lorenzo Cacaotepec; this was the geographically nearest source to San José Mogote.

THE EARLY FORMATIVE: MAGNETITE MIRROR PRODUCTION AND EXCHANGE

By far the majority of the Early Formative period archeological samples examined were either magnetites or mixed magnetite-ilmenites from geological sources in the Valley of Oaxaca. The bulk of the samples examined come from San José Mogote, the largest site in the Valley of Oaxaca during

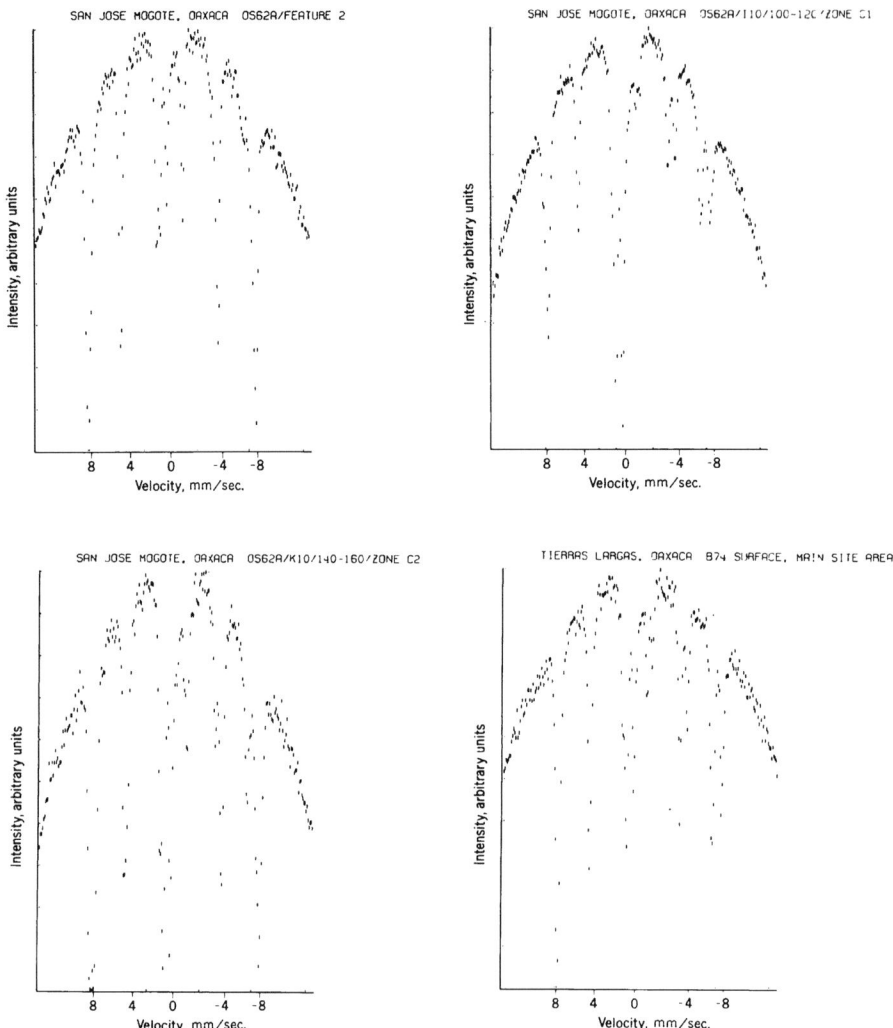

Fig. 25. Mössbauer spectra, samples of mixed magnetite and ilmenite from Group IV-A (Loma del Arroyo Terrero). Upper left, from Feature 2, Household Cluster C2, Area A, San José Mogote. Upper right, Household Cluster C1, Area A, San José Mogote. Lower left, Household Cluster C2, Area A, San José Mogote. Lower right, Tierras Largas, surface.

this period. The site is situated on a localized, noniron bearing zone of ignimbrite tuff. A surface survey of the site revealed a striking, one-hectare concentration of iron ores—more than 500 pieces which had evidently been collected from various iron sources in the valley. Excavations within this area (Area A) exposed a series of four superimposed household clusters (numbered C1 through C4) and associated midden deposits (D1-D3). Whole and broken magnetite mirrors, unfinished mirrors, and worked and unworked lumps of iron ore were found together in these household clusters. Comparative examination of the finished and unfinished mirrors reveals a similarity in size, shape, and grinding technique which indicates that mirror production was being carried out there. The typical products are thumbnail-size, flat-surface mirrors of various geometric forms, highly polished on one or both sides. Traces of multidirectional grind-

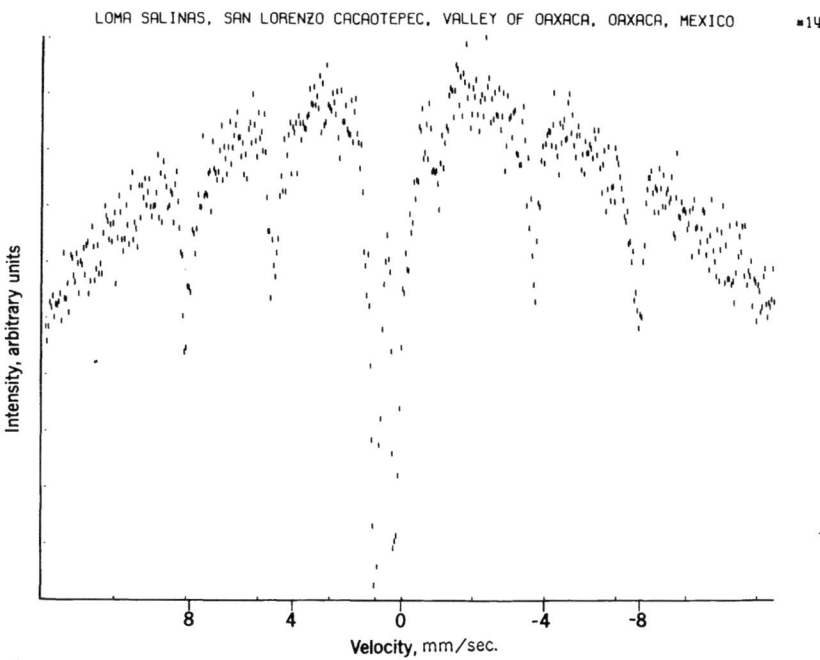

Fig. 26. Mössbauer spectrum, mixed magnetite-ilmenite source (Group IV-B), San Lorenzo Cacaotepec, Valley of Oaxaca. Mirrors made from this source were traded as far as San Lorenzo, Veracruz.

ing are discernible on the unfinished and roughly finished sides of the mirrors. Closer examination of the mirror surfaces reveals some traces of ochre in surface irregularities, indicating that this substance may have been used in order to obtain the high polish of the finished products.

Analysis of the ore lumps and unfinished mirrors from ths Area A households indicates that ore was collected from at least four sources. The Loma de Cañada Totomosle-Loma de la Visnagra magnetite source, 27 kilometers to the northwest of the site by air, is represented by ten samples. This source, located in the mountains just outside the valley, was exploited throughout the entire period of mirror production at San José Mogote. Although it is located slightly beyond the presently-known geographical limits of Early Formative settlement in the Valley of Oaxaca (Flannery, personal communication), it may have become known as the result of exploitation of the pine forest which grows both at the site of this probable source and on other high mountains surrounding the valley. Ample evidence of importation of pine charcoal and construction poles was obtained in the Early Formative levels at San José Mogote (Flannery et al., 1970:41). The second major source of magnetite ore was Loma los Sabinos, located on the edge of the valley floor, 33 kilometers south of San José Mogote by air, within an area of known Early Formative occupation (Flannery et al., 1970). The ore obtained from these two sources is the most inclusion-free and unweathered, and gives spectra most closely approximating those of pure magnetite of all the sources collected in and around the valley. Clearly there was a demand for high-quality magnetite ore, for many nearer ore sources of lower quality were passed over in favor of these.

In one case, however, ore lumps from such an intermediate source of mixed magnetite and ilmenite were collected, but apparently never worked into finished mirrors.

Three samples from the Loma del Arroyo Terrero source—14 kilometers from San José Mogote by air, and 17 kilometers distant if watercourses were followed along the most probable route to the Loma los Sabinos source (see Fig. 17)—were found in two separate household clusters. It seems not unlikely that ore from this source may have been collected while en route to or from the more important Loma los Sabinos source.

The final ore source represented is a mixed magnetite and ilmenite of somewhat lower quality from Loma Salinas near San Lorenzo Cacaotepec, only 6 kilometers south-southwest of San José Mogote. It is not surprising to find ore from this, the nearest source to San José Mogote, as the same area contains excellent pottery clay, as well as a large outcrop of mica which may have been utilized; mica fragments were common at San José Mogote. This was the ore source used for at least two small mirrors which reached San Lorenzo, Veracruz, during the Nacaste phase (perhaps as early as 900 B.C.).

Despite the large number of ore sources in the Valley of Oaxaca, distribution of iron ores and iron ore products in archeological sites of the Early Formative is very limited. At San José Mogote the ores are essentially limited to one mirror-making residential ward or *barrio,* where they are found in association with other exotic goods such as *Spondylus,* pearl oyster, freshwater mussel, and mica (see above).

Ore products have been found at only two other, smaller, sites in the Valley of Oaxaca. The ore lump from the site of San Bartolo Coyotepec was probably obtained directly from the Loma los Sabinos source, which is only 16 kilometers to the southwest across the flat valley floor. At Tierras Largas, an ore lump of probable Early Formative date was found to have come from the Loma del Arroyo Terrero source, which at 8 kilometers distance is the closest source to the site (Fig. 17).

Thus, the occupants of small hamlets in the Valley of Oaxaca picked up occasional lumps of iron ore from nearby sources but apparently did not work them. On the other hand, the mirror makers at San José Mogote concentrated on high-quality sources up to 30 kilometers away. It is not known what the mirrors served for, but evidence from figurines at Tlatilco and La Venta suggests they were worn on the chest, possibly by individuals of some special status. Some of the Oaxaca mirrors may have been worn as inlays in ornaments of pearl oyster shell, judging by some broken specimens found at Area A of San José Mogote.

Because of the restricted distribution of the San José Mogote mirrors both within that site and throughout the valley, and their possible association with individuals of some social rank, it was proposed by Flannery (1968) that the mirrors were part of an exchange network which linked Oaxaca with San Lorenzo and the Gulf Coast, as well as with other regions of Mexico. This proposal is supported by two mirrors of Oaxaca ore which reached San Lorenzo during the Nacaste phase, although the mechanisms of the exchange are unknown. We have also been able to demonstrate that mirrors or lumps of Oaxaca ores were traded toward the northwest, possibly as a form of exchange between elites. One lump of high-quality Loma de Cañada Totomosle-Loma de la Visnagra ore was found in Early Formative levels at the site of San Pablo in the state of Morelos, 320 kilometers northwest of San José Mogote. The possible links between these two sites in the exchange of Barranca de los Estetes obsidian blades have been discussed in Chapter II. A finished mirror of Oaxaca ore with a presumed Early Formative date came from what appears to be an eroded Cruz phase platform at the site of Etlatongo in the Valley of Nochixtlán, located some 50 kilometers north of San José Mogote. The spectrum of this sample matches the Loma los Sabinos source. Although the limits of

Oaxacan iron ore distribution cannot be defined on the basis of present evidence, they apparently exceeded 300 kilometers to the northwest and 200 kilometers to the northeast. Because of our limited sample, it is not yet clear how often the trade involved unmodified ore (as in the case of the San Pablo lump) and how often it involved finished mirrors.

All of the small iron ore mirrors recovered *in situ* in Oaxaca date to the second half of the San José phase, or roughly 1000-850 B.C. A few ore lumps, however, occurred in early San José phase context (1150-1000 B.C.), suggesting that earlier mirrors may be found. All the flat mirrors recovered at San Lorenzo, including two from a source at Cacaotepec in the Valley of Oaxaca, date to the Nacaste phase (900-750 B.C.). A single concave mirror at San Lorenzo appeared in mound fill with mixed sherds of the San Lorenzo A and B phases, and thus cannot with certainty be dated earlier than San Lorenzo B (1000-900 B.C.) (see Table 18). It therefore seems reasonable to assume that the major period for exchanges of small, flat mirrors was roughly 1000-800 B.C. In our study, 5 out of a sample of 9 small, flat mirrors analyzed were made from Valley of Oaxaca magnetites or mixed magnetite-ilmenites, while 4 were made from hematites or ilmenites occurring elsewhere. Out of a sample of 20 unworked or partly-worked iron ore lumps, all were from Valley of Oaxaca sources. More than 500 additional ore lumps from the Valley of Oaxaca remain to be analyzed.

Two multi-drilled beads from the sites of San Lorenzo, Veracruz and Amatal, Chiapas were found to have been made of ilmenite ore from the same unidentified source. The ore from which these beads were made matches that used in two mirrors from La Venta, three from San Lorenzo, and one from Las Choapas, Veracruz. The function of these cubic objects, with holes drilled through four walls, remains unknown. Only at San Lorenzo, where multidrilled beads were found in a cache associated with Monument 17, a colossal head of the San Lorenzo phase (M. D. Coe, personal communication), are they firmly dated. The Amatal sample comes from an undated

TABLE 18

PROVENIENCE, DATE, CONTEXT, AND PROBABLE SOURCE FOR 7 IRON ORE MIRRORS FOUND BY M. D. COE AT SAN LORENZO, VERACRUZ

Type of Mirror	Provenience	Date	Archeological Context	Iron Group	Probable Source
Small, flat	SL-CC-13B	Prob. Nacaste phase	Redeposited in fill of Central Court	Ilmeno-magnetite (IV-B)	Loma Salinas, S. Lorenzo Cacaotepec, Valley of Oaxaca
Small, flat	SL-PNW-ST-IA	Prob. Nacaste phase	Redeposited in fill of Northwest Ridge	Ilmeno-magnetite (IV-B)	Loma Salinas, S. Lorenzo Cacaotepec, Valley of Oaxaca
Thick, flat	SL-PNW-I-1a	Prob. Nacaste phase	Redeposited in fill of Northwest Ridge	Hematite (II-A)	Cerro Prieto, Niltepec, near Tehuantepec
Thick, flat	SL-PNW-I-1b	Nacaste phase	In house mound, Northwest Ridge	Hematite (II-A)	Cerro Prieto, Niltepec, near Tehuantepec
Small, flat	SL-PNW-13e	Nacaste phase	In house mound, Northwest Ridge	Ilmenite (III-A)	Unknown, but same as some La Venta mirrors
Small, flat	SL-ONW-ST-IIc ⓑ	Nacaste phase	In house mound, Northwest Ridge	Ilmenite (III-A)	Unknown, but same as some La Venta mirrors
Small, concave	SL-NW-MI-2zc	San Lorenzo phase	In fill of pyramidal mound	Ilmenite (III-A)	Unknown, but same as some La Venta mirrors

cache found near the site of Chiapa de Corzo (T. Lee, personal communication). Because of their resemblance to the San Lorenzo specimens, a possible Early Formative date may be assigned the Amatal sample. Many more multi-drilled beads from San Lorenzo await analysis.

Turning to a consideration of the Valley of Mexico, where no magnetite mirrors of certain Early Formative date have been recovered as yet,[10] we may note that small worked and unworked natural parting fragments of crystalline hematite are found in association with Early Formative ceramics at Tlatilco. These roughly-formed "mirrors" (examined through the courtesy of R. García Moll) are probably made from locally-available crystalline hematite sources (José Luis Lorenzo, personal communication). The placement of mirrors on the chests of jade figurines is characteristic of the Olmec area (Plate 2a), and a similar placement of some of these pieces of crystalline hematite on figurines in the Valley of Mexico (Plate 2b) suggests that they were used in imitation of the magnetite mirrors. Because of the distinctive physical appearance of these mirrors and their restricted distribution, it was not necessary to use the Mössbauer technique to define this tradition of mirror making.

THE MIDDLE FORMATIVE: LOCALIZED IRON ORE MIRROR PRODUCTION

Sometime prior to 800 B.C., mirror production seems to have come to an end in the Valley of Oaxaca. Extensive excavation of Middle Formative (Guadalupe and Rosario phase) levels at the sites of Huitzo, San José Mogote, Fábrica San José, and Tierras Largas have failed to recover even one lump of ore. This same time period saw the defacement of monuments at San Lorenzo and the concomitant rise of La Venta. The small, flat magnetite mirrors disappear from the archeological inventory of the Gulf Coast, and are replaced by large concave mirrors which are most frequently made of ilmenite and hematite.

Samples of five of the Middle Formative La Venta concave mirrors in the collections of the Museo Nacional de Antropología e Historia in Mexico City were obtained through the courtesy of Arqueólogo Román Piña Chan. One of these mirrors, recovered from Mound A-2 fill during Stirling's 1942 excavations (Drucker, Heizer and Squier, 1959:182, Figure 50c) was made of magnetite. The spectrum of this sample did not match any of the geological sources examined in the study. This mirror from La Venta is a fragment, with one edge reworked.

The two hematite concave mirrors (group II-A) from La Venta are tentatively identified as made of ore from the Cerro Prieto source, which is located at Niltepec in the southern part of the Isthmus of Tehuantepec. It has been noted (Heizer, 1961:44) that Niltepec was the source of approximately 5,000 tons of serpentine found at the site of La Venta, and Williams and Heizer (1965:12) have suggested that Niltepec is also a probable source of iron for mirror making. As tempting as it is to make a positive identification of this source, the knowledge of other sources extant in the isthmus which were not sampled in our survey (Ojeda Rivera et al., 1965) prevents us from doing so. The two mirrors in question include one found in Offering #9, construction phase IV, during Drucker's 1955 excavation (Drucker, Heizer and Squier, 1959:180, Figure 49a), and a second, also from Drucker's 1955 excavation but not illustrated in the 1959 report. In form, both mirrors utilize the natural outline of the ore lump with the concavity fitted to the size of the piece. Both are highly polished across the entire concave surface, and roughly ground and shaped on the reverse side. The second mirror has a

---

[10]Paul Tolstoy recovered a badly-corroded possible mirror from Early Formative levels of his excavations at Tlapacoya. Unfortunately, the sample collected for analysis was too small for testing.

groove running diagonally across the back side. These two mirrors differ from the other La Venta mirrors in the Museo Nacional de Antropología e Historia collections, in that they are the only two which utilize the natural form of the ore lump from which they were made. The other La Venta mirrors are artificially shaped on all sides. It may have been the rounded appearance of these mirrors that led Curtis (*in* Drucker, Heizer and Squier, 1959:285) to suggest that some of the ore pieces may have been picked up in stream beds after eroding from the source. Our study of the fluvial dispersal and associated break-up of iron ore from the Cañada Carreta source in the Valley of Oaxaca, however, indicates that the ore is too soft to survive a journey of more than a few kilometers by riverine transport (see below).

The other La Venta mirrors came from an ilmenite source which was not among those examined in this study. One of these samples, excavated by Drucker in 1955 but not illustrated in the 1959 report by Drucker, Heizer and Squier, represents a fragment of a flat, poorly-polished (unfinished?) mirror. The second is a concave mirror, perforated for suspension, from Offering 1943-F (Drucker, Heizer and Squier, 1959:182, Figure 50*a*). A third concave mirror from Arroyo Pesquero at Las Choapas and presently in the collections of the museum of the Universidad Veracruzana—is made from the same ilmenite ore, and is so technologically similar to the La Venta mirrors that it could have been produced by the same craftsman.

Evidence of Middle Formative iron ore mirror production and exchange is incomplete, but the restricted Gulf Coast distribution of large concave mirrors suggests that they are a local product. The changes in both ore material and form of the mirrors reflect a localized development, distinct from the Early Formative iron ore exchange which extended over hundreds of kilometers and spanned many different culture areas.

CAÑADA CARRETA SURVEY: FLUVIAL DISPERSAL OF IRON ORE

In his report on the La Venta concave mirrors, Garniss Curtis (*in* Drucker, Heizer and Squier, 1959:287) observed: "The unpolished sides of the mirrors have the appearance of stream rounded boulders, and it is probable that the La Ventans obtained their material from streams after it had been eroded from its primary source." The possibility that iron ore lumps could be washed great distances from the original source presented a real complication for our model of Formative exchange. Therefore, in order to measure the effect of stream transport on iron ore lumps, a study of the fluvial dispersal of ore from the source of Cañada Carreta in the Valley of Oaxaca was undertaken.

The Cañada Carreta (or Cañada Peras source, as it is referred to in older publications) is located adjacent to a stream tributary of the Río Atoyac (Fig. 27). It is the only surface exposure of iron ore in the Cañada Carreta. A surface scatter of ore is found over an area fifteen by twenty meters on the lower slope of a hill some twenty-five meters above the stream bed on a 25° to 30° slope. In order to examine the quantity of ore at the source and at measured distances downstream, a bucket sampling system was utilized. Beginning at the source, and at distances of 100, 200, 400, 800, 1600 and 3200 meters along the river bed, bucketsful of the deposit were shoveled from the surface and sifted through a .05 centimeter screen until a minimum of one hundred pieces of iron ore were retained in the screen. The ore and bedrock fractions were bagged separately for analysis. The fine-sifted fraction was also retained for study by Dr. Michael Kirkby of the Department of Geography, Bristol University, England.

At the source, one-half a bucket provided an adequate sample of ore, but 100 meters downstream—at a point where the stream

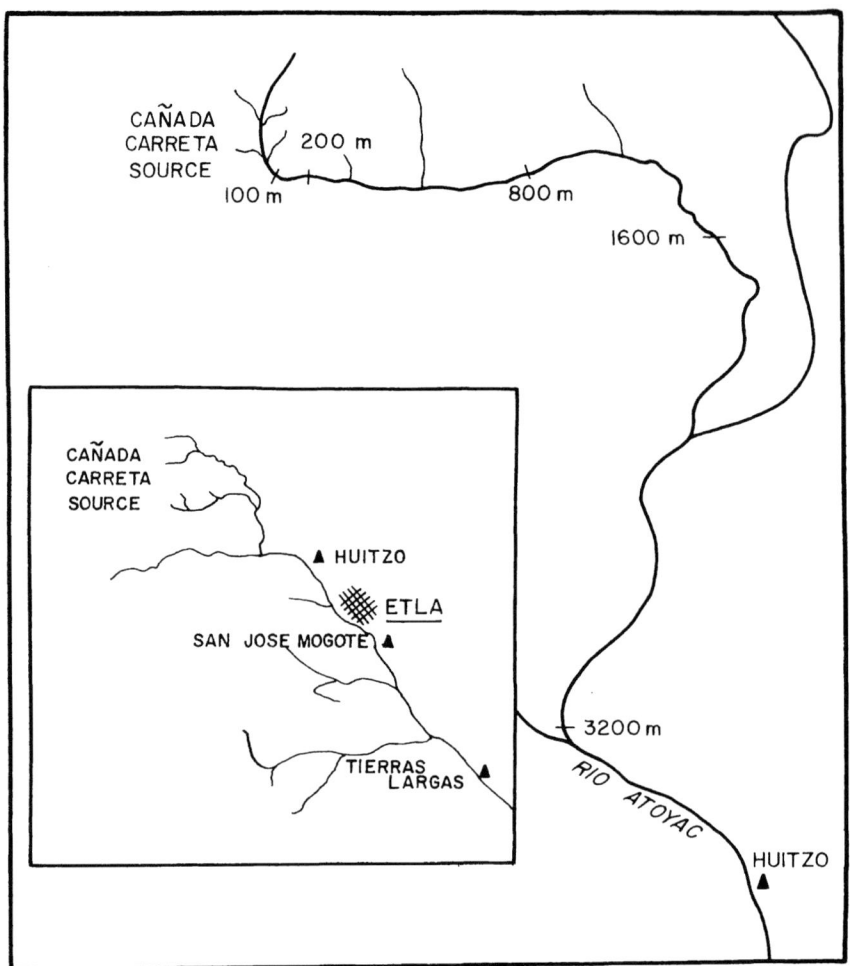

Fig. 27. Survey: Cañada Carreta fluvial dispersal of iron ore.

was cutting through bedrock—three bucketsful were required to obtain 100 pieces of ore. At 200 meters, in a boulder-strewn bed, a single bucket produced the necessary sample. At 400 meters, the stream was again cutting through bedrock and two buckets were required. By 800 meters, a black powder deposit had appeared in the river bed—this magnetic powder was a product of the disintegration of the ore as a result of the abrasion of stream transport. One bucket produced more than 100 small ore fragments. At 1600 meters, two buckets were required to obtain 100 ore samples, but by 3200 meters six bucketsful yielded only seven small pieces of ore.

The photographs (Figs. 28 and 29) of each of the samples, designated MAG-100, MAG-200, etc. to indicate the distance from the source, illustrate the gradual reduction in size and quantity of the ore as it was moved downstream. Figure 28, MAG-OA, illustrates the largest lumps of ore found on the surface of the source after the MAG-O sample had been taken. The overall reduction in the size of the samples as distance from the source increases is a result of breakup through abrasion by the much harder stream pebbles. The farther one moves from the source, the greater the percentage of magnetic fragments in the fine fraction of the sample. We also carried out analysis of the roundness and sphericity of the samples, using the procedures outlined in Krumbein and Pettijohn (1938:284-285). Utilizing the formula $\frac{\Sigma \frac{r}{R}}{N} = p$ where r is equal to the radius of curvature of the corner, R to the radius of the maximum incised circle, N to the number of corners, and p to total degree of roundness, this study revealed a slight tendency to increased angularity of the ore samples as distance from the source increased. MAG-0 to MAG-1600 represent samples taken within the Cañada Carreta; after the tributary stream enters the Río Atoyac at 2333 meters from the source, the remaining ore is quickly broken up and dispersed by the faster moving river. By 3200 meters from the source, the ore forms an insignificant fraction of the riverbed load.

The implications of this analysis are clear: even within the Valley of Oaxaca, the mirror makers could not have relied on stream action to bring the iron ore closer to their village. Formative period craftsmen had to know the source locations of the ore which they utilized for mirror making. However, within a few kilometers of each source, the presence of black powder in stream beds could be used as an indicator that a source lay not far upstream.

SUMMARY

This study has demonstrated, we hope, that Mössbauer spectroscopy can be an extremely useful technique in archeological investigations of iron containing artifacts. And while we have limited our present study to materials with substantial amounts of iron, this technique could be extended to other archeological elements, namely, tin and antimony. Most of these analyses were done with a transmission spectroscopic geometry which requires removal of material from the specimens, but the technique has since been adapted to a scattering geometry which is completely nondestructive of both the material and physical form of the artifact, which has made it possible to examine the mirrors from La Venta listed in the tables above. However, it is possible that the success of the present study may not be attainable in other areas, where very similar Mössbauer spectra are obtained for the different phases contained in the artifacts. Difficulties can also arise in cases for which there have not been a sufficient number of fundamental Mössbauer investigations of the materials contained in the artifacts. Such an unfavorable situation appears to exist for a recently-reported Mössbauer study of ancient pottery (Cousins and Dhwarmawardena, 1969).

In regard to the substantive and archeologically relevant conclusions of this study, analysis shows that during the latter part of the Early Formative period, magnetite mirrors produced at the site of San José Mogote in the Valley of Oaxaca were made from ore obtained at several different local sources, and that mirrors or ore lumps from these sources were exchanged at least as far as the Valley of Nochixtlán, the Valley of Morelos, and southern Veracruz. The Oaxacan mirror industry seems to have disappeared around 800 B.C., and was followed by the development of localized Gulf Coast concave mirror production which utilized primarily ilmenite and hematite ores. We have tentatively identified the Cerro Prieto, Niltepec hematite source as the raw material for two La Venta mirrors and have shown that two others (as well as a third from Las Choapas, Veracruz) were made of ore from a single, as yet unidentified, ilmenite source.

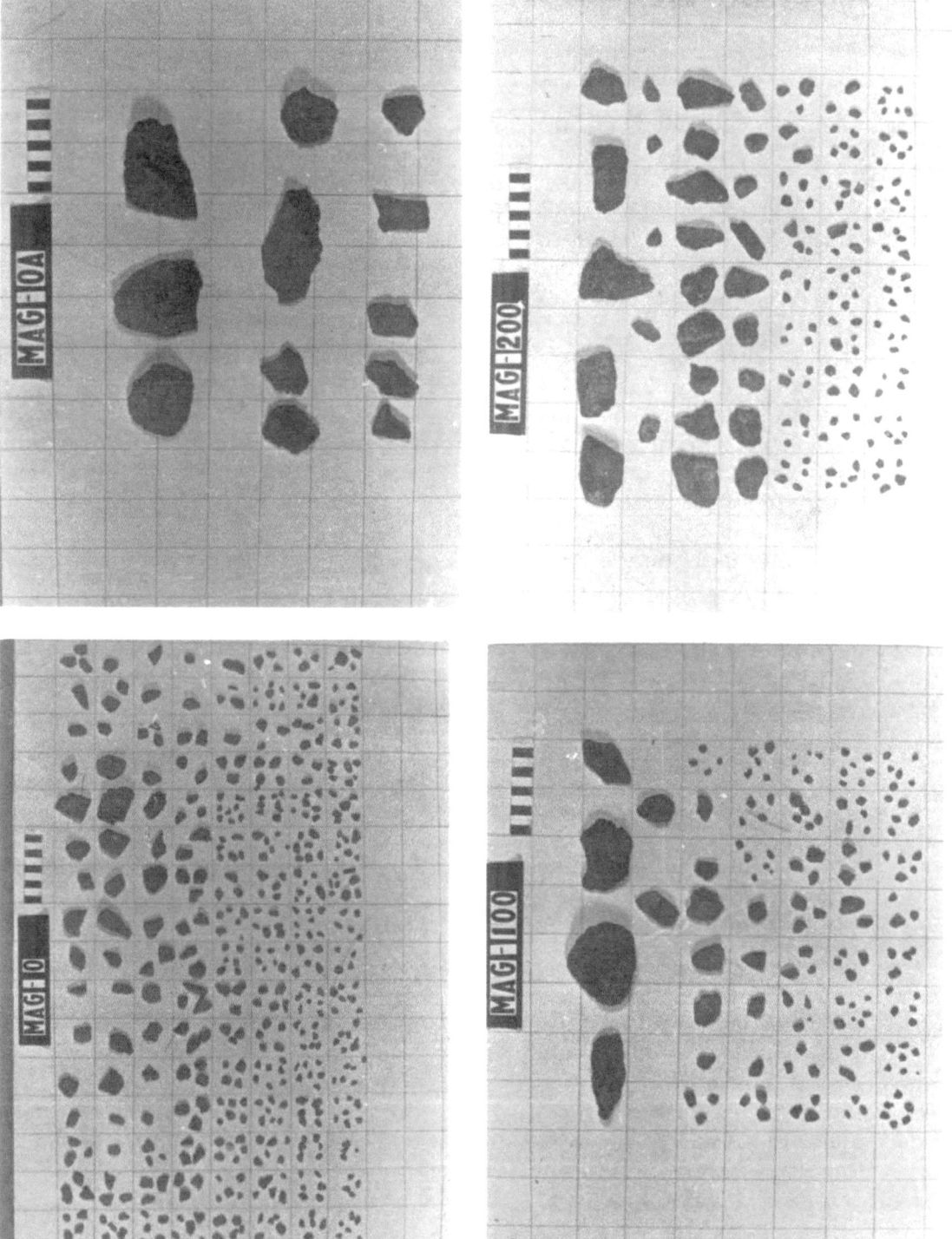

Fig. 28. Stages in the breakup of magnetite in the stream bed of the Cañada Carreta, Valley of Oaxaca (see text). MAG-O is a one-half bucket sample from the source, while MAG-OA illustrates the largest lumps of ore found on the surface after MAG-O was taken. MAG-100 and MAG-200 are, respectively, parts of a 3-bucket sample 100 m. downstream, and a one-bucket sample from 200 m. downstream.

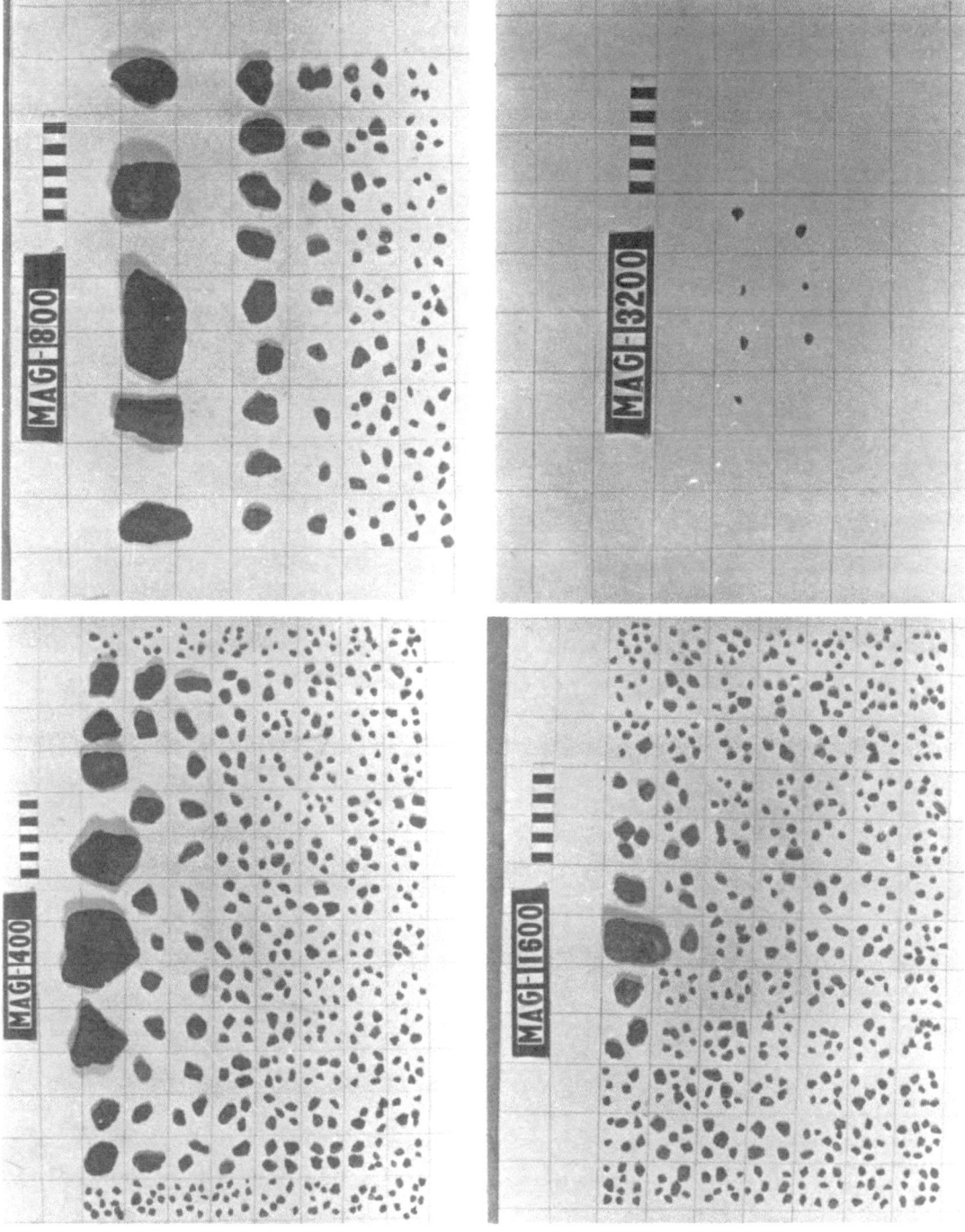

Fig. 29. Stages in the breakup of magnetite in the stream bed of the Cañada Carreta, Valley of Oaxaca (see text). MAG-400 is a two-bucket sample from 400 m. downstream. MAG-800 is part of a one-bucket sample from 800 m. downstream. MAG-1600 is a two-bucket sample from 1600 m. downstream. MAG-3200 shows the seven tiny pieces of ore produced by six bucketfuls of stream bed deposit 3200 m. downstream.

IV

SHELL EXCHANGE NETWORKS IN FORMATIVE MESOAMERICA

Highland and lowland Mesoamerica in the Early and Middle Formative were also linked by mollusk shell exchange. The tropical waters of coastal Mesoamerica are rich in mollusk species, many of which were used for food by the earliest villagers in the area. A few of these species, particularly pearl oyster, spiny oyster, and pearly fresh water mussel, have shells suitable for ornament manufacture; these were eagerly sought by the Formative peoples of the highlands. In addition, conch shells were used as trumpets by both highland and lowland peoples from the beginnings of the Formative to the time of the Spanish Conquest.

Examples of long-distance trade in marine shell are frequent in the ethnographic literature. One example is the exchange of gold-lip, sea-snail, and cowrie shells among villages in highland New Guinea (Rappaport, 1967). The use of such shells in building up bride wealth or dowries, or simply for personal adornment, is widespread. In the case of Formative Mesoamerica, it is interesting that the final conversion of this shell into ornaments (presumably further increasing their value) was not always done by the coastal villagers who had the best access to the shell; for example, unmodified *Spondylus* shells were traded to the Valley of Oaxaca where local part-time craftsmen cut, ground, and drilled them into pendants.

SHELLS: METHODOLOGY AND RAW DATA

The identification of shell materials from Early and Middle Formative Mesoamerican sites was completed by Dr. Joseph P. E. Morrison of the Smithsonian Institution, Washington, D.C. and the author. The extensive collection of Mesoamerican mollusks at the Smithsonian Institution provided comparative material for the analysis of archeological shell from the following sites: San José Mogote, Tierras Largas, Huitzo, Abasolo, and Laguna Zope, Oaxaca; Gamas, Tabasco; Nexpa and San Pablo, Morelos; and El Arbolillo East and West, Valley of Mexico. Additionally, excavation reports for Early and Middle Formative sites were reviewed and data on the shell material from the following sites were added to the list: La Victoria (Coe, 1961) and Salinas la Blanca (Coe and Flannery, 1967) in Guatemala, and Zacatenco (Vaillant, 1930) and El Arbolillo (Vaillant, 1935a) in the Valley of Mexico.

As the analysis proceeded it became clear that two major categories of shell material were to be found in Early and Middle Formative sites: Pacific coast marine and estuary shells, and Atlantic drainage freshwater shells. These categories are tentatively regarded as reflecting two different networks. In addition, one Atlantic marine shell has been reported in the Highland Mexican sites of these periods, a fragment of *Cassis* sp., or cameo shell, identified from Vaillant's excavations at El Arbolillo (Vaillant, 1935a:249); it is, however, the only example of an Atlantic marine shell. Tables 19-22 list the shells so far identified from a small sample of Early and Middle Formative period Mesoamerican sites. The tables are divided according to time periods and geographic origins of the shells.

TABLE 19

MOLLUSKS FOUND IN EARLY FORMATIVE CONTEXT: VALLEY OF OAXACA

Mollusk & Region of Origin	Site	Provenience	Total
1. Atlantic Marine			
Neritina usnea	S. J. Mogote	Area A, Zone D1 midden	1
2. Atlantic Estuary			
-none-			
3. Freshwater, Atlantic Drainage			
Actionaias sp.	S. J. Mogote	Area C, House 4	1
	T. Largas	Feature 141	1
	T. Largas	San José phase debris	6
Anadara incongrua	S. J. Mogote	Area C, House 4	1
Anodonta globosa	T. Largas	San José phase debris	1
Barynaias (= *Quadula*) sp.	S. J. Mogote	Area A, Household Cluster C2	1
	S. J. Mogote	Area A, Household Cluster C3	3
	S. J. Mogote	Area A, Household Cluster C4	3
	S. J. Mogote	Area A, Zone D1 midden	2
	S. J. Mogote	Area A, Zone D2 midden	2
	S. J. Mogote	Area A, San José phase debris	1
	S. J. Mogote	Area C, House 2	6
	S. J. Mogote	Area C, House 4	1
	S. J. Mogote	Area C, House 8	2
	S. J. Mogote	Area C, House 9	12
	T. Largas	Feature 4, House 1	2
4. Pacific Marine			
Anachis sp.	S. J. Mogote	Area C, House 4	1
Arca cf. *labiata*	T. Largas	Feature 160	1
Busicon cf. *columella*	T. Largas	Early Tierras Largas phase debris	1
Chione sp.	S. J. Mogote	Area A, Household Cluster C3	1
Anomalocardia (= *Chione*) *subrugosa*	S. J. Mogote	Area A, Zone D1 midden	2
	S. J. Mogote	Area A, Zone D2 midden	1
	S. J. Mogote	Area C, House 1	1
	S. J. Mogote	Area C, House 2	1
	S. J. Mogote	Area C, House 7	1
	S. J. Mogote	Platform 1 (redeposited San José phase debris	2
	T. Largas	San José phase debris	2
Neritina cassiculum	S. J. Mogote	Area C, House 4	1
Pinctada mazatlanica	S. J. Mogote	Area A, Household Cluster C1	1
	S. J. Mogote	Area A, Household Cluster C3	2
	S. J. Mogote	Area A, Zone D1 midden	3
	S. J. Mogote	Area A, Zone D2 midden	4
	S. J. Mogote	Area A, redeposited San José phase debris	5
	S. J. Mogote	Area C, House 1	1
	S. J. Mogote	Area C, House 2	10
	S. J. Mogote	Area C, House 4	19
	S. J. Mogote	Area C, House 5	1
	S. J. Mogote	Area C, House 6	2
	S. J. Mogote	Area C, House 7	1
	S. J. Mogote	Area C, House 8	8
	S. J. Mogote	Area C, House 9	4
	S. J. Mogote	Area C, House 10	1
	T. Largas	Early Tierras Largas phase	2
	T. Largas	Late Tierras Largas phase	5

TABLE 19 (Continued)

Mollusk & Region of Origin	Site	Provenience	Total
4. Pacific Marine (Continued)			
Pinctada mazatlanica (Continued)	T. Largas	San José phase	6
	Abasolo	Burial 1 (San José phase)	1
Spondylus calcifer	S. J. Mogote	Area A, Household Cluster C3	2
	S. J. Mogote	Area A, Zone D1 midden	1
	S. J. Mogote	Area A, redeposited San José phase debris	2
	S. J. Mogote	Area C, House 5	2
	S. J. Mogote	Area C, House 8	1
Spondylus cf. *pictorem*	T. Largas	San José phase debris	1
Strombus cf. *galeatus*	S. J. Mogote	Area A, Household Cluster C4	1 (?)
	S. J. Mogote	Platform 2, base of east wall	1
	S. J. Mogote	Area C, House 4	1
	T. Largas	San José phase debris	3
	Abasolo	San José phase debris	1 (?)
Pyrene sp.	S. J. Mogote	Area A, Household Cluster C3	1
	S. J. Mogote	Area A, Zone D1 midden	1
Thais biserialis	S. J. Mogote	Area A, Zone D2 midden	1
	S. J. Mogote	Area A, San José phase debris	1
Tivela cf. *gracilior*	T. Largas	Feature 159	1
5. Pacific Estuary			
Agaronia testacea	T. Largas	Feature 160/S	1
Cerithidea mazatlanica	S. J. Mogote	Area A, Household Cluster C3	1
	S. J. Mogote	Area A, Zone D1 midden	3
	S. J. Mogote	Area A, Zone D2 midden	2
	S. J. Mogote	Area C, House 2	2
	S. J. Mogote	Area C, House 4	2
Cerithium stercus-muscarum	S. J. Mogote	Area A, Household Cluster C3	1
	S. J. Mogote	Area A, Household Cluster C4	1
	S. J. Mogote	Area A, Zone D1 midden	1
	S. J. Mogote	Area A, redeposited San José phase debris	2
	S. J. Mogote	Area C, House 4	1
	T. Largas	Feature 160/S	1
Ostrea chilensis	T. Largas	Late T. Largas phase debris	1
6. Atlantic or Pacific Marine			
Cardata sp.	S. J. Mogote	Area A, Household Cluster C2	1
Strigilla sp.	S. J. Mogote	Area C, House 9	1
	T. Largas	Late T. Largas phase debris	1
7. Atlantic or Pacific Estuary			
Olivella sp.	S. J. Mogote	Area A, Feature 2, Household Cluster C3	1
	S. J. Mogote	Area C, House 8	1
Turritella sp.	S. J. Mogote	Area C, House 8	1
8. Freshwater, Atlantic or Pacific Drainage			
Anadonta sp.	S. J. Mogote	Area C, House 2	1
	T. Largas	San José phase debris	1 (?)

TABLE 20
MOLLUSKS FOUND IN EARLY FORMATIVE CONTEXT: OTHER REGIONS

Mollusk & Region of Origin	Site	Provenience	Total
1. Atlantic Marine			
Crassostrea virginica	Gamas, Tabasco	Excavation 1, Pit 1	±30
2. Atlantic Estuary			
Rangianella flaxuosa	Gamas, Tabasco	Excavation 1, Pit 1	6
Rangianella sp.	Gamas, Tabasco	Excavation 1, Pit 1	6
3. Freshwater, Atlantic Drainage			
Barynaias cf. *pigerrimus*	San Pablo, Morelos	H 17	1
Barynaias (= *Quadula*) sp.	San Pablo, Morelos	G 11	1
	San Pablo, Morelos	G 13	1
	Laguna Zope	Surface collection	Present
4. Pacific Marine			
Anadara grandis	La Victoria	Ocós phase debris	Present
	Salinas La Blanca	Jocotal phase debris	1
Anadara perlabiata	La Victoria	Ocós phase debris	Present
Anadara aequatorialis	Salinas La Blanca	Cuadros phase debris	5
Cardita laticostata	Salinas La Blanca	Cuadros phase debris	5
Chione gnidia	La Victoria	Ocós phase debris	Present
Harvella elegans	Salinas La Blanca	Cuadros phase debris	2
Iphigenia altior	La Victoria	Ocós phase debris	Present
	Salinas La Blanca	Cuadros phase debris	10
	Salinas La Blanca	Jocotal phase debris	1
Mulinia pallida	La Victoria	Ocós phase debris	Present
	Salinas La Blanca	Cuadros phase debris	2
	Salinas La Blanca	Jocotal phase debris	2
Mytella falcata	La Victoria	Ocós phase debris	1
	Salinas La Blanca	Cuadros phase debris	5
	Salinas La Blanca	Jocotal phase debris	1
Pinctada mazatlanica	Laguna Zope	Surface collection	Present
Pitar consanguineus	Salinas La Blanca	Cuadros phase debris	1
Pitar lupanaria	Salinas La Blanca	Jocotal phase debris	1
Strombus galeatus	La Victoria	Ocós phase debris	Present
	Salinas La Blanca	Cuadros phase debris	2
	Salinas La Blanca	Jocotal phase debris	1
	Laguna Zope	Surface collection	Present
Spondylus calcifer	Laguna Zope	Surface collection	Present
5. Pacific Estuary			
Agaronia testacea	La Victoria	Ocós phase debris	Present
	Salinas La Blanca	Cuadros phase debris	3
	Salinas La Blanca	Jocotal phase debris	27
Amphichaena kindermanni	La Victoria	Ocós phase debris	Present
	Salinas La Blanca	Cuadros phase debris	10
	Salinas La Blanca	Jocotal phase debris	5
Anomalocardia subrugosa	La Victoria	Ocós phase debris	Present
	Laguna Zope	Surface collection	Present
Cerithidea mazatlanica	Salinas La Blanca	Cuadros phase debris	41
	Salinas La Blanca	Jocotal phase debris	7
Cerithidea valida	Salinas La Blanca	Cuadros phase debris	2

TABLE 20 (Continued)

Mollusk & Reagion of Origin	Site	Provenience	Total
5. Pacific Estuary (Continued)			
Melampus tabogensis	Salinas La Blanca	Cuadros phase debris	2
Neritina luteofasciata	Salinas La Blanca	Cuadros phase debris	2
	Salinas La Blanca	Jocotal phase debris	1
Noetia reversa	Salinas La Blanca	Cuadros phase debris	4
Olivella semistriata	Salinas La Blanca	Cuadros phase debris	1
Ostrea columbiensis	La Victoria	Ocós phase debris	Present
	Salinas La Blanca	Cuadros phase debris	4
Polymesoda radiata	La Victoria	Ocós phase debris	Present
	Salinas La Blanca	Cuadros phase debris	486
	Salinas La Blanca	Jocotal phase debris	2
Sanguinolaria bertini	Salinas La Blanca	Jocotal phase debris	1
Thais melones	Salinas La Blanca	Jocotal phase debris	1
Ptotothaca asperrima	La Victoria	Ocós phase debris	Present
Trachycardium procerum	Laguna Zope	Surface collection	Present
6. Atlantic or Pacific Marine -none-			
7. Atlantic or Pacific Estuary -none-			
8. Freshwater, Atlantic or Pacific Drainage			
Nephronaias sp.	Salinas La Blanca	Jocotal phase debris	4

THE EARLY FORMATIVE: SHELL EXCHANGE NETWORKS LINKING VILLAGES

Precise identification of shell exchange networks is not possible because of the limited amount of data available from Early Formative sites, and the imprecise information on the areas inhabited by various shell species. In the first case, the lack of preservation of shell material at San Lorenzo and other Gulf Coast sites leaves a large gap in our understanding of shell exchange networks. In the second case, the wide natural distribution of the shell species which were exchanged makes identification of specific points of origin impossible. We are usually limited to generalizations such as "Pacific marine" or "Atlantic drainage." Despite these limitations, certain patterns of shell species distribution in the data do permit the tentative definition of two regionally distinct exchange networks: one transporting a small variety of Atlantic freshwater species for simple ornament manufacture, and one transporting a greater variety of Pacific marine species, including some for the manufacture of more complex ornaments. However, the presence of both kinds of shell on sites at the Isthmus of Tehuantepec suggests that both networks may have converged there on their way to the highlands.

The Pacific Coast Shell Exchange Network

Seventeen taxa of Pacific coast shells (including marine and estuary forms) have been recovered from three Early Formative sites (Abasolo, San José Mogote, and Tierras Largas) in the highland Valley of Oaxaca, while twenty-nine taxa come from three sites (Laguna Zope, La Victoria, and Salinas la Blanca) on the Pacific coast. Eleven of the species represent mollusks used for food at the coastal sites (and not occurring elsewhere); many of the remaining taxa are found at both highland and coastal sites (Tables 19, 20). It is the latter which provide the main basis for our discussion.

Of the shell species found at both Pacific coast and highland Early Formative sites, *Pinctada mazatlanica* (the Pacific pearl oyster) is the most frequent. Commonly found in shallow offshore water from lower California to Peru (Keen, 1958:58), these shells were one of the major materials used by Early Formative shell workers in the Oaxaca highlands. The shells of an adult animal are sufficiently thick and durable to permit cutting, grinding, and drilling into elaborate forms. The shape of these shells provides a relatively large flattish working surface, with waste limited to the marginal valve area. These characteristics differ from those exhibited by the fragile Atlantic freshwater shells, which could be drilled but not cut or ground into decorative forms (unpublished experimental data). At the sites of San José Mogote and Tierras Largas in the Etla region of the Valley of Oaxaca, abundant evidence of the working of *Pinctada mazatlanica* shells was found; at Abasolo in the Tlacolula region a finished pendant of pearl oyster was recovered with a burial, but no evidence of shell working was discovered.

The exchange links through which the unworked shell reached the Oaxacan craftsmen are not known. The possibility that they may have passed through the Tehuantepec region has been raised by surface shell material identified at the site of Laguna Zope near Juchitán, Oaxaca. This large Early and Middle Formative site was first reported by Delgado (1961 and 1965). A surface survey of the site in 1968 located quantities of shell in association with Early and Middle Formative period ceramics (Flannery, personal communication). Included among the shells were both worked and unworked *Pinctada mazatlanica* fragments. The most frequent worked form was a shell with the heavy valve section cut away. This indicates the existence of local shell working or the preparation of shell "blanks" for long-distance exchange. Examination of this hypothesis must await the analysis of more recent excavation at Laguna Zope by Robert and Judy Zeitlin (personal communication). So far the Zeitlins report abundant shell but no actual areas of ornament manufacture.

Two other Pacific marine shells found less frequently at both highland Mexican and Pacific coastal sites are *Spondylus calcifer* and *Strombus galeatus*. Both species are commonly found just below the low-tide line on beaches from California to Peru (Keen, 1958:336). The spiny oyster (*Spondylus calcifer*) was found among the shells at Laguna Zope and in association with shell-working areas of Early Formative households at San José Mogote. Unlike *Pinctada mazatlanica*, however, it appears that these shells were imported whole and trimmed to be used as large pendants, but not cut or worked into smaller ornaments. Also imported whole were conch shells, most commonly *Strombus galeatus* but also including *Malea ringens*. Fragments of presumed conch shell trumpets have been found in shell-working areas on house floors at San José Mogote and in association with public building at San José Mogote and Barrio del Rosario Huitzo. Fragments of *Strombus* have also been found at Laguna Zope, La Victoria, and Salinas la Blanca on the Pacific coast.

Two Pacific estuary shells have also been found in Early Formative sites in the Valley of Oaxaca on the Pacific coast. Fragments of *Agaronia testacea* occur at Tierras Largas and La Victoria, and *Anomalocardia subrugosa* is reported from San José Mogote, Tierras Largas, Laguna Zope, and La Victoria. It is interesting that *Anomalocardia*, which was used for food at La Victoria, became an ornament when it reached the highlands. Modification of these shells was by grinding or drilling of holes for suspension.

In addition to those already mentioned, more than a dozen other Pacific taxa have been identified at highland Mexican sites only (Table 19). The mechanics of the exchange which brought such a variety of shell into the Mexican highland area are not understood. Surface materials from Laguna Zope contain abundant shells, including four of the five Pacific marine genera found at both highland and lowland sites and the Atlantic freshwater genus *Barynaias*. Future excavations here and at other sites in the Tehuantepec region may show this area to be an important crossroads for the Pacific and Atlantic shell exchange networks. Within the highlands, access to the imported raw shell appears to have been limited—especially in the case of *Pinctada mazatlanica*—to shell working villages or residential wards within villages, which in turn passed on their finished shell ornaments to other sites. Pacific shell may have moved through the same "sphere of conveyence" which brought El Chayal obsidian to the Oaxaca highlands, the Isthmus, and the Gulf Coast, but full evaluation of this hypothesis must await both future Pacific coast excavations and the discovery of preserved Early Formative shell at Gulf Coast sites.

The Atlantic Drainage Shell Exchange Network

While Atlantic drainage freshwater shells were widely exchanged as ornaments during the Early Formative period, Atlantic marine and estuary shell resources were rarely traded or modified. Atlantic marine mollusks were collected and eaten, however; at the Tabasco coastal site of Gamas, some thirty fragments of the oyster *Crassostrea virginica* presumably represent food refuse. Two estuary clams, *Rangianella* sp. and *Rangianella flaxuosa petitiana* were also identified among the Gamas shells, and likewise were exploited for food.

The most widely distributed of the Atlantic mollusks at sites outside their native drainage area are the pearly fresh-water mussels (*Barynaias* sp. and *Barynaias* cf. *pigerrimus*). Native to the large river systems from Tampico to the Laguna de Términos (Morrison, personal communication), these mussels have been identified at the sites of San José Mogote and Tierras Largas in the Valley of Oaxaca; at Laguna Zope on the Pacific coast of the Isthmus of Tehuantepec; at El Arbolillo in the Valley of Mexico; and at San Pablo in Morelos. Apparently because of their fragility, these shells were not cut up into smaller ornaments; rather, when utilized, they were perforated for suspension as pendants. Three other taxa also found at the sites in the Valley of Oaxaca were *Actionaias* sp., *Anadara incongrua*, and *Anadonta globosa*. The native distribution of these mollusks is the same as for *Barynaias*.

The exchange of Atlantic drainage freshwater mussel shells is poorly understood, due to the widespread natural range of these four genera and the total absence of shell data from Early Formative Gulf Coast sites. It is possible that these shells were moved into the highlands along the same "sphere of conveyence" which brought Guadalupe Victoria obsidian to the Gulf. Also, there are differences in the distribution of Atlantic freshwater and Pacific marine shell among households at San José Mogote and Tierras Largas. These are commented on below, but can probably not be fully explained without further excavation.

THE MIDDLE FORMATIVE: SHELL EXCHANGE NETWORKS LINKING VILLAGES

Among the shells identified for seven Middle Formative sites, more than thirty taxa were recorded (Tables 21 and 22). In Oaxaca, only six Pacific marine and estuary taxa were found, compared with seventeen in the Early Formative. Similarly, the Atlantic freshwater drainage taxa dropped from six to one for the Middle Formative.

The Pacific Coast Shell Exchange Network

Pacific Coast shells from seven Middle Formative sites were considered. Five of the sites are located in the Mexican Highlands—Huitzo and Tierras Largas in the Valley of Oaxaca; El Arbolillo and Zacatenco in the Valley of Mexico; and Nexpa in Morelos. Two are on the Pacific coast of Guatemala, namely, La Victoria and Salinas la Blanca. However, nine marine and nine estuary species were found only at the coastal sites, and probably represent food refuse. The traded shells include five marine and five estuary species found so far at highland sites.

Only three of the thirteen Pacific coast shell species found at Early Formative highland Oaxacan sites continued to appear in Middle Formative layers. *Strombus galeatus,* found at La Victoria, Salinas la Blanca, and Tierras Largas, is

TABLE 21

MOLLUSKS FOUND IN MIDDLE FORMATIVE CONTEXT: VALLEY OF OAXACA

Mollusk & Region of Origin	Site	Provenience	Total
1. Atlantic Marine			
-none-			
2. Atlantic Estuary			
-none-			
3. Freshwater, Atlantic Drainage			
Barynaias (= *Quadula*) sp.	Huitzo	Area A, House 1	2
	Huitzo	Area A, Feature 1	1
	T. Largas	Guadalupe phase debris	1
4. Pacific Marine			
Pinctada mazatlanica	T. Largas	Guadalupe phase debris	3
Strombus galeatus	T. Largas	Guadalupe phase debris	1
Spondylus sp.	Huitzo	Zone F1 mound fill	1
Malea cf. *ringens*	Huitzo	Zone D2 (Guadalupe phase midden)	1
5. Pacific Estuary			
Amphichaena kindermanni	Huitzo	Zone D2 (Guadalupe phase midden)	3
Turritella jewettii	Huitzo	Guadalupe phase debris	1
6. Freshwater, Atlantic or Pacific Drainage			
Anadonta sp.	T. Largas	Feature 112 (late Guadalupe phase)	1

the only marine species found at both coastal and highland sites in our sample during both Early and Middle Formative periods. Presumably the importance of conch shell trumpets accounts for this. Other Pacific marine species exchanged during both periods include *Pinctada mazatlanica* (found at Middle Formative Zacatenco, Nexpa, and Tierras Largas) and *Spondylus* sp., found at Huitzo. The sample size for this period is small, and no evidence concerning the relation between shell import and shell craft production is available.

Two new Pacific estuary species appear at highland sites during the Middle Formative. *Amphichaena kindermanni,* a small marsh clam native to the estuary system of the Pacific coast (Clench, quoted in Coe, 1961), was eaten at both La Victoria and Salinas la Blanca and traded to Huitzo in the Valley of Oaxaca. A second estuary form, the snail *Neritina (Theodoxus) luteofasciata,* was found at both Salinas la Blanca and Zacatenco. This species is found from the Gulf of California to Panama (Keen, 1958:266).

The Atlantic Drainage Freshwater Shell Exchange Network

A decrease, similar to that seen in the number of Pacific coast species, is also recorded for Atlantic drainage shells during the Middle Formative period. Only four shells of *Barynaias* sp. (from Huitzo and Tierras Largas) have been identified in our sample of seven Middle Formative sites. This reduction in the exchange of freshwater clam shell is evidently not compensated for by the substitution of other Atlantic species, for only one fragment of Atlantic marine shell, *Cassis* sp. or cameo shell, has been identified (at El Arbolillo). The cause of the drop-off in the exchange of Atlantic drainage shell is probably also to be found in the trend towards regionalization already noted for the Middle Formative.

TABLE 22

MOLLUSKS FOUND IN MIDDLE FORMATIVE CONTEXT: OTHER REGIONS

Mollusk & Region of Origin	Site	Provenience	Total
1. Atlantic Marine			
Cassis sp.	El Arbolillo		1
2. Atlantic Estuary			
-none-			
3. Freshwater, Atlantic Drainage			
-none-			
4. Pacific Marine			
Anadara aequatorialis	La Victoria	Conchas I debris	Present
Anadara grandis	La Victoria	Conchas II debris	Present
Anadara obesa	La Victoria	Conchas I debris	Present
Anadara perlabiata	La Victoria	Conchas I & II debris	Present
Cardita laticostata	La Victoria	Conchas I & II debris	Present
Chione pulicaria	La Victoria	Conchas I debris	Present
Iphigenia altior	La Victoria	Conchas I & II debris	Present
Lunarca brevifrons	La Victoria	Conchas I debris	Present
Mytella falcata	La Victoria	Conchas I debris	Present
Pinctada mazatlanica	Zacatenco	E Trenches	1
	Zacatenco	Middle Period debris	1
	Nexpa, Morelos	Burial NA-2	1
Strombus galeatus	La Victoria	Conchas I & II debris	Present
Melogena cf. *patula*	El Arbolillo	Tolstoy dig: West, E172N1	1
5. Pacific Estuary			
Agaronia testacea	La Victoria	Conchas I & II debris	Present
Amphichaena kindermanni	La Victoria	Conchas I & II debris	Present
Anomalocardia subrugosa	La Victoria	Conchas I & II debris	Present
Cerithidea valida	La Victoria	Conchas I debris	Present
Natica chemnictzii	La Victoria	Conchas I debris	Present
Neritina luteofasciata	Zacatenco	E Trenches	1
Neritina usnea	El Arbolillo	Tolstoy dig: East, L28N1	1
Ostrea columbiensis	La Victoria	Conchas I & II debris	Present
Polinices bifasciatus	La Victoria	Conchas I debris	Present
Polymesoda radiata	La Victoria	Conchas I & II debris	Present
Thais kiosquiformis	La Victoria	Conchas I debris	Present
Trachycardium senticosum	La Victoria	Conchas I debris	Present
6. Altnatic or Pacific Estuary			
Neritina sp.	El Arbolillo	Skeleton 129 (necklace)	20

THE DISTRIBUTION OF SHELL AMONG FORMATIVE HOUSEHOLDS: AN EXAMPLE FROM OAXACA

Tierras Largas and San José Mogote are unique among Early Formative villages so far excavated in Oaxaca: every house of that period at each site contains some shell, and usually evidence of shell-working. Similar evidence has not appeared at Huitzo, Abasolo, Fábrica San José, or Tomaltepec. It would thus appear that a very high proportion of the shell ornaments made during the Early Formative were turned out by part-time craftsmen in this one localized area of the Valley of Oaxaca.

Evidence from three house floors of the Tierras Largas phase at the site of Tierras Largas indicates that the importation of Pacific marine

TABLE 23
NUMBERS OF IDENTIFIED SHELL TAXA, BY REGION OF ORIGIN, FOR THE VALLEY OF OAXACA AND A SMALL SAMPLE OF OTHER REGIONS: EARLY AND MIDDLE FORMATIVE

Region of Origin	Early Formative		Middle Formative	
	Oaxaca	Other Regions	Oaxaca	Other Regions
1. Atlantic Marine	1	1	–	1
2. Atlantic Estuary	–	2	–	–
3. Freshwater, Atlantic Drainage	4	2	1	–
4. Pacific Marine	13	14	4	12
5. Pacific Estuary	4	15	2	12
6. Atlantic or Pacific Marine	2	–	–	–
7. Atlantic or Pacific Estuary	2	–	–	1
8. Freshwater, Atlantic or Pacific Drainage	1	1	1	–
Totals	27	35	8	26

shell goes back before 1300 B.C. (Winter, 1972:181). The shell appears to be evenly distributed among all the houses, and no Atlantic drainage shells are found.

The importance of Pacific coast shell, both marine and estuary, grew during the San José Phase (1150 to 850 B.C.). Data from thirteen house floors or household clusters at San José Mogote suggest that Pacific coast shell was the primary object of local shell ornament production (Table 24). Twenty-three Pacific coast shell ornaments and finished pieces are present, compared to two freshwater Atlantic drainage shell ornaments; 23 Pacific coast shell unfinished pieces, or waste products, are present, compared to 16 Atlantic drainage shells in this same category. However, the numbers of unmodified shells are approximately equal, with 24 from the Pacific coast and 26 from the Atlantic drainage.

Examination of the worked shell indicates that *Pinctada mazatlanica*, the Pacific pearl oyster, was the preferred raw material for ornament production at San José Mogote. This shiny shell not only presents a relatively large and flattish working area, but also holds up during cutting, grinding and drilling, the basic ornament production procedures. Experiments in working both *Pinctada mazatlanica* and the freshwater clam shells by these techniques showed the latter to be too brittle for ornament manufacture (unpublished data).

There are variations in shell content of the thirteen household areas at San José Mogote which are intriguing, but the samples are too small to be conclusive, usually because whole houses were rarely recovered. Tentatively, it appears that some houses may have worked primarily Pacific shell while others worked primarily Atlantic shell—perhaps indicating different networks of trade partners. Extensive concentrations of Atlantic coast waste products or unworked shell fragments occurred in House 9 (Area C) and Household Cluster C3 (Area A); House 4 (Area C) had a similar concentration of Pacific coast waste products.

One can also cite households which had finished ornaments from one coast, but primarily waste products from the other coast. House 9 had two elaborate finished Pacific shell products, including a pendant with an Olmec paw-wing motif, but there was no evidence for Pacific coast shell working; the householders were mainly involved in working Atlantic freshwater mussel. Similarly, Household Cluster C3 had three finished Pacific coast products including a fragment of mother-of-pearl mirror holder for a magnetite mirror (see above), while its waste products were mainly from *Barynaias*. On the other hand, the residents of House 4 had clearly been working Pacific shell (10 unfinished pieces or waste products), but there was little to indicate the working of Atlantic drainage mussel although four unworked whole shells were present. House 2 had six finished products and five

TABLE 24

SOURCES AND UTILIZATION OF SHELLS: EARLY FORMATIVE HOUSE FLOORS OR HOUSEHOLD CLUSTERS AT SAN JOSÉ MOGOTE, OAXACA

San José Mogote, Early Formative Households	Ornaments and Finished Pieces, Including Fragments			Unfinished Pieces and Waste Products			Unworked Shell Fragments			Unworked Whole Shells			Shell Tools			Subtotal			Total
	P	A	U	P	A	U	P	A	U	P	A	U	P	A	U	P	A	U	
Area A																			
H.C. C1	2		1	1												3		1	4
H.C. C2	1				2			1	4							1	3	4	8
H.C. C3	3	1	1	3	9		4	1	2							10	11	3	24
H.C. C4			2	2	3		1	3								3	6	2	11
Area C																			
House 1	2						1		1							3		1	4
House 2	6			5	1			6	2	2						13	7	2	22
House 4	3	1		10			7	2		4			1			25	3		28
House 5				1			2									3			3
House 6							2									2			2
House 7	1									1						2			2
House 8	2		1	1			5	2					1	1		9	2	2	13
House 9	2		1		1	1	2	11	2							4	12	4	20
House 10	1															1			1
Total	23	2	6	23	16	1	24	26	11	7		1	2	1		79	44	19	142

Key: H.C. = Household Cluster
P = Pacific Marine and Estuary
A = Atlantic Drainage
U = Unidentified

unfinished fragments or waste products of Pacific coast shell, accompanied by scantier evidence for Atlantic drainage mussel working. In Household Cluster C4, the working of shells from both regions was well documented. Less variation from house to house in shell ornament manufacture was found at the smaller site of Tierras Largas, where Winter (1972:181) notes an even distribution of shell and shell working evidence among the three San José phase household clusters he excavated (Tables 25 and 26).

The mechanism by which finished ornaments were distributed both within San José Mogote and to other sites in the valley is not understood. Nor is it clear if the distribution of Atlantic drainage clams is a function of technical unsuitability for ornament manufacture, or of social status, or both.

It may be that the freshwater clam shells were obtained from the Papaloapan river via the nearby Cañada Tomellín and used in imitation of higher-status marine shell ornaments. A similar situation involving the manufacture from wood of imitation stone axes by Mt. Hagen natives in New Guinea has been reported by Strathern (1969:327). These shells may also, however, have been obtained through exchange with Gulf Coast sites. If the shell was imported through the same "sphere of conveyence" in which the Guadalupe Victoria obsidian, Xochiltepec white pottery, and other Gulf Coast items moved, a far different value might have been attached to it. But full understanding of the value of Atlantic drainage shell and the way in which it was obtained in Early Formative Oaxaca will only come with future excavations.

Data from only one Middle Formative household is available. The total of six shells recovered

TABLE 25

SOURCES OF EARLY AND MIDDLE FORMATIVE SHELL FOUND AT TIERRAS LARGAS, OAXACA
BY NUMBER OF SPECIMENS

Time Period	Pacific Marine	Pacific Mangrove	Pacific Estuary	Atlantic Drainage Freshwater	Atlantic or Pacific Drainage Freshwater	Atlantic or Pacific Marine	Marine ?	?	Total
Mixed Formative	11	1		2			1	3	18
Rosario Phase	2							1	3
Guadalupe Phase	4			1	1				6
Late San José Phase	16		1	13	2			1	33
Early San José Phase	2			3					5
Late Tierras Largas Phase	7					1		1	9
Early Tierras Largas Phase	2								2
Total	44	1	1	19	3	1	1	6	76

TABLE 26

UTILIZATION OF SHELLS: EARLY AND MIDDLE FORMATIVE HOUSEHOLD CLUSTERS AT
TIERRAS LARGAS, OAXACA

Time Period	Ornaments and Finished Pieces, Including Fragments	Unfinished Pieces and Waste Products	Unworked Fragments	Unworked Whole Shells	Tools	Total
Mixed Formative	6	4	7	1		18
Rosario Phase	1	2				3
Guadalupe Phase	2	1	2		1	6
Late San José Phase	12	5	13	3		33
Early San José Phase	1	2	1	1		5
Late Tierras Largas Phase	4	2	2		1	9
Early Tierras Largas Phase	2					2
Total	28	16	25	5	2	76

from Household Cluster G-3 at Tierras Largas includes four Pacific marine, one Atlantic drainage and one Atlantic or Pacific drainage shell. Winter (1972:181) has suggested that this reflects a reduction in exchange contacts with the Gulf Coast area. If this is indeed the case, it would agree well with our evidence for the reduction in the number of Atlantic drainage shell species in highland sites, the breakdown of the Guadalupe Victoria obsidian exchange network (Chapter II), and the end of Oaxacan magnetite mirror exchange with the Gulf Coast (Chapter III).

SUMMARY

Two possible shell exchange networks have been proposed for the Early and Middle Formative periods. The first, based on Pacific coast marine and estuary shells, involved the movement of raw material from the coast to part-time craftsmen in the highlands who manufactured ornaments for local distribution. The various links in this network cannot be specified because of a lack of excavated Pacific coast sites (although the area near Tehuantepec may have been important), nor is the mechanism by which the finished products were distributed understood. A different network may have brought to the highlands unworked Atlantic drainage shell, which was turned into much simpler ornaments involving less expertise. Reduction in the amount and variety of shell during the Middle Formative suggests a period of centralization and associated reduction in long-distance exchange.

V

ADDITIONAL COMMODITIES WHICH FIGURED IN EARLY AND MIDDLE FORMATIVE EXCHANGE

Many other commodities were exchanged during Early and Middle Formative times, but our data are, for the most part, inadequate to trace them to their ultimate sources, or pinpoint the villages and regions which made up the exchange network. However, a few observations on some of these commodities can be made.

RITUAL PARAPHERNALIA

Fish spines, sting ray spines, shark teeth, and turtle shell drums figured importantly in the ritual life of Mesoamerican Formative peoples. The first three items are presumed, on the basis of ethnohistorical evidence, to have been used in ceremonial bloodletting; the drums were probably used to accompany dancers at ceremonies of various kinds. Flannery (n.d.) and Drennan (n.d.) have discussed the occurrence and excavation context of such items in the Valley of Oaxaca. Drums made from the lowland river turtle *Dermatemys mawii* would have their origin in the same Gulf Coast rivers from which *Barynaias* mussel shells were taken. The sting ray spines, although not identifiable as to species, are also considered most probably to originate in the Gulf Coast region. However, most of the fish spines are from marine genera which occur on both the Atlantic and Pacific sides of Mesoamerica.

"SPECULAR HEMATITE" PIGMENT

An extremely extensive deposit of ocherous red oxide containing iron crystals—the kind of pigment usually referred to (erroneously) in the literature as "specular hematite"—occurs at Ejido Almagres near San Lorenzo, Veracruz. Such ocherous pigment with sparkling iron crystals was used widely on pottery of the Early Formative period. Unfortunately, our techniques are not yet refined to the point where we can trace such iron oxide to its source. However, the proximity of this large deposit to San Lorenzo makes it a likely source for many regions of Mesoamerica.

CERAMICS

Many villages in Mesoamerica made pottery wares which were traded outside their area of origin. For the most part, however, the evidence for this kind of trade has been circumstantial. That is, archeologists have identified rare or "trade" sherds on the basis of their resemblance to pottery from other regions, but usually have not confirmed their suspicions by petrographic analysis. In addition, even petrographic analysis is sometimes not sufficient to identify the point of origin of a ceramic type, unless the clay contains some rare mineral which is highly localized. The major components of most Formative pottery are minerals like quartz and feldspar, which are extremely widespread and occur to a degree in all suitable pottery clays.

Delfina Fine Gray is a pottery type which was manufactured in the Valley of Oaxaca during the San José phase (1150-850 B.C.). The parent material was an alluvial clay, the weathering product of locally-occurring gneisses and Miocene volcanic tuffs (ignimbrites) which had been washed down from the mountains and deposited in the alluvial valley center. One of the commonest shapes in which Delfina Fine Gray occurred was a cylindrical bowl with a carved representation of the Olmec "fire-serpent" motif (Coe, 1965a). Vessels of Delfina Fine Gray were evidently traded as far north as the Valley of Mexico; Muriel Porter Weaver (1967) discovered a carved cylinder at Tlapacoya and, noting its similarity to the later gray pottery of Monte Albán, had it thin-sectioned and petrographically examined by Howell Williams, a vulcanologist who was extremely familiar with the ignimbrites of the Valley of Oaxaca. Williams compared it to a sherd of Oaxaca gray ware from Monte Albán, with the following results:

> *Monte Albán (Sherd No. 1)* "Temper consists of minute, angular chips, none more than 0.2 mm. long, of quartz, sodic plagioclase (oligoclase and sodic andesine) and sanidine, with a few flakes of biotite, and abundant, very small glass shards showing typical curved vitroclastic textures. The temper is thus a biotite rhyolite or rhyodacite tuff, and it may well be an ignimbrite (*i.e.* a flowing avalanche deposit) similar to those widespread around the southern end of the Vale of Oaxaca, as around Mitla. The temper differs radically from all those seen by me from the Valley of Mexico, almost all of which are pyroxene, and/or hornblende andesites and dacites."
>
> *Tlapacoya (Sherd No. 3)* "Again, essentially similar to No. 1, the principal differences being that the temper is slightly coarser, and the small arcuate glass shards are accompanied by many bits of colorless pumice, up to 0.3 mm. across. The cellular and fibrous pumice-glass is perfectly fresh.
>
> If, as I think, the parent deposit is an ignimbrite, it must be of the poorly consolidated, *sillar* type, such as is to be found near the bottoms of some ignimbrite sheets near Mitla." (Williams, quoted by Weaver, 1967:29-30)

In 1970, William O. Payne of Orange Coast College, a ceramic technologist affiliated with the University of Michigan's Oaxaca Project, examined more fine gray sherds from Tlapacoya which had been excavated by Christine Niederberger for the Instituto Nacional de Antropología e Historia. All proved, under the binocular microscope, to be indistinguishable from Delfina Fine Gray specimens made in the Valley of Oaxaca. The characteristic Oaxaca ignimbrites had also left their stamp on fine gray sherds from Aquiles Serdán, Chiapas, a site excavated by Carlos Navarrete for the New World Archaeological Foundation (Payne, personal communication). In 1972 Nanette Pyne was able to examine a large collection of Calzadas Carved pottery from San Lorenzo, Veracruz, through the courtesy of Michael D. Coe. Pyne instantly recognized a series of "fire-serpent" designs on fine gray pottery which appeared to be in the Valley of Oaxaca style rather than the more common San Lorenzo style. Samples from these sherds were sent to Payne, and he reports that several are indistinguishable from Delfina Fine Gray (personal communication). The implications of this discovery are two-fold. First, it appears that Delfina Fine Gray was traded by its makers in the Valley of Oaxaca to villages as far away as the Valley of Mexico, the Gulf Coast, and the Pacific Coast of Chiapas. Second, it becomes clear that not all "Olmec" pottery was radiating out from some cultural epicenter on the Gulf Coast to eager recipients in the highlands. Rather, a number of centers in the highlands were making their own varieties of pottery with Olmec designs, and some of these were even traded to the major centers of the Gulf Coast.

The Gulf, of course, had its own export wares. Chief among these was probably Xochiltepec White, a pottery type defined by Coe at San Lorenzo, but recognized earlier under the name "kaolin ware" by Román Piña Chan at Tlatilco. This extremely fine pottery, which is "white clear through" (MacNeish, Peterson, and Flannery, 1970), is most abundant at San Lorenzo and is presumed to be locally made (Coe, personal communication). However, it forms a small percentage of the sherds at Tlatilco; Tlapacoya; Ajalpan and Moyotzingo in Puebla; San José Mogote in Oaxaca; and David Grove's sites in Morelos. Examination of Xochiltepec White sherds from Oaxaca has convinced Payne (personal communication) that most could not have been made in Oaxaca because their mineral consistency does not correspond to any of the known local clays. In fact, it is possible that this pure white luxury ware was one of the Gulf Coast products most in demand in the highlands; Flannery (personal communication) suspects that it was in imitation of Xochiltepec White that highland villagers began coating vessels of local clay with a white kaolinite slip during the Early Formative. Such white-slipped wares became extremely abundant by 900 B.C. in the Valleys of Mexico, Tehuacán, Oaxaca, and the Grijalva.

Neither the networks nor the mechanisms by which this interregional exchange of pottery went on are known. Xochiltepec White pottery, albeit in low frequency, occurs almost everywhere during the time period under discussion. The known distribution of traded Delfina Fine Gray ceramics corresponds roughly to the area of the combined Barranca de los Estetes and Guadalupe Victoria obsidian exchange networks.

VI

SUMMARY AND CONCLUSIONS

Formative Mesoamerican exchanges of obsidian, iron ore mirrors, and mollusk shell have been examined on the regional, local, and site levels. Four different types of exchange have been distinguished in an effort to provide some insight into both the form in which a commodity is traded, and the relationship between the various commodity exchange networks. Neutron activation analysis of obsidian, Mössbauer spectral analysis of iron ore, and species determination of shell have provided the data on which definition of the networks is based.

The Early Formative period in Mesoamerica was characterized by four major obsidian exchange networks. The first, referred to as the Barranca de los Estetes network, linked the Central Highlands of Mexico with the Oaxaca Highlands. This network brought to Oaxaca prismatic blades of Barranca de los Estetes obsidian, some of which probably were passed on to Veracruz via the second major network. The latter, referred to as the Guadalupe Victoria network, linked the Oaxacan Highlands with the Gulf Coast and the source in eastern Puebla. This network circulated most of the Guadalupe Victoria obsidian, little or none of which was passed on by Oaxaca to the Central Highlands of Mexico. The third, or El Chayal network, linked the Gulf Coast with the Guatemalan Highlands and the Chiapas-Guatemalan Pacific Coast. The fourth, or Zinapécuaro network involved the movement of prismatic blades of Zinapécuaro obsidian to the Oaxaca area. At areas of overlap between networks—such as Oaxaca—obsidian from one system passed to another, albeit at low frequency.

Shell and iron ore mirror exchange networks are less clearly defined for the Early Formative. Preliminary definition of Central Highland ties with a Pacific Coast shell exchange network and an Atlantic drainage freshwater shell network has been made. Two links in the iron ore mirror exchange network have been demonstrated, joining Oaxaca with Morelos to the northwest and southern Veracruz to the southeast.

It has been suggested that despite differences among our four types of exchange, several kinds of products may have moved together within the same "sphere of conveyence." Thus, another product which may have moved through the same network of villages as the Barranca de los Estetes obsidian is Oaxacan-made Delfina Fine Gray ceramics. Because of its position at the overlap between several networks, Oaxaca may have passed Gulf Coast sting ray spines, turtle shell drums, and Xochiltepec White ceramics on to the Central Highlands. The presence of some of these Gulf Coast goods in Oaxaca may in turn be related to the latter's participation in the Guadalupe Victoria obsidian exchange network. Other items which may have moved in that same sphere of conveyence include Delfina Fine Gray ceramics, and, possibly, Barranca de los Estetes prismatic obsidian blades. The interrelation, if any, between the El Chayal obsidian exchange network and the Oaxacan and Central Mexican Highland Pacific Coast shell exchange network is unclear. The presence of Oaxacan-made Delfina Fine Gray ceramics on the Chiapas coast may indicate stronger exchange relationships between these two areas than the obsidian data alone indicates.

The distribution of exchange items among households in Oaxacan villages provides some information on the type of exchange involved, and may even suggest relative values for various products at that specific point within the networks. Variation in obsidian utilization by Early Formative households at the sites of Tierras Largas and San José Mogote suggests that two types of obsidian exchange may have been in existence. Households at Tierras Largas show such variability in obsidian sources used (and percentages from each) that we suspect these obsidian exchanges were individually obtained by households or kin-groups from trade partners in other regions. In contrast, data from houses of the same period in one residential ward at nearby San José Mogote show no such variability. The uniform mixture of obsidian source utilization from house to house suggests that some form of "pooling" of the imported obsidian was taking place prior to distribution to the households. This pooling, which appears to be associated with the beginning of prismatic blade importation around 1000 B.C., becomes common even at small hamlets like Tierras Largas by the Middle Formative period. We suspect, therefore, that prismatic blades were so much more valued than obsidian flakes that their importation was taken over by important families, who in turn redistributed the blades to their relatives and affines.

The conversion of Oaxacan iron ore into a small number of small, flat mirrors for local use, as well as for exchange with other regions, appears to be restricted to one *barrio* at the largest Early Formative site in the valley, San José Mogote. This long-distance trade, presumed to reflect an exchange of sumptuary goods between elites, represents a different type of exchange.

Finally, Pacific marine and Atlantic freshwater mollusk shells were imported by villagers in the Etla region of the Valley of Oaxaca for ornament manufacture. Villages in other parts of the valley have shell ornaments, but lack evidence of shell-working areas like those seen at San José Mogote and Tierras Largas. In addition, although the sample is limited, it is possible that an even smaller number of households worked *Spondylus* and pearl oyster shell than fresh water mussel.

The defacement of monuments at San Lorenzo, Veracruz about 900 B.C., as well as contemporaneous signs of political evolution in the Central Mexican and Oaxacan Highlands, suggests widespread changes which are also reflected in breakdowns and realignments of these exchange networks. The Middle Formative was a period of regionalization, with a reduction in long-distance exchange. The Guadalupe Victoria obsidian exchange network, linking the Gulf Coast and the Oaxacan Highlands, weakened as prismatic blademaking became important and as contact between the two areas was greatly reduced. The manufacture of iron ore mirrors ceased in Oaxaca. The concave iron ore mirrors found at La Venta are apparently a regional product, made from nearby sources of ilmenite and hematite. The accumulation of sumptuary goods, such as the serpentine at La Venta, became a matter of intensified regional exploitation rather than long-distance exchange. Increasing regionalization in ceramics also took place.

Increasing demand for well-made prismatic obsidian blades presumably was one cause for an increase in direct exchange of Barranca de los Estetes obsidian (which is appropriate for such blade production) between the Central Highlands and the Gulf Coast. In addition to decreasing the importance of the Guadalupe Victoria source, this marked the beginning of a process which led to the monopolization of obsidian blade production by the Valleys of Mexico and Guatemala City, a phenomenon which characterizes the later periods of Mesoamerican prehistory.

APPENDIX I

OTHER REPORTED MESOAMERICAN OBSIDIAN SOURCES

This list has been compiled over several years from information kindly supplied by Arqueólogo José Luis Lorenzo, Dr. Jeffrey R. Parsons, Dr. Michael Spence, and Mr. Robert Cobean. Sources listed in Weaver and Stross (1965) are also included in this list.

GUERRERO

1. El Ocotito—Obsidian is found at a source 9 kilometers west of the village.
2. Taxco—Poor quality obsidian (unsuitable for most tool making) is reported, but information on the locality is incomplete.
3. Zumpango del Río—Twenty kilometers north of Chilpancingo on the highway between Mexico City and Acapulco, red and blue obsidian is found in barrancas adjacent to the highway.

HIDALGO

1. Huayacocota—A small cut exposing abundant obsidian exists on the road from Pachuca to Zacualtipan, at the turn off to Huayacocota to the east.
2. Zacualtipan—Red and blue obsidian is reported from this village, but precise information on the locality is lacking.

MICHOACAN

1. Ucareo—Abundant obsidian deposits are reported to exist at the turn-off to Ucareo, on the road from Zinapécuaro to Acámbaro. "On highway from Zinapécuaro to Ciudad Hidalgo; just south of Zinapécuaro, Michoacán. This locality is called Sierra de San Andres, near Ucareo, N.E. Michoacán..." (Weaver and Stross, 1965:99).

QUERETARO

1. El Colorado—Red and blue obsidian is found 14 kilometers east of Querétaro, on the highway to San Juan del Río.
2. El Paraíso—High quality black obsidian is found on the highway from Bernal to El Paraíso, about 7 kilometers northeast of El Paraíso and 28 kilometers east of the city of Querétaro.
3. Cadareyta de Montes—A low quality obsidian is found about 20 kilometers northeast of San Juan del Río, on the highway to Cadareyta de Montes and approximately three kilometers south of the village of Fuentezuelas.
4. An unnamed source is reported between San Pedro Escobedo and San Antonio, near the highway to San Juan del Río.

VERACRUZ

1. Mecacelco—An obsidian source is reported to exist a four-hour horseback ride north of the village of Las Vigas, near Perote.
2. An unnamed source is located adjacent to the highway between Tulancingo and Tuxpan, at kilometers 144 to 146.
3. Large obsidian deposits are reported along the old mule trail between Teziutlán and Papantla.
4. Following the road from Puebla to Veracruz via Perote, at a place known as Ensalado (which is about 15 minutes drive after the village of San Salvador el Seco), turn right on a dirt road to Ciudad Guzmán. This road passes through a dry riverbed which is filled with obsidian pebbles.

APPENDIX II

MÖSSBAUER SPECTROSCOPY

B. J. Evans

Department of Geology and Mineralogy
University of Michigan

For extended discussions on nuclear gamma-ray resonance (NGR) spectroscopy, commonly known as Mössbauer spectroscopy in honor of its Nobel Prize-winning discoverer (Mössbauer, 1958) and more recently as NGR spectroscopy, the reader is referred to the bounty of reviews (Greenwood and Gibb, 1971, Goldanskii and Herber, 1968). Only those aspects having direct pertinence to the present investigation are summarized here.

But for one important exception, the physics of NGR spectroscopy are very similar to those of atomic resonance spectroscopy for which the classical illustration is the absorption of the D lines of a sodium vapor lamp, or of common salt placed in the flame of a bunsen burner by sodium vapor contained in an appropriately placed tube. Nuclear gamma-ray resonance differs from atomic resonance absorption, however, inasmuch as the ratio of the recoil energy, E_R, to the energy breadth, Γ_γ, of the emitted or absorbed radiation, i.e. E_R/Γ_γ, is much larger in the former case than in the latter (Fig. A1 and Table A1). In order for there to be resonant emission and absorption of the nuclear gamma-rays, the recoil process must be suppressed and this is done by incorporating the atoms into a solid substance; therefore, this technique is not generally applicable to liquids. On the other hand, the solid need not be crystalline, and glasses can also be studied.

For iron-containing specimens, such as the mirrors of Mesoamerica, nuclear gamma-ray resonance can be observed for the ^{57}Fe isotope, which has a natural abundance of 2.19 percent. The resonance absorption corresponds to the nuclear transition from the ground state to the lowest-lying excited state, which has an energy of 14.4 keV. This lowest-lying excited state is populated by the electron capture decay of ^{57}Co ($t_{1/2}$ = 270 days) (see Fig. A2).

A radioactive source of ^{57}Co is used to provide the 14.4 keV gamma-rays; this source is usually in the form of radioactive ^{57}Co plated onto another metal, such as Cu, Cr, or Pd.

TABLE A1

ATOMIC RESONANCE VERSUS NUCLEAR GAMMA-RAY RESONANCE

Transition Parameter	Atomic Transition (Sodium D Line)	Nuclear Gamma-ray Transition (^{57}Co)
Transition energy	2.1 eV	14,400 eV
Natural width, Γ, of excited level	4.4×10^{-8} eV	4.7×10^{-9} eV
Doppler width, 2Δ, at room temperature	3.3×10^{-6} eV	1.4×10^{-2} eV
Recoil Energy, E_R	10^{-10} eV	2.0×10^{-3} eV
E_R/Γ	2.5×10^{-3}	5×10^5

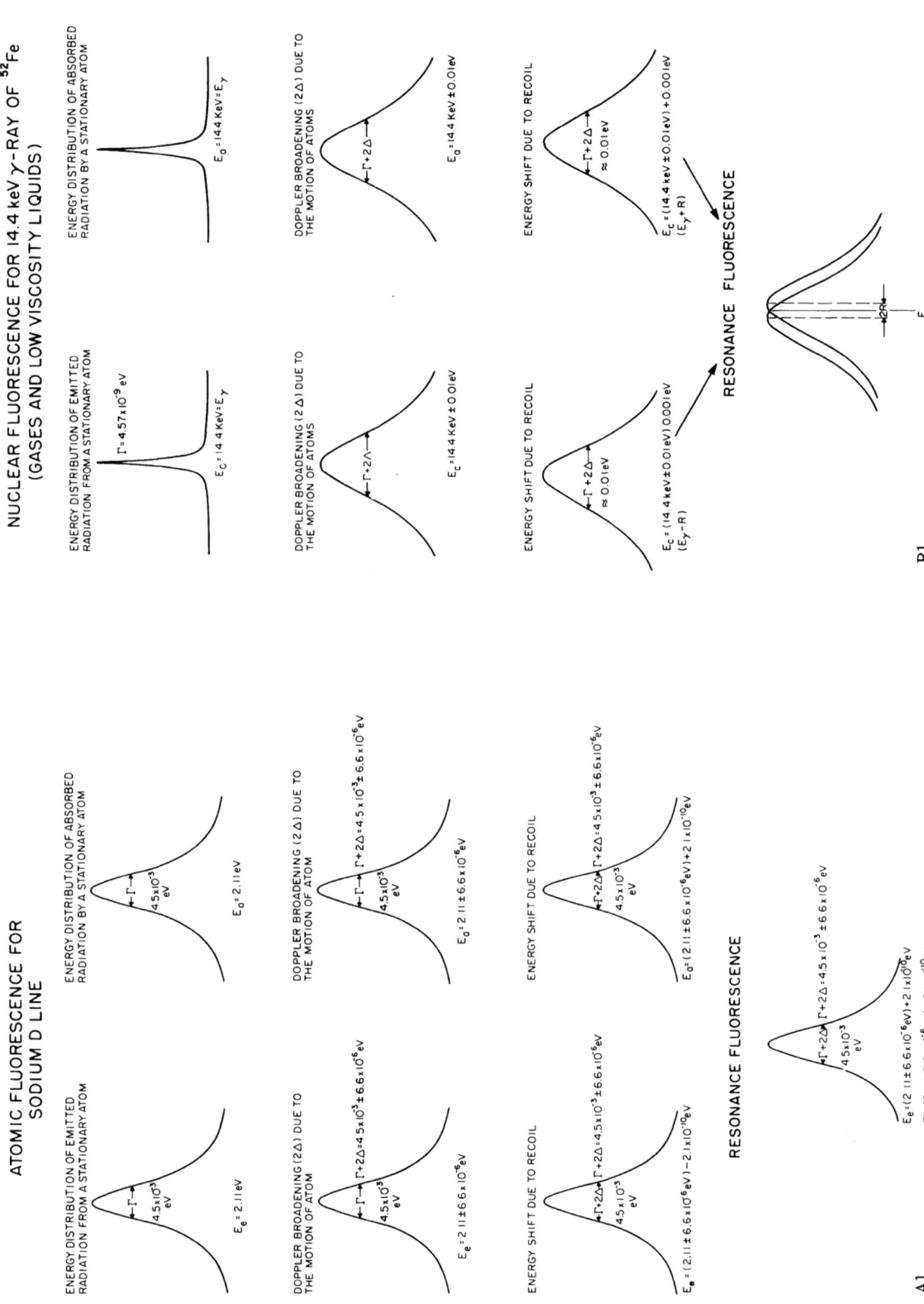

Fig. A1. Line profiles and relative energies of emitted and absorbed radiation for atomic resonance (visible and ultraviolet radiation) and nuclear resonance. Note the much smaller recoil shift of the lines for atomic resonance compared to nuclear resonance. The overlap is much less than that shown in the bottom profile of B1 since Doppler broadening does not occur for a stationary atom.

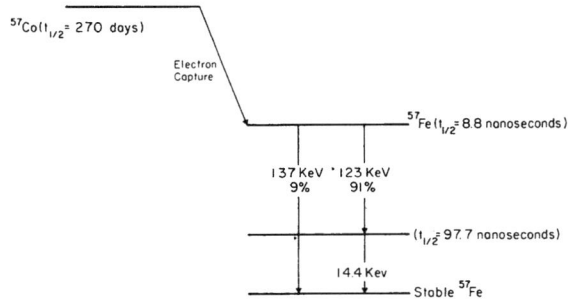

Fig. A2. Nuclear level diagram for ^{57}Co.

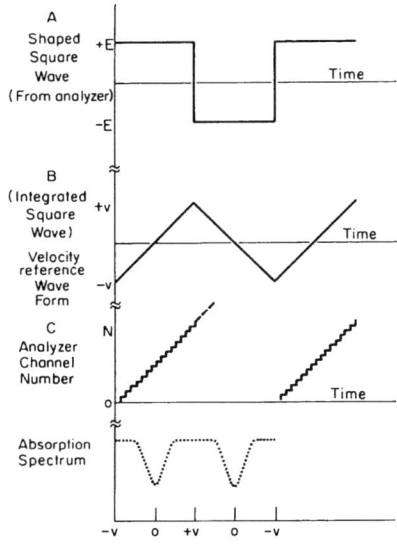

Fig. A3. Schematic of time-amplitude relationship between different components of a Mössbauer spectrometer. The square wave in A is used to synchronize the motion of the velocity transducer with the sweep through the memory of the multi-channel analyzer and is also used to provide a reference signal (B) for the velocity waveform. The points A, B and C are also indicated in Fig. A4.

Because of the very narrow emission lines of the source and the absorber, nuclear gamma ray resonance is possible only if the absorber is identical to the source. If this condition is fulfilled, the resonance absorption is indicated by the decrease in count rate (below that expected for mass absorption) when the absorber is placed between the source and the detector. The detector is usually a proportional counter, but scintillation and semiconductor detectors are also used. At this stage, however, we do not have a spectroscopic technique.

In most spectroscopic techniques, it is desirable to obtain the resonance absorption as a function of energy or wave length; and for this purpose there must be some means of changing the energy of the gamma-ray emitted by the radioactive ^{57}Co source. The energy of the gamma ray is varied by means of the *Doppler Effect*, that is, the source is moved relative to the absorber. The same result can be accomplished by moving the absorber relative to the source. The spectra are constructed by plotting the count-rate at the detector as a function of the Doppler velocity of the source. For thin absorbers, the line shapes are Lorentzian, that is

$$[I(V) = I(O)/[1+(V-V_0)/(\Gamma/2)^2]$$

where $I(V)$ is the absorption at Doppler velocity V, $I(O)$ is the maximum absorption, V_0 is the Doppler velocity at maximum absorption, and Γ is the width of the absorption line, e.g. full-width-at-half-maximum intensity.

The spectrum can be obtained point-by-point using a *constant velocity* Doppler shifter and counting for a sufficiently long time (on the order of 5 to 10 minutes) at a given velocity setting, manually changing the velocity setting and counting at the new velocity until a complete spectrum has been obtained. These operations can also be automated. At the present time, it is more usual to have a *constant acceleration* Doppler shifter and to synchronize the motion of the Doppler shifter (or velocity transducer) with the address of a multichannel analyzer operating in the multiscaling model (see Figs. A3 and A4). With this technique counts are collected at each velocity for only 1×10^{-5} to 1×10^{-3} sec for each sweep through the complete velocity range. However, there is little significant reduction in the total time spent to collect a spectrum since the velocity range is swept through repetitively at least 10^4 times.

In general, the Mössbauer spectra will show a shift of the absorption maximum from zero velocity, or various splittings of the single line into many absorption lines. These shifts and splittings arise from the hyperfine interactions of

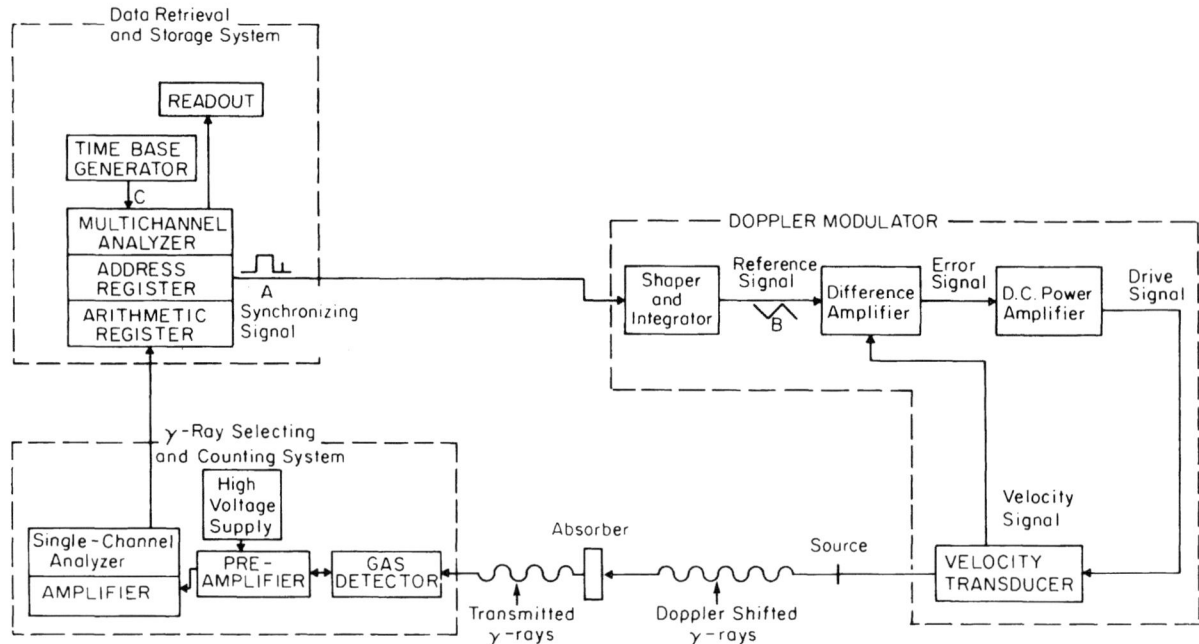

Fig. A4. A schematic diagram of a typical, constant acceleration Mössbauer spectrometer. The counter-absorber-source configuration is for transmission spectrometry.

the nuclear charge and electric quadrupole and magnetic dipole moments with the charge and the electric and magnetic fields of the electrons respectively, at the nuclear site in the crystal. A particular combination of magnitudes and signs of these hyperfine interactions is sometimes unique to a given material. The hyperfine interactions include:

Electrostatic Interaction Between the Electronic Charge Density at the Nucleus and the Nuclear Charge Distributions in the Ground and First Excited States

The ^{57}Fe nucleus has different radii in its ground and first excited states. Consequently, its charge density is different in these two states and so is its interaction with the electronic charge density at the nucleus. This leads to a shift in the energy of the excited state relative to the ground state (see Fig. A5). Furthermore, since the electronic charge density at the nucleus depends upon the electronic structure of the atom and its neighboring atoms, the relative shift in the energy of the excited state will be different for different materials. Therefore, when the source and absorber are not identical the center of gravity of the spectrum does not occur at zero Doppler velocity. The centers of gravity of ^{57}Fe Mössbauer spectra in different materials or at inequivalent sites in the same material will not, in general, be the same. The shift of the center of gravity of the spectrum from zero velocity, known as the *isomer shift,* is usually referred to a *standard absorber* such as iron metal, stainless steel, or sodium nitroprusside. The isomer shifts of Fe^{2+} oxides are in general different from those of Fe^{3+} oxides, typical values for the former being 1 mm/sec and for the latter 0.5 mm/sec with respect to an iron metal absorber.

Interaction Between the Gradient of the Electric Field at the Nucleus and the Electric Quadrupole Moment of the Nucleus

Since the spin quantum number of the ground state of ^{57}Fe is less than 1, its electric quadrupole moment is zero and so is its interaction with the electric field gradient. However, the 14.4 keV excited state of ^{57}Fe has nuclear spin quantum number of 3/2 and a non-zero value for

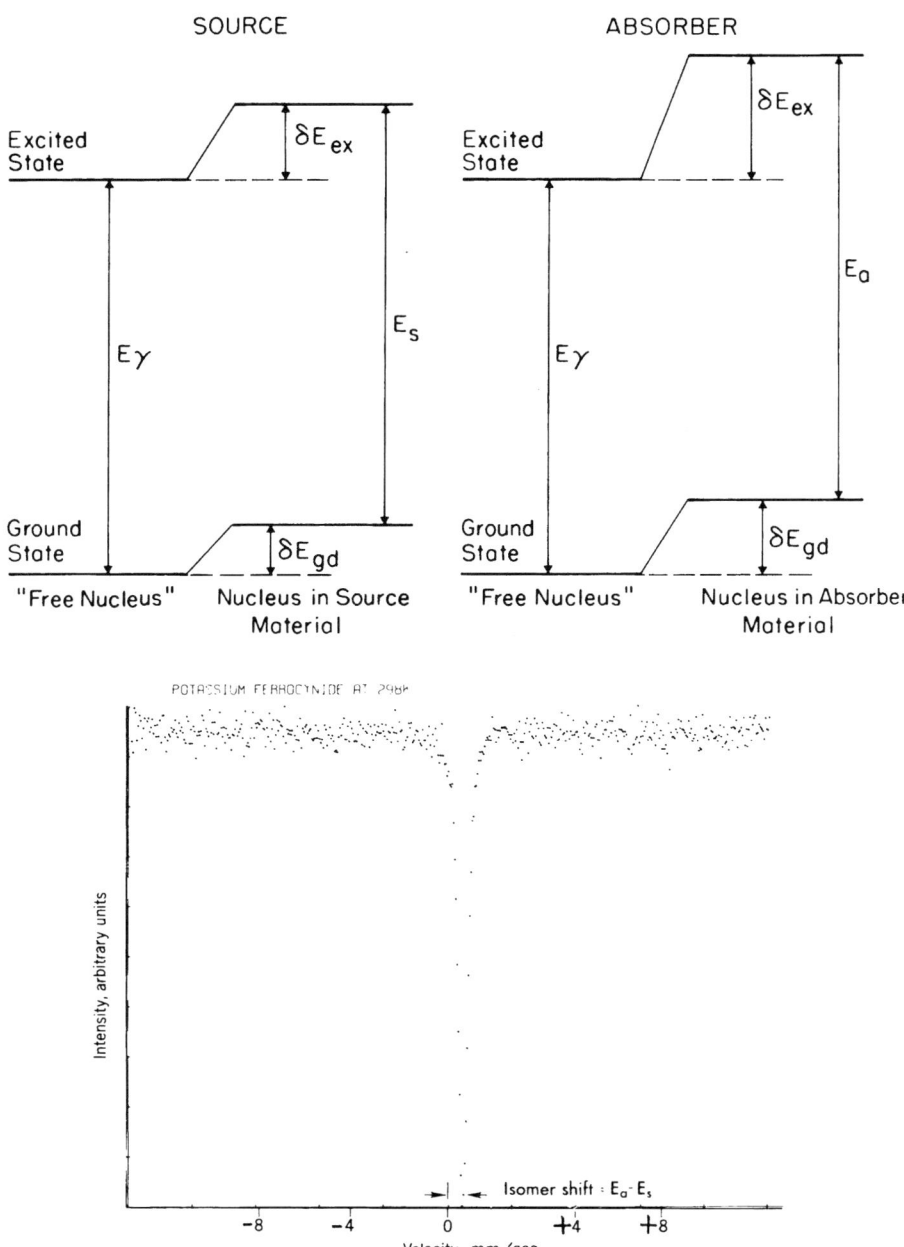

Fig. A5. Electric monopole interaction or isomer shift for ^{57}Fe. The isomer shift is E_a-E_s. The spectrum arising from a material in which only the electric monopole interaction is present is shown in the bottom of the figure. Note that the isomer shift of $K_4Fe(Cn)_6 \cdot 3H_2O$ is positive-a characteristic of the ferrous ion.

its electric quadrupole moment. The spin degeneracy of the excited state is partially lifted by the electric quadrupole interaction, and the excited state is split into two levels (see Fig. A6). Any time the symmetry of the site occupied by the iron atom is less than cubic, a non-zero electric field gradient is possible.

Magnetic Dipole Interaction

In magnetically ordered materials there is a further splitting of the nuclear levels resulting from the interaction between the nuclear magnetic dipole moment and the *internal* magnetic fields generated by the electronic spin and orbital

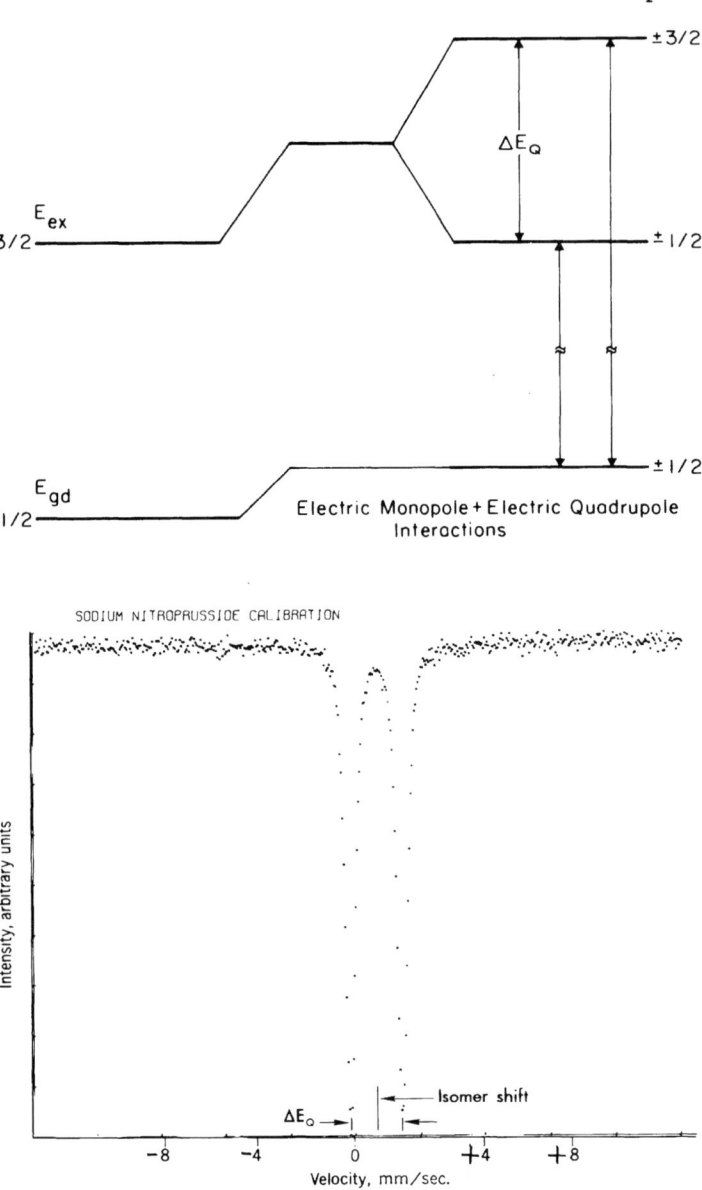

Fig. A6. Electric quadrapole interaction for ^{57}Fe.

moments. For ^{57}Fe the magnetic dipole interaction splits the ground state (I=1/2) into two levels and the excited state (I=3/2) into four levels (see Fig. A7). If the ^{57}Fe atom occupies a lattice site with less than cubic symmetry in a magnetically ordered material, then both the electric quadrupole and magnetic dipole interactions can have non-zero values; and further shifts in the energies of different levels will take place (see Fig. A8). As in the case of the isomer shifts, the magnetic dipole interaction is different, in general, for different materials and also for inequivalent atoms in the same material.

MÖSSBAUER SPECTRA OF SELECTED IRON OXIDES

The predominant iron oxides in the mirrors of Early and Late Formative sites in Mesoamerica are magnetite (Fe_3O_4), ilmenite ($FeTiO_3$), and

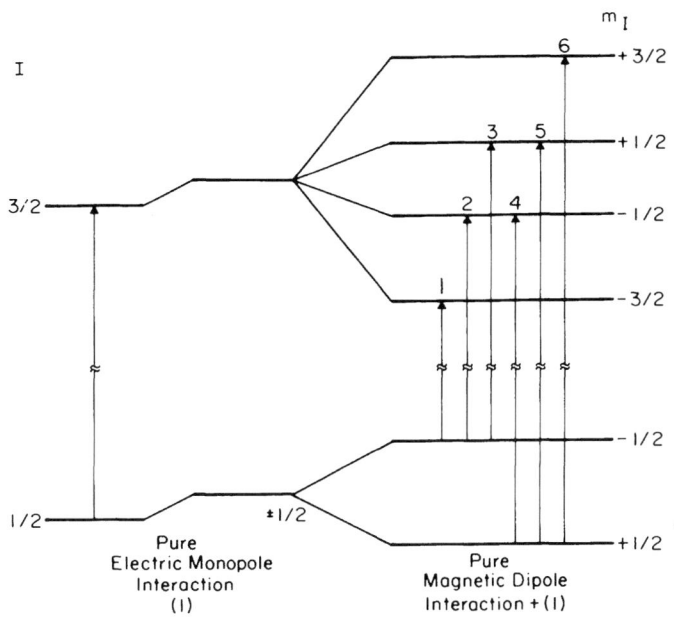

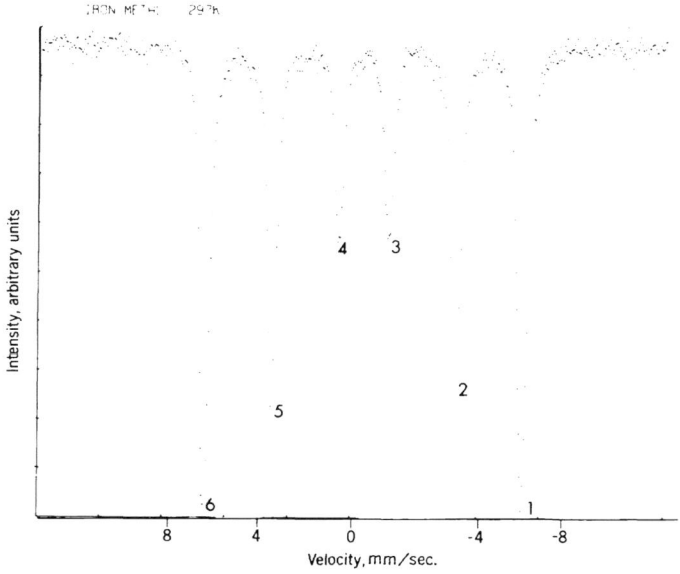

Fig. A7. Magnetic dipole interaction ^{57}Fe. The arabic numerals for the lines in the spectrum correspond to the transitions with the same numbers in the energy level diagram in the upper part of the figure.

hematite (Fe_2O_3); there may also be some titano-magnetite ($Fe_{3-x}Ti_xO_4$) and titano-hematite ($Fe_{2-x}Ti_xO_3$) phases contained in the mirrors (Evans, 1968; Gibb, Greenwood and Twist, 1969; Shirane et al., 1972; Van der Woude, 1966; Ono et al., 1968). Ilmenite has a rhombohedral structure with Fe and Ti atoms being located in sites having six oxygen nearest neighbors; even though the sites have approximately octahedral symmetry, the site symmetry is less than cubic (Garg and Puri, 1971). Above 55°K ilmenite is not magnetically ordered, and the magnetic dipole splitting of the ^{57}Fe nuclear levels is expected to be absent at 300°K. The

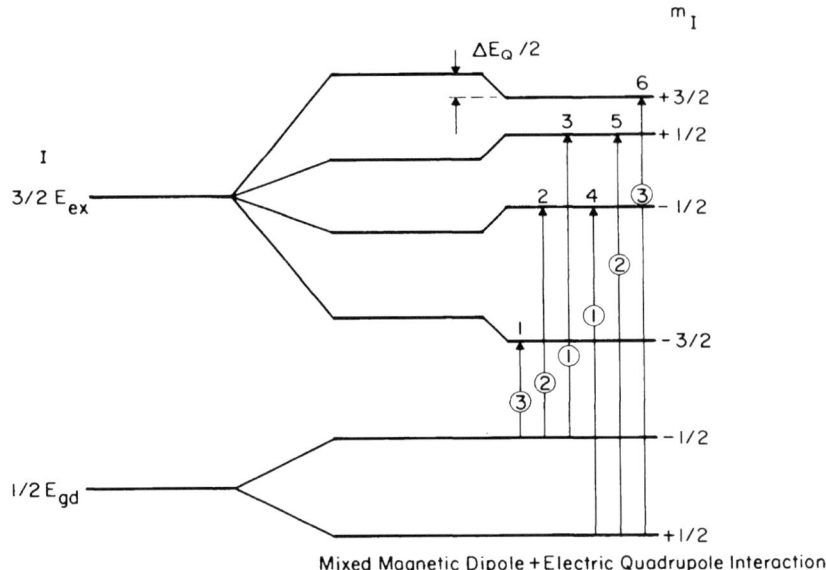

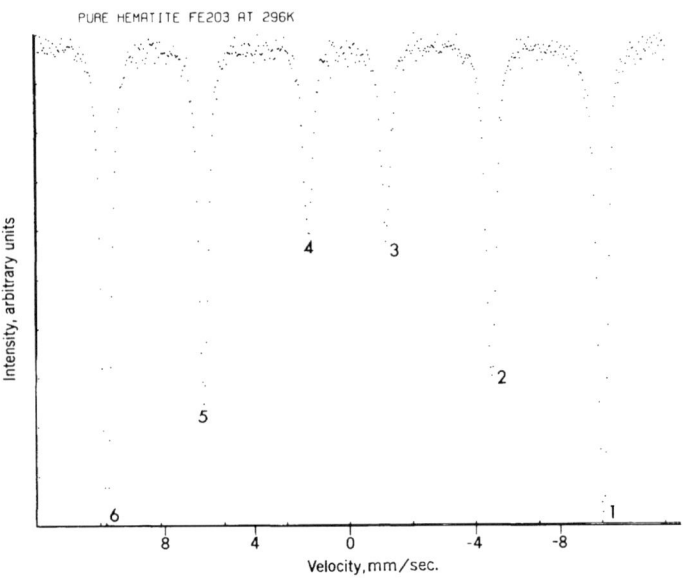

Fig. A8. Mixed magnetic dipole plus electric quadrapole interaction. This spectrum differs from that in Fig. A7 inasmuch as the separations between lines 1&2, 2&3, 4&5 and 5&6 are the same as in Fig. A7, but the separations between lines 1&2 and lines 5&6 are different in the above spectrum. The numbers in the circles in the upper part of the figure refer to the relative intensities of the lines.

electric quadrupole splitting and isomer shift are clearly evident, however, in the NGR spectrum of $FeTiO_3$ (see Fig. A9). Ulvospinel also has a spectrum (see Fig. A10) qualitatively similar to that of $FeTiO_3$, but the quadrupole splittings are sufficiently different to permit a clear distinction to be made. Fe_2O_3 has a structure very similar to that of ilmenite but differs from $FeTiO_3$ inasmuch as the Ti sites of $FeTiO_3$ are occupied by Fe in Fe_2O_3. However, hematite is magnetically ordered at 300°K, being antiferromagnetic and having a magnetic ordering temperature of

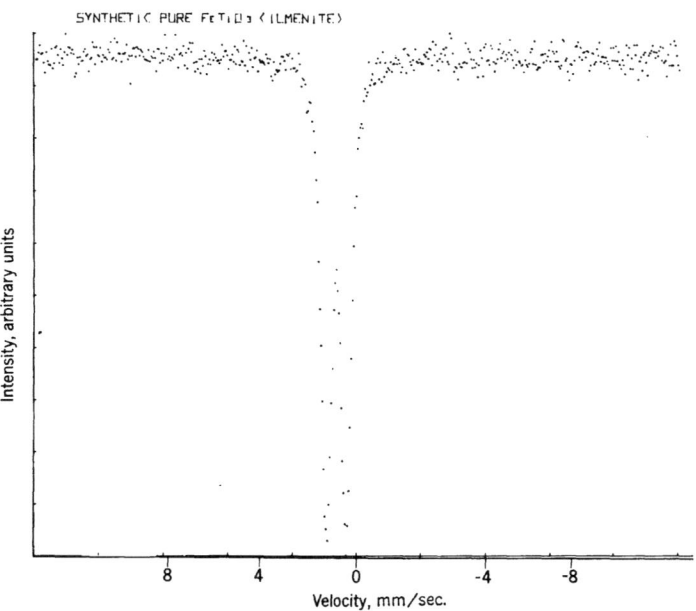

Fig. A9. ^{57}Fe NGR spectrum of ilmenite (FeTiO$_3$). Note the positive isomer shift and quadrapole splitting of about 0.7 mm/sec.

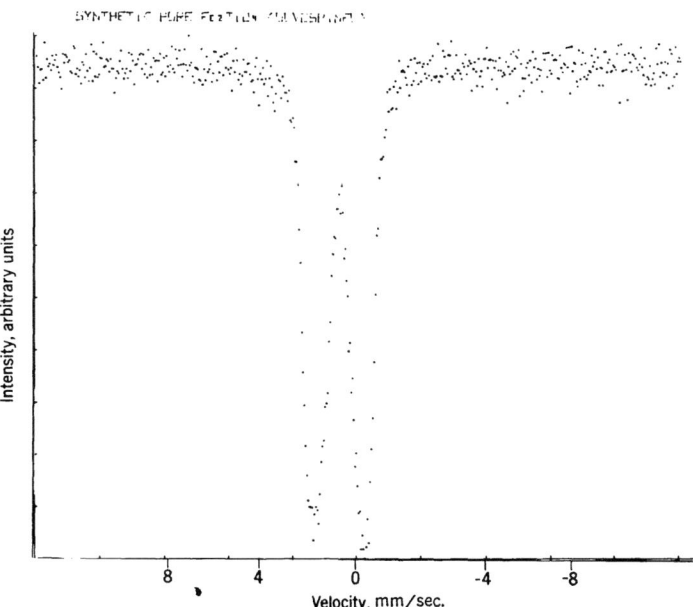

Fig. A10. ^{57}Fe NGR spectrum of ulvöspinel (Fe$_2$TiO$_4$). This spectrum is similar to that for FeTiO$_3$ but the quadrapole splitting is much larger, being about 2 mm/sec. This difference in quadrapole splitting can be used to distinguish FeTiO$_3$ from Fe$_2$TiO$_4$.

950°K (Schieber, 1967). As expected, its spectrum exhibits all three interactions with values characteristic of an Fe^{3+} oxide (see Fig. A8).

Titano-hematites will have ^{57}Fe Mössbauer spectra intermediate between those of hematite and ilmenite (Shirane et al., 1962). For small values of x in $Fe_{2-x}Ti_xO_3$, the Mössbauer spectra will resemble that of Fe_2O_3, with the separation between the outermost lines decreasing more rapidly than any of the other line separations with increasing x. The width of the outermost lines and the relative intensity (*raw depth*) of the innermost pair of lines will also increase with increasing x (Fig. A11).

Magnetite has the spinel structure and contains three inequivalent iron atoms, (1) 8 Fe^{3+} ions in 4-coordinated, perfect oxygen coordination, (2) 8 Fe^{3+} ions in 6-coordinated oxygen polyhedra, and (3) 8 Fe^{2+} ions in 6-coordinated oxygen polyhedra. The 6-coordinated polyhedra are only approximately octahedral. There is a reduction in the number of time-averaged inequivalent iron atoms in magnetite due to rapid electron exchange among the 6-coordinated Fe^{2+} and Fe^{3+} ions at 300°K. The rapid electron exchange has the effect of reducing the two inequivalent 6-coordinated ions to a single, time-averaged species during the characteristic measurement time of the ^{57}Fe Mössbauer measurement (Fig. A12). The doublet structure in the absorption peaks in the negative velocity region are due to the different spectra arising from the tetrahedrally coordinated Fe^{3+} and the time-averaged ($Fe^{3+}-Fe^{2+}$) 6-coordinated ions. The more intense members of the doublets are due to the time-averaged ($Fe^{3+}-Fe^{2+}$) species.

Titano-magnetites will exhibit spectra having a relationship to pure Fe_3O_4 in a manner similar to that expected for hematites and titanohematites (Banerjee et al., 1967) (Fig. A12).

From the Mössbauer spectra shown here it is clear that a straightforward distinction can be made between materials that consist of different amounts of $FeTiO_3$, Fe_2O_3, and Fe_3O_4. For the massive iron oxide deposits from which the source materials for the mirrors were extracted, the relative amounts of the different iron oxides are not expected to vary greatly over regions of

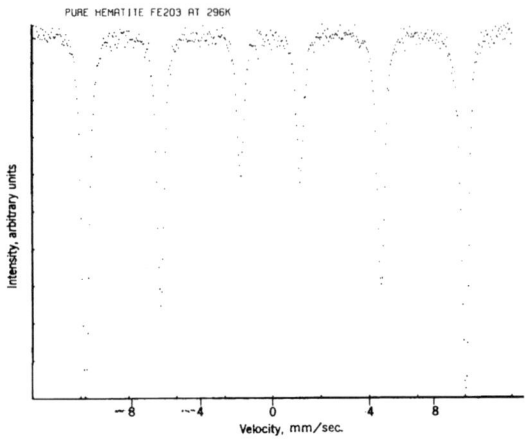

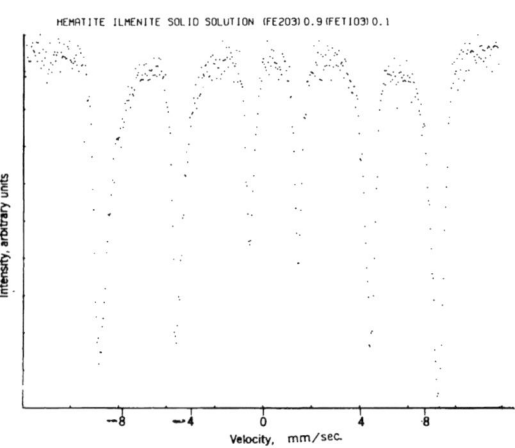

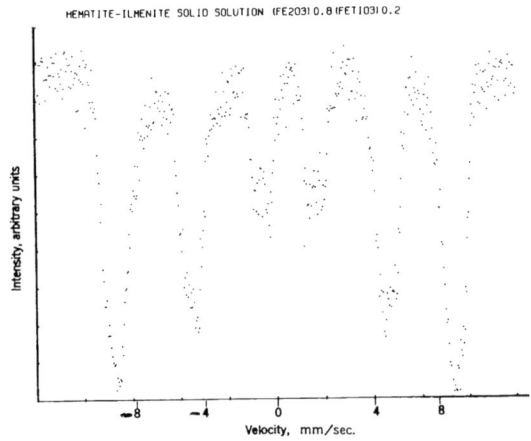

Fig. A11. ^{57}Fe NGR spectrum of titanohematites. Note the broadening of the lines for the small concentration of titanium.

APPENDIX II

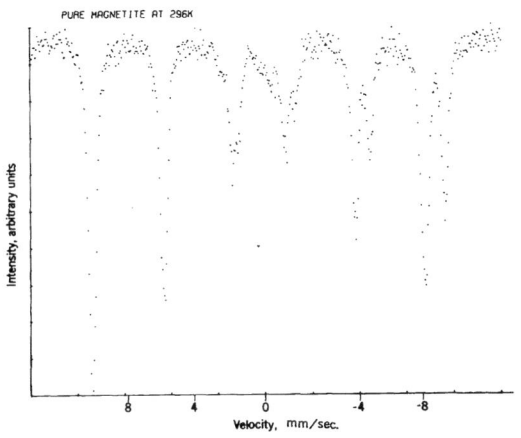

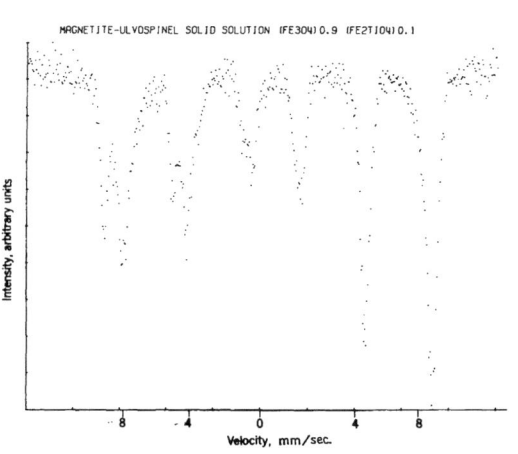

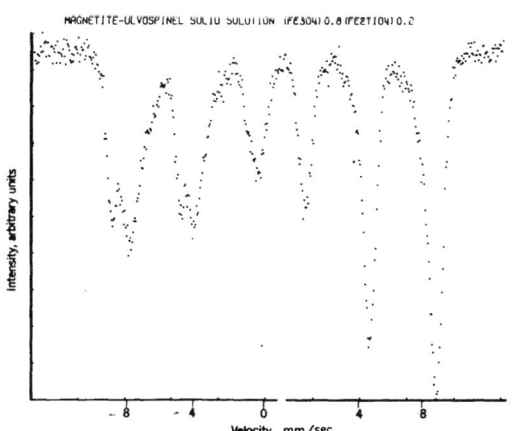

Fig. A12. ^{57}Fe NGR spectrum of titanomagnetites. Note the broadening of the lines as the titanium content increases. Note also that the last two spectra are plotted in an opposite sense to the first one.

the size of the finished mirrors. Therefore, a determination of the relative amounts of the iron oxides in small samples might serve to distinguish between mirrors from different sources. Because the spectra of each of these iron oxides are also sensitive to impurities, especially titanium impurities, the character of *each* of the *spectra* of each individual phase in a multiphase mirror can also be used as an indicator of differences and similarities among the source materials for different mirrors. The present technique differs from the traditional chemical methods since differences in both chemical composition and structure are directly manifest in the spectra and a *single* analysis of the data permits definitive conclusions to be drawn regarding both structure and composition without introducing further assumptions. It is also clear from the spectra presented that conclusions can be drawn concerning the mirrors and their possible source materials by visual inspection of the primary data. In this respect we were particularly fortunate in this study. Ordinarily a useful data analysis would require a fitting of the spectra by least-mean-squares techniques. We have, in all probability, only utilized a small fraction of the information contained in the spectra with the visual inspection technique employed in this study. Such least-squares fitting of the data is quite expensive, however, about ten dollars per spectrum, and should be attempted only when significantly improved conclusions are expected.

EXPERIMENTAL METHOD

A systematic survey of all potential iron-bearing geologic zones in the Valley of Oaxaca, the Isthmus of Tehuantepec, central Chiapas, and Morelos was carried out by Jane W. Pires-Ferreira. A sampling procedure designed to test physical variation within the iron ore at each source was used for all sources examined. Archeological samples were obtained from the collections of museums and from various individuals.

Material for the Mössbauer analysis was obtained with a diamond or tungsten stylus from a 1 cm^2 area. For the highly polished mirrors absorber material was removed from the unpolished rear surface. Absorbers were prepared by mixing 50 milligrams of the powdered sample with thinned Duco cement and forming the slurry into a one inch diameter disc on a .005 inch thick Mylar sheet. The slurry was permitted to dry into a thin flexible film and, without being removed from the Mylar supporting sheet, was covered with a layer of adhesive plastic tape.

The spectra presented in the body of this book were obtained from samples prepared as above in the so-called "transmission geometry." In this configuration, the rays that are counted have passed through or been "transmitted" through the sample. In this geometry, the order of components is *source-absorber-counter* as shown in Fig. A4. There are two ways of obtaining motion of the absorber relative to the source in this configuration: the source can be moved and the absorber held stationary or the absorber can be moved and the source held stationary. The first of these possibilities has been used in our transmission measurements. In this instance, significant geometrical distortions of the spectrum can result from the varying distance between the source and the counter. This is the source of the parabolic distortion of many of the spectra presented in this dissertation.

The Mössbauer spectra were obtained with a constant acceleration, electromechanical drive which is similar in design to those in use at the U.S. National Bureau of Standards (DeVoe, 1970). The 14.4 keV gamma-rays were detected with a proportional counter filled with a 90% Argon-10% CO_2 gas mixture. The 14.4 keV pulses were selected using a single-channel analyzer and stored in a 1024 channel analyzer operating in the multiscaling mode; only 256 or 512 channels of the analyzer memory were used to store the spectrum. A seven milliCurie source of ^{57}Co in a copper matrix was employed as the Mössbauer source and typically a spectrum with an off-resonant count per channel of 5×10^5 was obtained in 12 hours. The counts per channel were obtained using a teletype printer/punch and were plotted without further data analysis on a computer controlled digital plotter.

As the bulk of the measurements for this book were being completed, a new, non-transmission technique became available in our laboratories. This technique, known as *Mössbauer Backscatter Spectroscopy,* does not require the removal of material from the artifact for the preparation of an absorber and in many cases requires little or no sample preparation. The basic requirement is that there be an approximately flat surface on the artifact. In Mössbauer backscatter spectroscopy, the configuration of components is source-counter-absorber and the γ-rays that are counted are those scattered back into the counter by the sample. (The term scatter does not actually describe the complexity of the phenomena involved and refers only to apparent phenomena.) A typical, commercially-available backscatter detector is shown in Fig. A13. This detector is a windowless flow counter and, because it is a flow counter, it need not be leak proof. Since the interface between the rear of the counter and the sample (see Fig. A13) need not be free of leaks, the sample need not be perfectly flat.

The important advantages of this technique are the following:

1. It is a non-destructive analysis technique. There is no need to remove material from the specimen or to alter the surface of the specimen.
2. Macroscopic areas, 1 square inch, can be sampled in one measurement and errors and uncertainty due to poor sampling techniques involved in removing materials from a specimen are avoided.
3. The surface material and material in the body of an artifact can be sampled. This is particularly important in investigations of glazed ceramic bodies.

Item 3 listed above results from the fact that not only can the 14.4 keV γ-ray be counted but the conversion electrons and the 6.3 keV x-ray associated with the production of the conversion electrons can also be used to obtain the Mössbauer spectrum. The conversion electrons are used for surface studies since those conversion electrons arriving in the backscatter detector have not penetrated more than a 300 mm thickness of material; and the spectrum must, therefore, arise

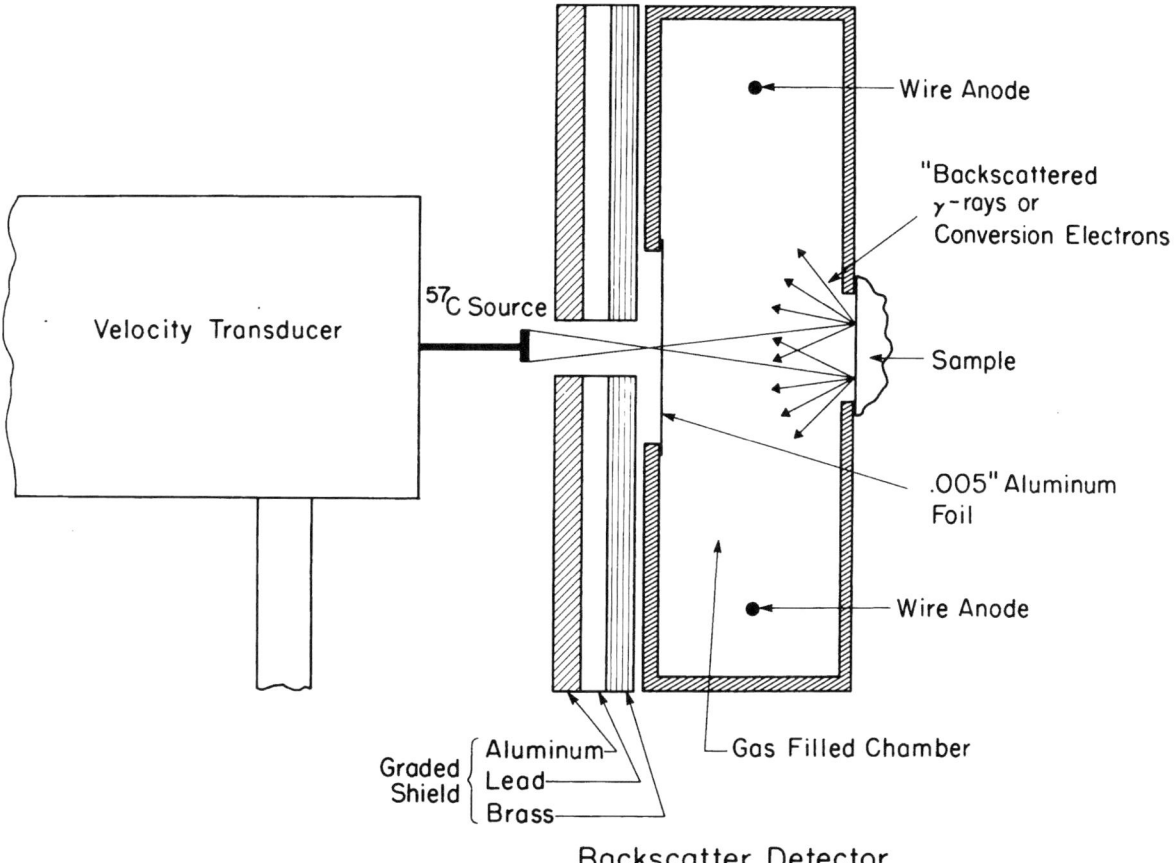

Fig. A13. Commercial backscatter detector showing relative positions of source, detector and absorber.

from material contained within this thickness of the artifact. On the other hand, the penetration depth of the 6.3 keV x-ray and the 14.4 keV γ-ray is greater than 0.01 mm. For most materials, there is little variation in the chemical and phase composition of the artifact once it has been penetrated to a depth of 0.01 mm; thus, the Mössbauer spectrum is likely to be characteristic of the bulk material (Swanson and Spjikerman, 1969).

Backscatter spectra obtained from the polished front surface of a finished iron oxide mirror are shown in Fig. A14. A transmission spectrum is also shown for comparison. These spectra indicate that the mirror consists exclusively of hematite and that the hematite did not arise from oxidation of the iron ore during or subsequent to the manufacture of the mirror.

This conclusion would not have been possible on the basis of either the transmission or backscatter spectrum alone. The powdered sample used to collect the transmission spectrum could have been obtained from a locally oxidized region of the mirror, from a region rich in hematite in a multiphase but unoxidized or the hematite could have resulted from oxidation during the removal of the powder from the mirror. Similarly, the backscatter spectrum could have resulted from an oxidized surface. However, the fact that hematite is the only phase observed for a thin surface layer, a thick surface layer and bulk material establishes the fact that this mirror consists almost exclusively of hematite.

Backscatter Mössbauer spectra from an unusual iron ore artifact are shown in Fig. A15; this artifact, which is a 2″ × 3/8″ × 1/4″ rectangular

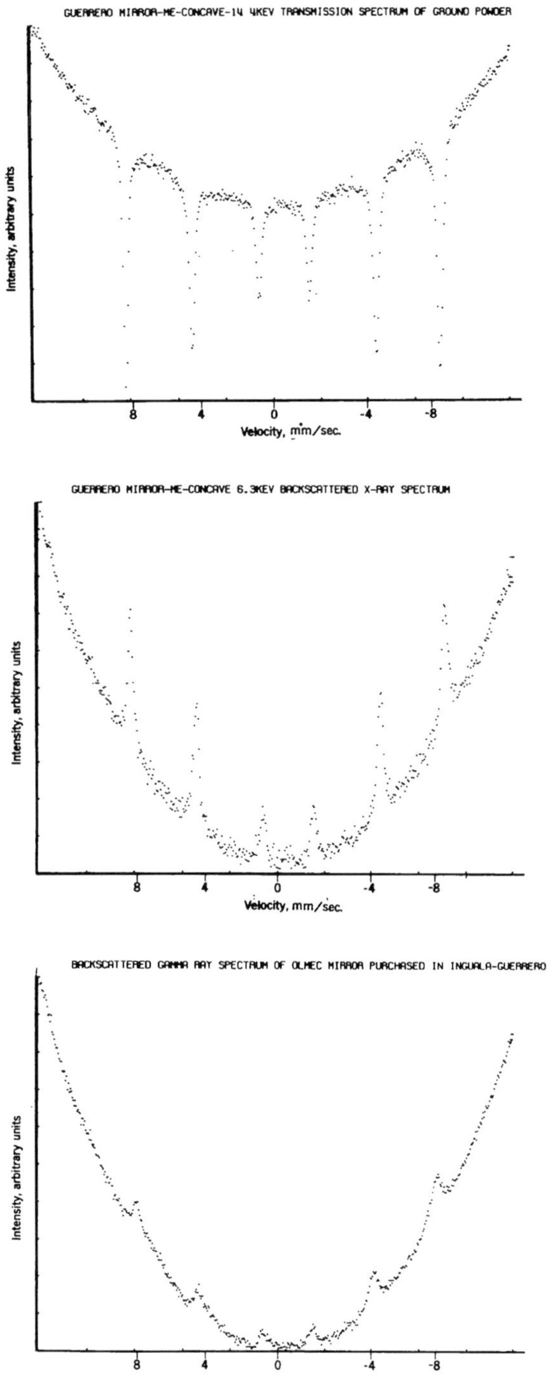

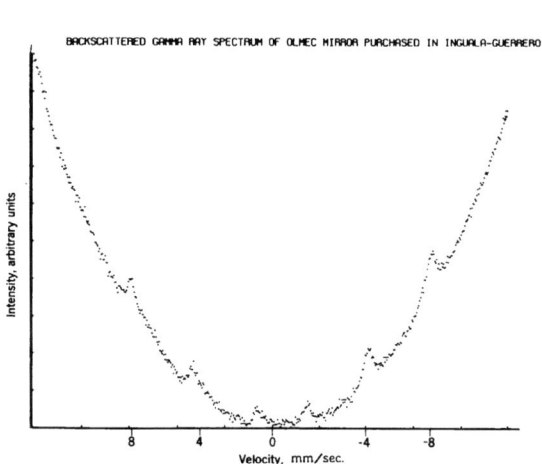

Fig. A14. ^{57}Fe transmission and backscatter spectra of a polished iron ore mirror. Note the similarity among these spectra—except for the opposite sense of the absorption peak—as well as with those of Fig. A11.

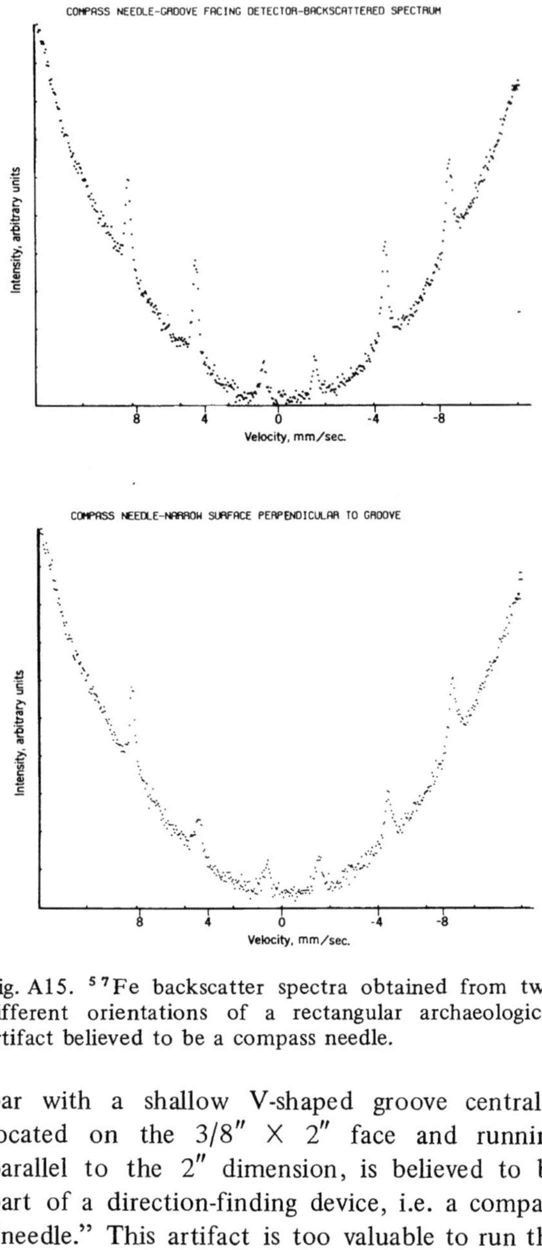

Fig. A15. ^{57}Fe backscatter spectra obtained from two different orientations of a rectangular archaeological artifact believed to be a compass needle.

bar with a shallow V-shaped groove centrally located on the 3/8″ × 2″ face and running parallel to the 2″ dimension, is believed to be part of a direction-finding device, i.e. a compass "needle." This artifact is too valuable to run the risk of destroying it during the removal of material. In addition, the removal of material could also alter its magnetic properties to such an extent that its possible use as a compass needle could never be established. Then too, Mössbauer Backscatter measurements on the artifact, when it is oriented in different directions with respect to the source-detector line, can be used to establish, in part, its possible use as a compass needle. This is so because the Mössbauer effect can be used to determine the remanent magnetization in certain iron oxides; and the presence of magnetic remanence is a necessary condition for the use of this artifact as the indicator of a direction-finding device.

Such oriented Backscatter spectra have been obtained (cf. Fig. A15) and while the details of the data analysis cannot be fully presented here, there is clear evidence of remanence. It should be noted, however, that this conclusion with respect to the remanence could not be reached by visual inspection of the spectra but required a full least-squares analysis of the data. On the basis of this rough, qualitative result from Mössbauer spectroscopy, considerably more tedious, time-consuming and expensive paleomagnetic measurements are being pursued: a pursuit which should lead to a definite confirmation of the possible use of this artifact in a direction-finding device.

From a technological and cultural point of view, it is intriguing that this artifact consists entirely of hematite (obvious from visual inspection), which has a remanent magnetization which is weak compared to that of magnetite. This suggests that either some unique techniques or highly fortuitous circumstances are needed to explain its deliberate (?) use in a direction-finding device by a people primitive in magnetic and electrical technology.

REFERENCES

Banerjee, S. K., W. O'Reilly, T. C. Gibb and N. N. Greenwood
    1967   The Behavior of Ferrous Ions in Iron-Titanium Spinels. The Journal of the Physics and Chemistry of Solids, 28:1323-1335.

DeVoe, J. R., ed.
    1970   NBS Technical Note 501. Washington, D.C.: U.S. Government Printing Office.

Evans, B. J.
    1968   Order, Disorder and Hyperfine Interactions in Spinal Ferrites. Unpublished Ph.D. dissertation, University of Chicago.

Garg, V. K. and S. P. Puri
    1971   Quadrupolar Hyperfine Anisotropy in Ilmenite. Physica Status Solidi (B), 44:K45-K47.

Gibb, T. C., N. N. Greenwood and W. Twist
    1969   The Mössbauer Spectra of Natural Ilmenites. Journal of Inorganic Nuclear Chemistry, 31:947-954.

Goldanskii, V. I. and R. H. Herber
    1968   Chemical Applications of Mössbauer Spectroscopy. New York: Academic Press.

Greenwood, N. N. and T. C. Gibb
    1971   Mössbauer Spectroscopy. London: Chapman and Hall.

Mössbauer, R. L.
    1958   Kernresonanz-fluoreszenz von Gammastrahlung in ^{191}Ir. Zeitschrift für Physik, 151:124-143.

One, K., L. Chandler and A. Ito
    1968   Mössbauer Study of the Ulvöspinel (Fe_4TiO_4). Technical Report of the Institute of Solid State Physics. Tokyo: University of Tokyo.

Schieber, M. M.
    1967   Experimental Magnetochemistry. New York: Interscience.

Shirane, G., D. E. Cox, W. J. Takei and S. L. Ruby
    1962   A Study of the Magnetic Properties of the $FeTiO_3$-Fe_2O_3 System of Neutron Diffraction and the Mössbauer Effect. Journal of the Physical Society of Japan, 17:1598-1611.

Swanson, K. R. and J. J. Spjikerman
    1970   Analysis of Thin Surface Layers by Fe-57 Mössbauer Backscattering Spectrometry. Journal of Applied Physics, 41:3155-3158.

Van der Woude, F.
    1966   The Mössbauer Effect in Fe_2O_3. Physica Status Solidi, 17:417-432.

RESUMEN EN ESPAÑOL

(por *David J. Wilson*)

Los períodos del Formativo Temprano y Medio en Mesoamérica (1500-500 a. de C.) vieron muchos cambios significativos del período Precerámico en el aumento de población, arquitectura, patrones de asentamiento y categorías de artefactos. Sin embargo, uno de los cambios más notables fue con respecto a la cantidad enormemente expandida de material, tanto materia prima como materia trabajada, que se movía entre las regiones culturales y entre las zonas ambientales. El movimiento interregional de la alfarería, obsidiana, jade, turquesa, pigmentos férreos, menas de hierro, mica, conchas de molusco, corazas de tortuga, espinas de pescado y raya, dientes de tiburón y otros productos llegaron con frecuencia a proporciones impresionantes. Muchos de estos artículos se destinaron al uso ritual, y probablemente reflejan un papel cada vez más importante para las actividades rituales por parte de las gentes Formativas. Otros fueron de índole utilitaria, aunque la línea divisoria entre utilitario y no utilitario frecuentemente se obscurece. Aun los artículos destinados al rito, hasta el punto que fortalecieron la integración de las comunidades Formativas e hicieron que se estrecharan las conexiones entre las familias quienes también intercambiaron los bienes comestibles y cosas de subsistencia, pudieran considerarse en parte de índole utilitaria.

En este estudio, la Dra. Jane Pires-Ferreira primero define cuatro especies de intercambio que pueden vislumbrarse tanto con los datos etnográficos como con los datos arqueológicos relativos a la Mesoamérica Formativa. Estos son:

1. *El intercambio recíproco de productos utilitarios (exceptuando los bienes comestibles) a los cuales cada aldeano tuvo acceso.* Un ejemplo de tal intercambio sería el movimiento de lascas y pedazos de obsidiana durante el período del Formativo Temprano. A pesar de la abundancia de pedernales nativos en la región montañosa de Mesoamérica, casi no existe ninguna casa entre las que se han excavado cuidadosamente que no tenga obsidiana; mientras que algunos pueblos de tierra baja, que carecían de depósitos locales de pedernal, usaron exclusivamente la obsidiana.

El intercambio de obsidiana probablemente se relacionó tanto a (1) *la densidad y distribución de la población,* ya que la cantidad que se movía en cualquier dirección fue en parte una función del número de pueblos en esa área; como a (2) *la distancia,* ya que la cantidad en cualquier pueblo también fue en parte una función de la distancia a la fuente más cercana. Este intercambio probablemente fue análogo a los cambios de obsidiana etnográficamente documentados de la gente de las Islas de Siassi, en que el recurso natural se disminuía en cantidad y se aumentaba en cuanto a su valor mientras se aumentaba la distancia de la fuente.

2. *El amontonamiento de los productos utilitarios para distribuirlos más tarde a todos los miembros de la comunidad.* Un ejemplo de esta especie de intercambio sería el movimiento de hojas prismáticas de obsidiana, comenzando alrededor de 1000-900 a. de C. en Mesoamérica. Aunque la cantidad de hojas prismáticas que se intercambiaron presumiblemente se relacionara a los mismos factores de población y distancia que afectaron el intercambio recíproco de productos utilitarios, el tipo de intercambio fue diferente. A diferencia de la variación en la utilización de la fuente casa por casa que caracteriza el cambio interrecíproco, la distribución uniforme de la obsidiana de varias fuentes entre todas las casas de grandes centros cívico-ceremoniales como San José Mogote, Oaxaca, sugiere el amontonamiento de obsidiana por alguna agencia central antes de distribuirla a otros miembros de la comunidad (véase abajo).

3. *Intercambios de materias primas no utilitarias y no trabajadas para su conversión por especialistas trabajando sólo una parte del tiempo, con la mayoría de los aldeanos teniendo acceso al producto terminado.* Las conchas no modificadas movieron desde la costa del Pacífico y los estuarios de agua de marea hasta las casas en ciertas pueblos de Oaxaca (v.gr., San José Mogote y Tierras Largas) donde se convertieron en adornos. La variedad de artefactos encontrados en los pisos de las casas donde se hallaron las conchas sugiere que sus habitantes fueron

labradores con una especialidad durante parte del tiempo, o sea que no trabajaron las conchas todo el tiempo. Por otro lado, los adornos terminados se han encontrado en pequeños yacimientos cercanos donde no se encontró ninguna señal de trabajar las conchas. No se entiende por completo ni el mecanismo por el cual la materia prima llegó a los trabajadores de concha ni el mecanismo por el cual los productos terminados llegaron a las personas que los utilizaron. Pero puede que esta situación sea semejante a la que se describió para algunos habitantes de las Islas de Siassi quienes trabajan la materia prima recibida por medio del trueque de otra isla, y que ellos mismos utilizan y luego la pasan a una tercera isla.

4. *La conversión de la materia prima exótica en productos aún más exóticos para el intercambio entre los élites cacicales.* La producción de espejos de magnetita durante el período del Formativo Temprano, en uno de los barrios residenciales de un sitio de Oaxaca, evidentemente para intercambiar con sitios en Morelos, Nochixtlán y San Lorenzo (Veracruz) provee un ejemplo de este tipo. La distribución de estos espejos indica un tipo de intercambio que *no* es una función de distancia de la fuente. Un número muy reducido de sitios (y casas dentro de estos sitios) tuvieron acceso a espejos que, basado en los datos de ciertas figurillas, pudieran llevarse en los pechos de induvuos élites. Situaciones etnográficas análogas podrían ser la fabricación de peines de coraza de tortuga en Truk para llevarse por miembros de los linajes de alto rango, o los intercambios de jade en Burma entre los caciques de Kachin y los aristócratas de Shan. El mecanismo para tal especie de intercambio pudo haber sido los regalos entre los élites, quizá arreglados a veces por alianzas de matrimonio.

Después de definir estos tipos de intercambio, Pires-Ferreira selecciona tres productos para un estudio más detallado: la obsidiana (estudiada por medio de la activación de neutrones), los espejos de mena de hierro (estudiados por medio del análisis Mössbauer del espectro) y la concha del molusco marítimo. Los análisis de elementos de traza, que identifican las regiones desde las cuales procedieron los ejemplares, le ayuda a definir las redes de intercambio. Los datos obtenidos del estudio casa por casa en los sitios Formativos del Valle de Oaxaca le ayudan a sacar unas conclusiones acerca de la naturaleza de este intercambio. Aunque la mayoría de sus datos vienen del Valle de Oaxaca, ella también trata acerca de los Valles de México, Puebla y Morelos, las costas del Golfo y el Pacífico, Chiapas y Guatemala.

El período del Formativo Temprano en Mesoamérica se caracterizó por cuatro redes mayores de intercambio de obsidiana. La primera, designada como la red de la Barranca de los Estetes, ligó la Sierra Central de México con la Sierra de Oaxaca. Esta red llevó a Oaxaca las hojas prismáticas de obsidiana de la Barranca de los Estetes, algunas de las cuales probablemente se pasaron luego a Veracruz por medio de la segunda red mayor. Esta última, conocida como la red de Guadalupe Victoria, ligó la Sierra de Oaxaca con la costa del Golfo y la fuente en el este de Puebla. Esta red hizo circular la mayoría de la obsidiana de Guadalupe Victoria, poca o ninguna de la cual fue pasada luego por los de Oaxaca a la Sierra Central de México. La tercera red, o sea la de El Chayal, ligó la costa del Golfo con la sierra guatemalteca y la costa del Pacífico de Chiapas-Guatemala. La cuarta, a sea la red de Zinapécuaro, también tuvo que ver con el movimiento de hojas prismáticas de obsidiana de Zinapécuaro al área de Oaxaca. En las áreas que solapan por entre las redes—tal como Oaxaca—la obsidiana de un sistema pasó al otro, aunque con una frecuencia poco elevada.

Las redes de intercambio de concha y mena de hierro se definen en forma menos clara para el Formativo Temprano. Ya se ha realizado la definición preliminar de los vínculos de la Sierra Central y una red de intercambio de conchas de la costa del Pacífico con una red de conchas de agua fresca del litoral Atlántico. Dos vínculos en la red de intercambio de los espejos de mena de hierro se han demonstrado, ligando Oaxaca con Morelos al noroeste y con el sur de Veracruz al sudeste.

Se ha sugerido que a pesar de las diferencias entre nuestros cuatro tipos de intercambio, varias clases de productos pudieran moverse juntos dentro de la misma "esfera de conducción." De esta manera otros productos que pudieran haberse movido por la misma red de aldeas que la obsidiana de la Barranca de los Estetes incluyen la cerámica llamada "Delfina Fine Gray" (Delfina Gris Fino) hecha en Oaxaca. A causa de su colocación en el área que solapa entre varias redes, es posible que Oaxaca pasara a la Sierra Central las espinas de raya de la costa del Golfo, tambores de coraza de tortuga y la cerámica Xochiltepec White (Xochiltepec Blanco). La presencia de algunos de estos productos procedientes de la costa del Golfo en Oaxaca pudiera relacionarse en cambio a la participación de Oaxaca en la red de intercambio de obsidiana de Guadalupe Victoria. Otros artículos que pudieran moverse en esta misma esfera de conducción incluyen la cerámica Delfina Fine Gray, y posiblemente las hojas prismáticas de obsidiana de la Barranca de los Estetes. La interrelación, si ésta de veras existe, entre la red de intercambio de obsidiana de El Chayal y la red de intercambio de conchas de Oaxaca y la costa del Pacífico de la Sierra Central todavía no se ha clarificado. La presencia de la cerámica Delfina Fine Gray hecha en Oaxaca en la costa de Chiapas tal vez indique que las relaciones de intercambio entre estas dos áreas fueran más fuertes que los datos de obsidiana indican.

La distribución de artículos de intercambio entre las casas en las aldeas oaxaqueñas provee algunos datos

RESUMEN EN ESPAÑOL

sobre el tipo de intercambio de que se trata, y aún más puede que sugiera los valores relativos para varios productos en ese punto específico dentro de las redes. La variación en el utilizaje de obsidiana por casas del Formativo Temprano en los yacimientos de Tierras Largas y San José Mogote sugiere que dos tipos de intercambio de obsidiana pudieran haber existido. Las casas de Tierras Largas demuestran tanta variabilidad en las fuentes de obsidiana utilizadas (y en los porcentajes de cada una) que sospechamos que los intercambios de obsidiana se arreglaron individualmente por las casas o linajes, quizá con socios de trueque en otras regiones. En cambio, los datos de otras casas del mismo período en un barrio residencial de San José Mogote (cerca de Tierras Largas) no demuestran tal variabilidad; más bien, la mezcla uniforme de utilización de la fuente de obsidiana casa por casa sugiere que alguna especie de "amontonamiento" de la obsidiana importada ocurriera antes de distribuirla a las casas. Este amontonamiento, que parece asociarse con el comienzo de la importación de hojas prismáticas alrededor de 1000 a. de C., llega a ser común aun en pequeñas aldeas como Tierras Largas en el período del Formativo Medio. Por eso, sospechamos que las hojas prismáticas se valoraron tanto más que las lascas de obsidiana que su importación llegó a ser controlada por las familias importantes, quienes luego redistribuían las hojas a sus parientes y afines. Las conchas de molusco del Océano Pacífico y de agua fresca del litoral Atlántico fueron importados por los aldeanos de la región de Etla del Valle de Oaxaca para la fabricación de adornos. Los pueblos en otras partes del valle tienen adornos de concha, pero carecen de indicios de áreas para el trabajo de las conchas como las que sí se encuentran en San José Mogote y Tierras Largas. Además de esto, aunque la muestra es limitada, es posible que una cantidad aún más pequeña de casas trabajaran conchas de *Spondylus* y ostra que de almeja de agua fresca.

Finalmente, la conversión de mena de hierro oaxaqueña en pequeños espejos planos para la utilización limitada local, tanto como el intercambio igualmente limitado con otras regiones, parece limitarse a un sólo barrio en el sitio Formativo Temprano más grande del valle, o sea San José Mogote. Este trueque de larga distancia, que presumiblemente refleja un intercambio de bienes suntuosos entre "élites," representa un tipo distinto de intercambio.

La mutilación de monumentos en San Lorenzo, Veracruz alrededor de 900 a. de C., tanto como las indicaciones contemporáneas de la evolución política de la Sierra Central de México y Oaxaca, sugiere unos cambios muy esparcidos que también se reflejan en derrumbamientos y realineamientos de estas redes de intercambio. El período del Formativo Medio fue uno de regionalización, con una efectiva reducción en el intercambio de larga distancia. La red de intercambio de obsidiana de Guadalupe Victoria, que liga la costa del Golfo y la sierra oaxaqueña, se debilitaba mientras se hacía importante la fabricación de hojas prismáticas y el contacto entre las dos áreas llegó a ser muy reducido. La fabricación de espejos de mena de hierro cesó en Oaxaca. Los espejos de mena de hierro cóncavos hallados en La Venta aparentemente son un producto regional, hechos de fuentes cercanas de ilemita y hematita. La acumulación de bienes suntuosos, tal como la serpentina en La Venta, llegó a ser un asunto de intensificada explotación regional en vez de un intercambio de larga distancia. Al mismo tiempo, también ocurrió la regionalización de la cerámica.

La creciente demanda para hojas prismáticas de obsidiana bien hechas presumiblemente fuera una de las causas del aumento en el intercambio directo de la obsidiana de la Barranca de los Estetes (que es apropiado para tal producción de hojas) entre la Sierra Central y la costa del Golfo. Además de disminuir la importancia de la fuente de Guadalupe Victoria, esto marcó el comienzo de un proceso que llevó a la monopolización de la producción de hojas de obsidiana por los Valles de México y Ciudad Guatemala, un fenómeno que caracteriza los períodos tardíos de la prehistoria mesoamericana.

REFERENCES

Acosta Saignes, Miguel
    1945 Los Pochteca: Ubicación de los Mercaderes en la Estructura Social Tenocha. Acta Antropológia, I(1).

Artman, J. O., A. H. Muir, Jr. and H. Wiedersich
    1970 Determination of the Nuclear Quadrupole Moment of Fe^{57m} from a-Fe_2O_3 Data. The Physical Review, 173(2):337-343.

Aufdermauer, Jörg
    1970 Excavaciones en dos sitios preclásicos de Moyotzingo, Puebla. Communicaciones, Proyecto Puebla-Tlaxcala, I: 9-24. Fundación Alemaña para la Investigación Científica, Puebla.

Aveleyra A. de Anda, Luis y Manuel Maldonado-Koerdell
    1952 Asociación de artefactos con mamut en el Pleistoceno superior de la Cuenca de Mexico. Revista Mexicana de Estudios Antropológicos, 8(1):3-29.

Benson, Elizabeth, ed.
    1968 Dumbarton Oaks Conference on the Olmec. Washington, D.C., Dumbarton Oaks.

Bernal, Ignacio
    1968 El Mundo Olmeca. Mexico, Editorial Porrúa, S.A.
    1969 The Olmec World. Berkeley, University of California Press.

Blom, Franz and Oliver LaFarge
    1926 Tribes and Temples. 2 Vols. New Orleans, Carnegie Institution.

Caso, Alfonso
    1964 Existió un Imperio Olmeca? Memoria del Colegio Nacional, V(3). Mexico.

Chapman, Anne
    1957 Port of Trade Enclaves in Aztec and Maya Civilizations. *In*: Trade and Market in the Early Empires, Karl Polanyi, Conrad M. Arensberg and Harry W. Pearson, eds. Glencoe, The Free Press.

Cobean, Robert H., et al.
    1971 Obsidian Trade at San Lorenzo Tenochtitlán. Science, 174(4010):666-671.

Coe, Michael D.
    1961 La Victoria, an Early Site on the Coast of Guatemala. Papers of the Peabody Museum of Archaeology and Ethnology, 53. Cambridge.
    1965a The Jaguar's Children: Pre-classic Central Mexico. New York, Museum of Primitive Art.
    1965b The Olmec Style and its Distribution. Handbook of Middle American Indians, 3(2). R. Wauchope and G. Willey, eds. Austin, University of Texas Press.
    1965c Archaeological Synthesis of Southern Veracruz and Tabasco. Handbook of Middle American Indians, 3(2). R. Wauchope and G. Willey, eds. Austin, University of Texas Press.
    1968a America's First Civilization. New York, American Heritage Publishing Company.
    1968b San Lorenzo and Olmec Civilizaiton. *In*: Benson, 1968.
    1970 The Archaeological Sequence at San Lorenzo, Veracruz, Mexico. Contributions of the University of California Archaeological Research Facility, 8:21-34.

Coe, Michael D. and Kent V. Flannery
    1964 The Pre-Columbian Obsidian Industry of El Chayal, Guatemala. American Antiquity, XXX(1):43-49.
    1967 Early Cultures and Human Ecology in South Coastal Guatemala. Smithsonian Contributions to Anthropology, 3. Washington, D.C.

Cousins, D. R. and Dhwarmawardena, K. G.
    1969 Use of Mössbauer Spectroscopy in the Study of Ancient Pottery, Nature (London), 223:772.

Covarrubias, Miguel
    1950 Tlatilco: el arte y la cultura preclásica del Valle de México. Cuadernos Americanos, LI(3):149-162.
    1957 Indian Art of Mexico and Central America. New York, Alfred Knopf.

Delgado, Agustín
   1961   La sequencia arqueológica en el Istmo de Tehuantepec. *In*: Los Mayas del Sur y sus Relaciones con los Nahuas Meridionales. Mexico, Sociedad Mexicana de Antropología.
   1965   Archaeological Research at Santa Rosa, Chiapas and in the Region of Tehuantepec. Papers of the New World Archaeological Foundation, 12/13. Provo, Brigham Young University.

Diehl, Richard
   1969   An Evaluation of Cultural Evolution in the Formative Period in Mesoamerican Prehistory. Unpublished Ph.D. dissertation, Pennsylvania State University.

Drennan, R. D.
   n.d.   Religion and Social Evolution in Formative Mesoamerica. *In*: The Early Mesoamerican Village, Kent V. Flannery, ed. New York, Academic Press.

Drucker, Philip and Robert F. Heizer
   1965   Commentary on W. R. Coe and Robert Stuckenrath's review of Excavations at La Venta, Tabasco, 1955. Kroeber Anthropological Society Papers, XXXIII:37-40.

Drucker, Philip, Robert F. Heizer and Robert J. Squier
   1959,   Excavations at La Venta, Tabasco, 1955. Bureau of American Ethnology, Bulletin 170. Washington, D.C., Smithsonian Institution.

Ekholm, Susanna M.
   1969   Mound 30a and the Early Preclassic Ceramic Sequence of Izapa, Chiapas, Mexico. Papers of the New World Archaeological Foundation, 25. Provo, Brigham Young University.

Evans, B. J.
   1968   Order, Disorder and Hyperfine Interactions in Spinel Ferrites. Unpublished Ph.D. dissertation, University of Chicago.

Flannery, Kent V.
   1968   The Olmec and the Valley of Oaxaca: A Model for Interregional Interaction in Formative Times. *In*: Benson, 1968.

Flannery, Kent V., et al.
   1970   Preliminary Archaeological Investigations in the Valley of Oaxaca, Mexico, 1966-1969. A report to the National Science Foundation and the Instituto Nacional de Antropología e Historia, Mexico. (Mimeographed).
   n.d.   Early and Middle Formative Ceramics from the Etla Valley, Oaxaca, Mexico. In preparation.

Ford, James A.
   1969   A Comparison of Formative Cultures in the Americas. Smithsonian Contributions to Anthropology, 11. Smithsonian Institution, Washington, D.C.

Fried, M.
   1967   Evolution of Political Society. New York, Random House.

Garcia Payon, José
   1966   Prehistoria de Mesoamerica: Excavaciones en Trapiche y Chalahuite, Veracruz, Mexico, 1942, 1951 y 1959. Cuadernos de la Faculdad de Filosofía, Ciencias y Letras, 31. Xalapa, Universidad Veracruzana.

Gordus, A. A. et al.
   1967   Identification of the Geologic Origins of Archaeological Artifacts: An Automated Method of Na and Mn Neutron Activation Analysis. Archaeometry, 10:87-96.

Gordus, A. A., Gary A. Wright, and James B. Griffin
   1968   Obsidian Sources Characterized by Neutron Activation Analysis. Science, 161:382-384.

Green, Dee F. and Gareth W. Lowe
   1967   Altamira and Padre Piedra, Early Preclassic Sites in Chiapas, Mexico. Papers of the New World Archaeological Foundation, 20. Provo, Brigham Young University.

Greenwood N. N. and T. C. Gibb
   1971   Mössbauer Spectroscopy. London, Chapman and Hall.

Grove, David C.
   1968a   The Morelos Preclassic and the Highland Olmec Problem. Unpublished Ph.D. dissertation, University of California at Los Angeles.
   1968b   The Preclassic Olmec in Central Mexico: Site Distribution and Inferences. *In*: Benson, 1968.
   1968c   Informe: A Final Report on Archaeological Excavations Carried Out in 1967 in Morelos, Mexico. Report submitted to the Instituto Nacional de Antropología e Historia, Mexico. (Mimeographed.)
   1968d   Chalcatzingo, Morelos, Mexico: A Re-appraisal of the Olmec Rock Carvings. American Antiquity, XXXIII(4):486-491.

1970a The Morelos Formative: Cultural Stratigraphy and Implications. Paper read at the 35th Annual Meeting of the Society for American Archaeology, Mexico.

1970b The San Pablo Pantheon Mound: A Middle Preclassic Site in Morelos, Mexico. American Antiquity, XXXV(1):62-73.

1972a *Review of* Materiales para la Arqueología de Teotihuacán, by José Luis Lorenzo. American Anthropologist, 74(1/2):122-123.

1972b The Highland Olmec Manifestation: A consideration of what it is and isn't. Paper presented at the Symposium on Recent Research in Mesoamerican Archaeology, Cambridge, England.

n.d. The Mesoamerican Formative and South American Influences. Primer Simposio de Correlaciones Antropológicas Andino-Mesoamericanas. Salinas, Ecuador, 1972.

Hammond, Norman
 1972 Obsidian Trade Routes in the Mayan Area. Science, 178:1092-1093.

Harding, Thomas G.
 1967 Voyagers of the Vitiaz Strait. Seattle, University of Washington Press.

Heizer, Robert F.
 1961 Inferences on the Nature of Olmec Society Based Upon Data From the La Venta Site. Kroeber Anthropological Society Papers, XXV:43-57.
 1968 New Observations on La Venta. *In*: Benson, 1968.

Heizer, Robert F. and Howell Williams
 1965 Geological Notes on the Ruins of Mitla and Other Oaxacan Sites. Contributions of the University of California Archaeological Research Facility, 1.

Heizer, Robert F., Philip Drucker and John A. Graham
 1968a Investigations at La Venta, 1967. Contributions of the University of California Archaeological Research Facility, 5:1-34.

Heizer, Robert F., John A. Graham and L. K. Napton
 1968b The 1968 Investigations at La Venta. Contributions of the University of California Archaeological Research Facility, 5:101-203.

Jack, R. N. and Robert F. Heizer
 1968 "Finger-Printing" of Some Mesoamerican Obsidians. Contributions of the University of California Archaeological Research Facility, 5:81-99.

Jiménez Moreno, W.
 1966 Mesoamerica Before the Toltecs. *In*: Ancient Oaxaca, John Paddock, ed. Stanford, Stanford University Press.

Jones, Julie
 1963 Bibliography for Olmec Sculpture. New York, Museum of Primitive Art.

Keen, A. Myra
 1958 Sea Shells of Tropical West America. Stanford University Press.

Kidder, Alfred V., Jesse D. Jennings and Edwin M. Shook
 1946 Excavations at Kaminaljuyú, Guatemala. Carnegie Institution of Washington, Publication 561.

Kirkby, M. J.
 n.d. Past and Present Physical Environment of the Valley of Oaxaca. Memoirs of the Museum of Anthropology, University of Michigan. Ann Arbor. (In preparation.)

Krumbein, W. C. and F. J. Pettijohn
 1938 Manual of Sedimentary Petrography. New York, Appleton-Century-Crofts, Inc.

Leach, Edmund R.
 1964 Political Systems of Highland Burma: A Study of Kachin Social Structure. London, The London School of Economics and Political Science. G. Bell and Sons, Ltd.

Lowe, Gareth W., et al.
 1960 Excavation at Chiapa de Corzo, Chiapas, Mexico. Papers of the New World Archaeological Foundation, 8/11. Provo, Brigham Young University.

MacNeish, Richard S.
 1954 An Early Archaeological Site Near Pánuco, Vera Cruz. Transactions of the American Philosophical Society, 44(5).

MacNeish, Richard S. and Frederic A. Peterson
 1962 The Santa Marta Rockshelter, Ocozocoautla, Chiapas, Mexico. Papers of the New World Archaeological Foundation, 10. Provo, Brigham Young University.

MacNeish, Richard S., Frederick A. Peterson and Kent V. Flannery
  1970 The Prehistory of the Tehuacán Valley, III. Austin, University of Texas Press.

Melgar y Serrano, José María
  1869 Antigüedades Mexicanas. Boletín de la Sociedad Mexicana de Geografía y Estadística, Epoca 2, Vol. 1:292-297.
  1871 Estudio sobre la antigüedad y el origin de la Cabeza Colosal de tipo etiópico que existe en Huayapam. Boletín de la Sociedad Mexicana de Geografía y Estadística, Epoca 2, Vol. 2:104-109.

Ojeda Rivera, Jesus et al.
  1965 Geología Regional y Yacimientos Minerales de la Porción Meridional del Istmo de Tehuantepec, Mexico. Mexico, Consejo de Recursos Naturales No Renovables.

Peterson, Fredrick A.
  1963 Some Ceramics from Mirador, Chiapas, Mexico. Papers of the New World Archaeological Foundation, 11. Provo, Brigham Young University.

Piña Chán, Roman
  1952 Tlatilco y la cultura Preclásica del Valle de México. Anales del Instituto Nacional de Antropología e Historia, 4(32). Mexico.
  1955 Chalcatzingo, Morelos. Informe, 4. Instituto Nacional de Antropología e Historia. Mexico.
  1958a Tlatilco. Investigaciones I, Instituto Nacional de Antropología e Historia. Mexico.
  1958b Tlatilco. Investigaciones, II, Instituto Nacional de Antropología e Historia, Mexico.

Piña Chán, Roman, Arturo Romano Pacheco and Pareyón Moreno
  1952 Tlatilco: nuevo sitio preclásico del Valle de México. Tlatoani, 1(3/4):9-13.

Pires-Ferreira, Jane W.
  1973 Formative Mesoamerican Exchange Networks. Unpublished Ph.D. dissertation, University of Michigan.

Rappaport, Roy A.
  1967 Pigs for the Ancestors. New Haven, Yale University Press.

Renfrew, Colin A., J. E. Dixon and J. R. Cann
  1966 Obsidian and Early Culture Contact in the Near East. Proceedings of the Prehistoric Society, XXXII:30-72.
  1968 Further Analysis of Near Eastern Obsidians. Proceedings of the Prehistoric Society, XXXIV:319-331.

Sahagún, Fray Bernardino
  1959 Florentine Codex, Vol. 9. Translated by C. E. Dibble and A. J. Anderson. Monographs of the School of American Research and the Museum of New Mexico. Santa Fe.

Sahlins, Marshall D.
  1965 On the Sociology of Primitive Exchange. In: The Relevance of Models for Social Anthropology, M. Banton, ed. ASA Monographs 1. London, Tavistock; New York, Praeger.
  1972 Stone Age Economics. Chicago/New York, Aldine/Atherton.

Sanders, William T.
  1961 Ceramic Stratigraphy of Santa Cruz, Chiapas, Mexico. Papers of the New World Archaeological Foundation, 13, Provo, Brigham Young University.

Sanders, William T. and Barbara J. Price
  1968 Mesoamerica: The Evolution of a Civilization, New York, Random House.

Service, Elman R.
  1962 Primitive Social Organization. New York, Random House.

Shirane, G. et al.
  1962 A Study of the Magnetic Properties of the $FeTiO_3-\alpha Fe_2O_3$ System by Neutron Diffraction and the Mössbauer Effect. Journal of the Physical Society of Japan, 17(10).

Shook, Edwin and Tatiana Proskouriakoff
  1956 Settlement Patterns in Mesoamerica and the Sequence in the Guatemala Highlands. In: Prehistoric Settlement Patterns in the New World, Gordon R. Willey, ed. Viking Fund Publications in Anthropology, 23. New York.

Sisson, Edward B.
  1970 Settlement Patterns and Land Use in the Northwestern Chontalpa, Tabasco, Mexico: A Progress Report. Cerámica de Cultura Maya, 6:41-55.

Sociedad Mexicana de Antropología
  1942 Mayas y Olmecas. Segunda Reunión de Mesa Redonda. Sociedad Mexicana de Antropología.

REFERENCES

Spores, Ronald
    1969   Exploraciones arqueológicas en el Valle de Nochiztlán. Boletín del Instituto Nacional de Antropología e Historia, 37:35-43.

Stirling, Matthew W.
    1942a   An Initial Series from Tres Zapotes, Veracruz. National Geographic Society Contributed Technical Papers: Mexican Archaeology Series, 1(1). Washington, D.C.
    1942b   La Venta's Green Stone Tigers. National Geographic Magazine, LXXXIV:321-332.
    1942c   Recientes Hallazgos en La Venta. Mayas y Olmecas. Mexico, Sociedad Mexicana de Antropología.
    1947   On the Trail of La Venta Man. National Geographic Magazine, XCI:137-172.
    1955   Stone Monuments of the Río Chiquito, Veracruz, Mexico. Smithsonian Institution Anthropological Papers, 43:1-23.

Strathern, Marilyn
    1969   Stone Axes and Flake Tools: Evaluations From New Guinea. Proceedings of the Prehistoric Society, XXXV:330-344.

Stross, F. H. et al.
    1968   Analysis of American Obsidian by X-Ray Fluorescence and Neutron Activation Analysis. Contributions of the University of California Research Facility, 5:59-79.

Tolstoy, Paul
    1971   Recent Research into the Early Preclassic of the Central Highlands. *In*: Observations on the Emergence of Civilization in America, Robert F. Heizer and John A. Graham, eds. Berkeley, Contributions of the University of California Archaeological Research Facility, 11.

Tolstoy, Paul and André Guénette
    1965   Le Placement de Tlatilco dans le cadre du Préclassique du Bassin de Mexico. Journal de la Société des Américanistes de Paris, LIV(1):47-91.

Tolstoy, Paul and Louise I. Paradis
    1970   Early and Middle Preclassic culture in the Basin of Mexico. Science, 167:344-351.

Vaillant, George C.
    1929   On the Threshold of Native American Civilization. Natural History, XXIX(5):530-542.
    1930a   Notes on the Middle Cultures of Middle America. Proceedings, 23rd International Congress of Americanists, pp. 74-81. New York.
    1930b   Reconstructing the Beginning of a History. Natural History, XXX(6):606-616.
    1930c   Excavations at Zacatenco. Anthropological Papers of the American Museum of Natural History, XXXII(1). New York.
    1932a   Stratigraphical Research in Central Mexico. Proceedings, National Academy of Sciences, XVIII(7):487-490. Washington, D.C.
    1932b   Some Resemblances in the Ceramics of Central and North America. Globe, Medallion Papers, 12.
    1935a   Excavations at El Arbolillo. Anthropological Papers of the American Museum of Natural History, XXXV(2). New York.
    1935b   Early Cultures in the Valley of Mexico: Results of the Stratigraphical Project of the American Museum of Natural History in the Valley of Mexico 1928-1933. Anthropological Papers of the American Museum of Natural History, XXXV(3). New York.

Weaver, J. R. and F. H. Stross
    1965   Analysis by X-Ray Fluorescence of Some American Obsidians. Contributions of the University of California Archaeological Reserach Facility, 1:89-103.

Weaver, Muriel P.
    1967   Tlapacoya Pottery in the Museum Collection. Indian Notes and Monographs. Miscellaneous Series, 56.

Williams, H. and Robert F. Heizer
    1965   Sources of Rocks Used in Olmec Monuments. Contributions of the University of California Archaeological Research Facility, 1:1-39.

Winter, Marcus C.
    1972   Tierras Largas: A Formative Community in the Valley of Oaxaca, Mexico. Unpublished Ph.D. dissertation, University of Arizona.

Wright, Gary A.
    1969   Obsidian Analysis and Prehistoric Near Eastern Trade: 7500 to 3500 B.C. Anthropological Papers, 37. Museum of Anthropology, University of Michigan.

Wright, Henry T. and M. A. Zeder
    1973   The Simulation of a Linear Exchange System Under Equilibrium Conditions. Museum of Anthropology. University of Michigan. (Mimeographed.)

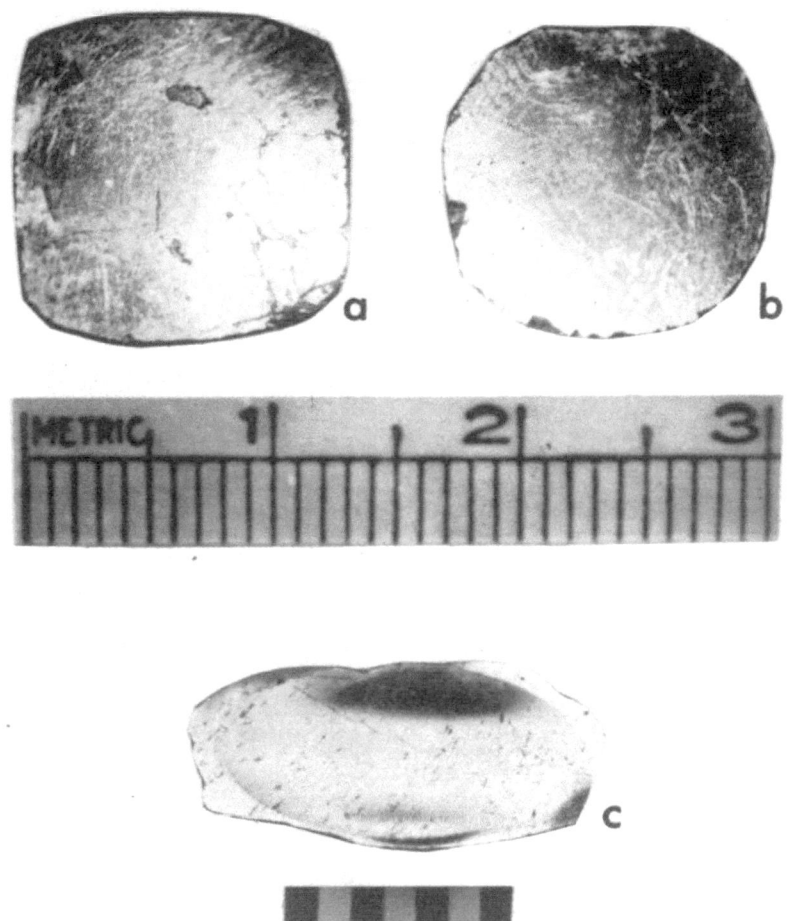

Plate 1. Examples of iron-ore mirrors from Formative Mesoamerica. *a*, small flat mirror from Zone B, Area A, San José Mogote. *b*, small flat mirror from magnetite working area in Household Cluster C3, Area A, San José Mogote. *c*, large concave ilmenite mirror from offering no. 11, La Venta. (Scale in cm.)

Plate 2. Figurines in the Museo Nacional de Antropología e Historia, Mexico City, wearing metal mirrors. *a*, jade figurine from La Venta, dusted with red hematite pigment, wearing iron ore mirror. *b*, ceramic figurine from Tlatilco wearing crystalline hematite mirror.

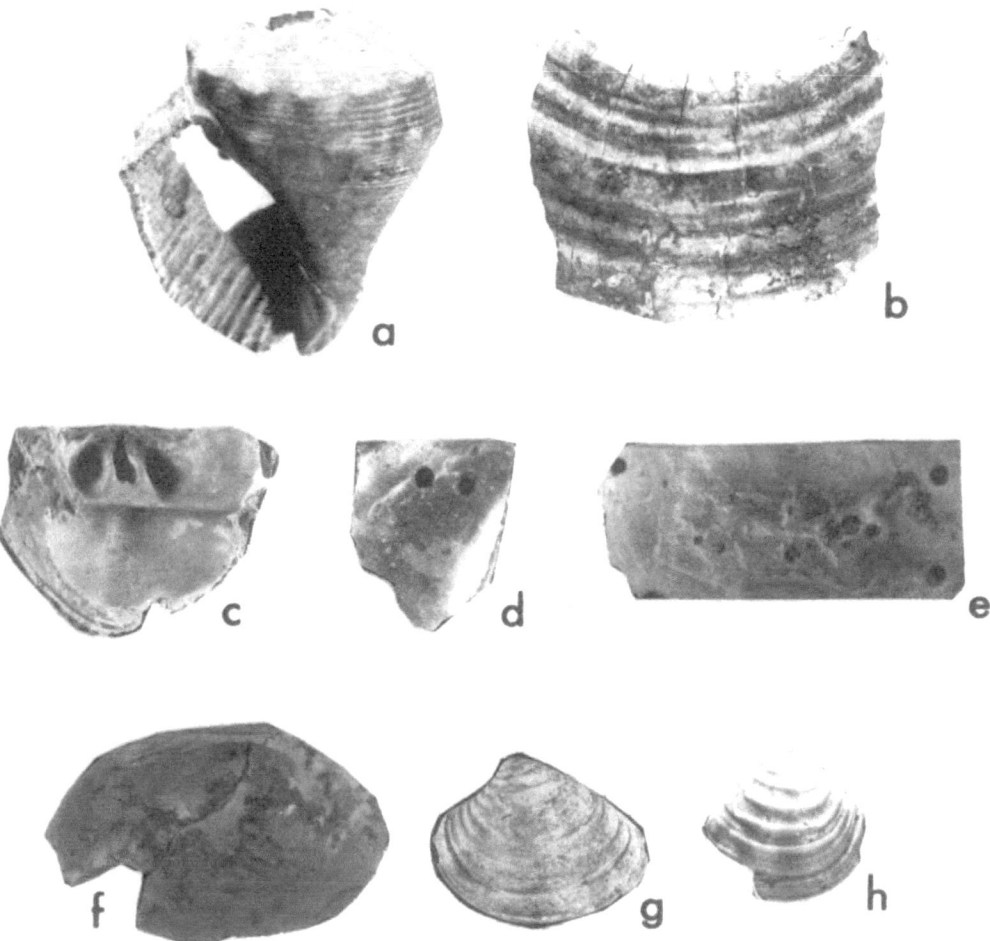

Plate 3. Examples of shells and shell ornaments from Formative sites in Oaxaca (not all to same scale). *a*, conch shell (*Strombus* cf. *galeatus*) from east wall of Platform 2, Area A, San José Mogote. *b*, charred fragment of conch shell (*Malea* cf. *ringens*) from Zone D2 midden, Area C, Huitzo. *c*, trimmed-off valve area from *Spondylus calcifer*, Household Cluster C3, Area A, San José Mogote. *d*, broken fragment of drilled pearl oyster (*Pinctada mazatlanica*), Household Cluster C2, Area A, San José Mogote. *e*, drilled shell pectoral, House 1, Tierras Largas. *f*, pearly freshwater mussel (*Baryonaias* sp.), Feature 4, House 1, Tierras Largas. *g-h*, *Chione* (=*Anomalocardia*) *subrugosa*; *g*, Zone D1 midden, Area A, San José Mogote; *h*, Platform 1, Stages II-III, Area A, San José Mogote.